THE COMPLETE
JON SABLE FREELANCE

San Diego, CA

book design:
Robbie Robbins

production:
Tom B. Long

www.idwpublishing.com

HARDCOVER ISBN: 1-933239-52-2
SOFTCOVER ISBN: 1-933239-39-5

08 07 06 05   1 2 3 4 5

IDW Publishing is:

Ted Adams, Publisher
Chris Ryall, Editor-in-Chief
Robbie Robbins, Design Director
Kris Oprisko, Vice President
Alex Garner, Art Director
Dan Taylor, Editor
Aaron Myers, Distribution Manager
Tom B. Long, Designer
Chance Boren, Editorial Assistant
Yumiko Miyano, Business Development
Rick Privman, Business Development

NightSky Sable LLC
in association with
Kickstart Investment Partners
and
IDW Publishing
present

The Complete
Jon Sable, Freelance™
Volume Three

Ken F. Levin — Producer
Mike Gold — Executive Producer and Editor

Mike Grell — Creator, Writer, Artist, Cover Artist

Jason Netter — Co-Producer
John C. Hoff — Co-Producer

Glenn Hauman — Webmaster and Assistant Editor
George Hagenauer — Research
Mario Moreno — Film Master

Film Provided Under License From First Comics, Inc.

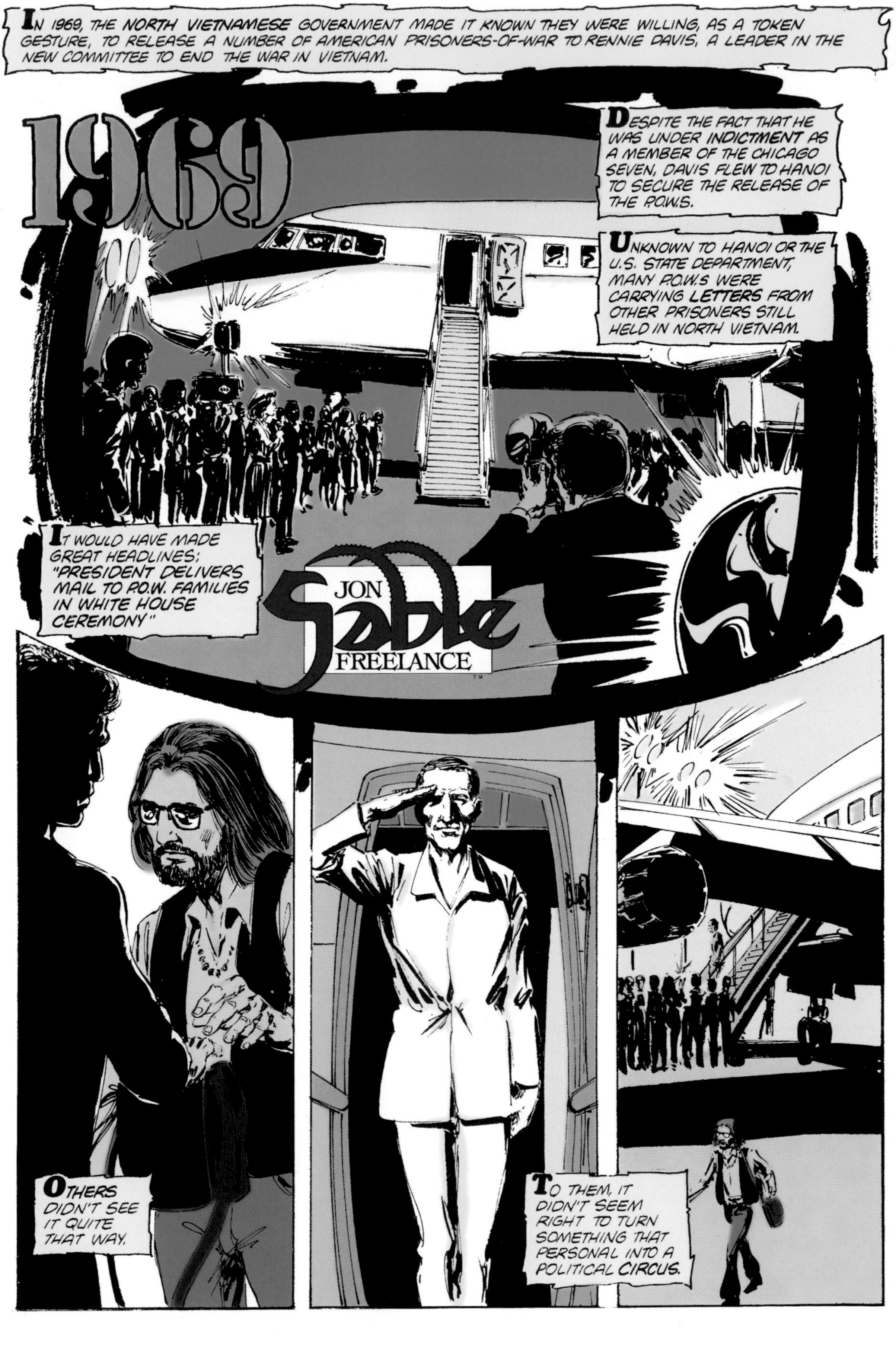
In 1969, the NORTH VIETNAMESE government made it known they were willing, as a token gesture, to release a number of American prisoners-of-war to Rennie Davis, a leader in the New Committee to End the War in Vietnam.
1969
Despite the fact that he was under INDICTMENT as a member of the Chicago Seven, Davis flew to Hanoi to secure the release of the P.O.W.s.
Unknown to Hanoi or the U.S. State Department, many P.O.W.s were carrying LETTERS from other prisoners still held in North Vietnam.
It would have made great headlines: "PRESIDENT DELIVERS MAIL TO P.O.W. FAMILIES IN WHITE HOUSE CEREMONY"
JON Sable FREELANCE
Others didn't see it quite that way.
To them, it didn't seem right to turn something that personal into a political CIRCUS.

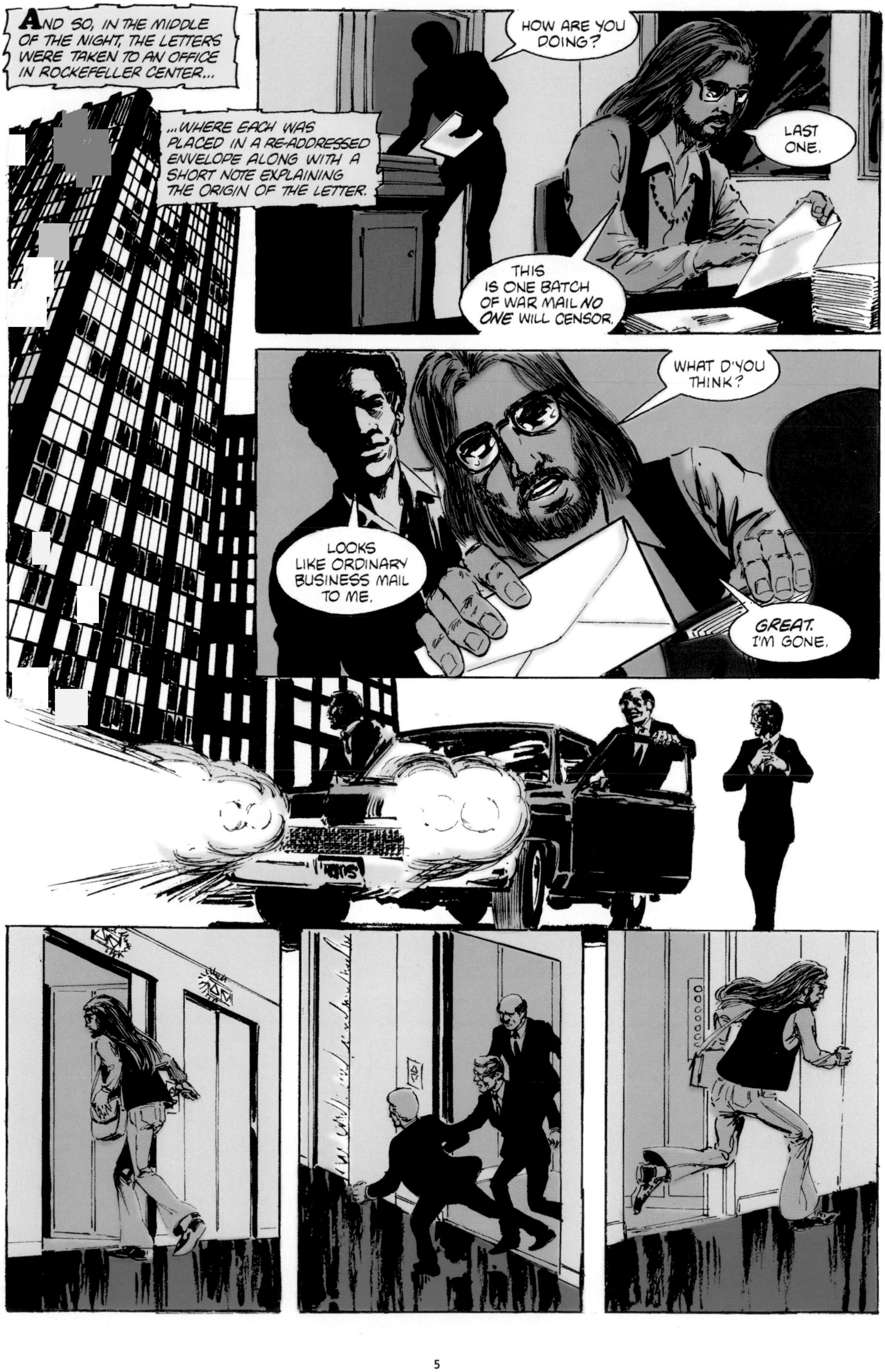
AND SO, IN THE MIDDLE OF THE NIGHT, THE LETTERS WERE TAKEN TO AN OFFICE IN ROCKEFELLER CENTER...
...WHERE EACH WAS PLACED IN A RE-ADDRESSED ENVELOPE ALONG WITH A SHORT NOTE EXPLAINING THE ORIGIN OF THE LETTER.
HOW ARE YOU DOING?
LAST ONE.
THIS IS ONE BATCH OF WAR MAIL NO ONE WILL CENSOR.
WHAT D'YOU THINK?
LOOKS LIKE ORDINARY BUSINESS MAIL TO ME.
GREAT. I'M GONE.

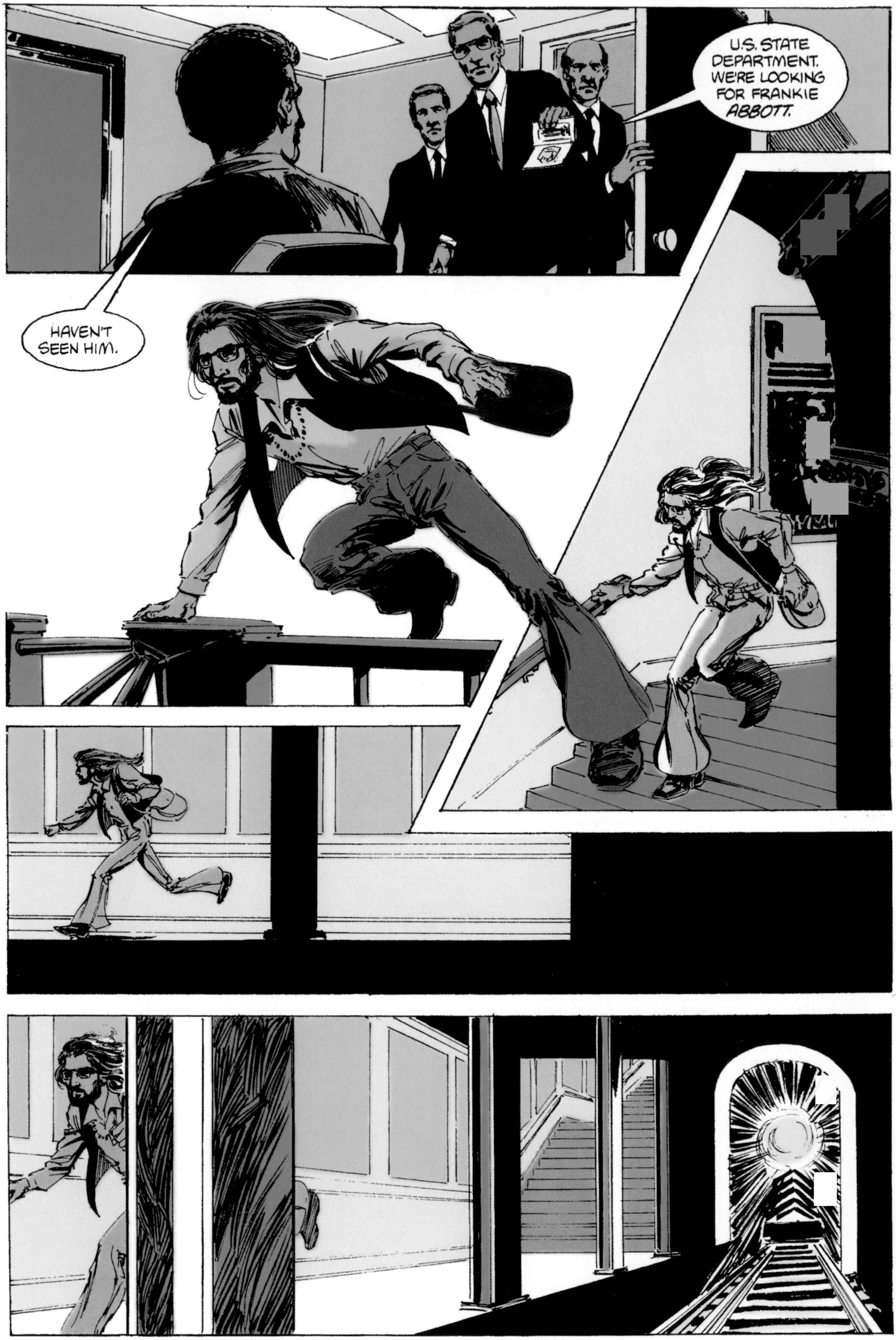
U.S. STATE DEPARTMENT. WE'RE LOOKING FOR FRANKIE ABBOTT.
HAVEN'T SEEN HIM.

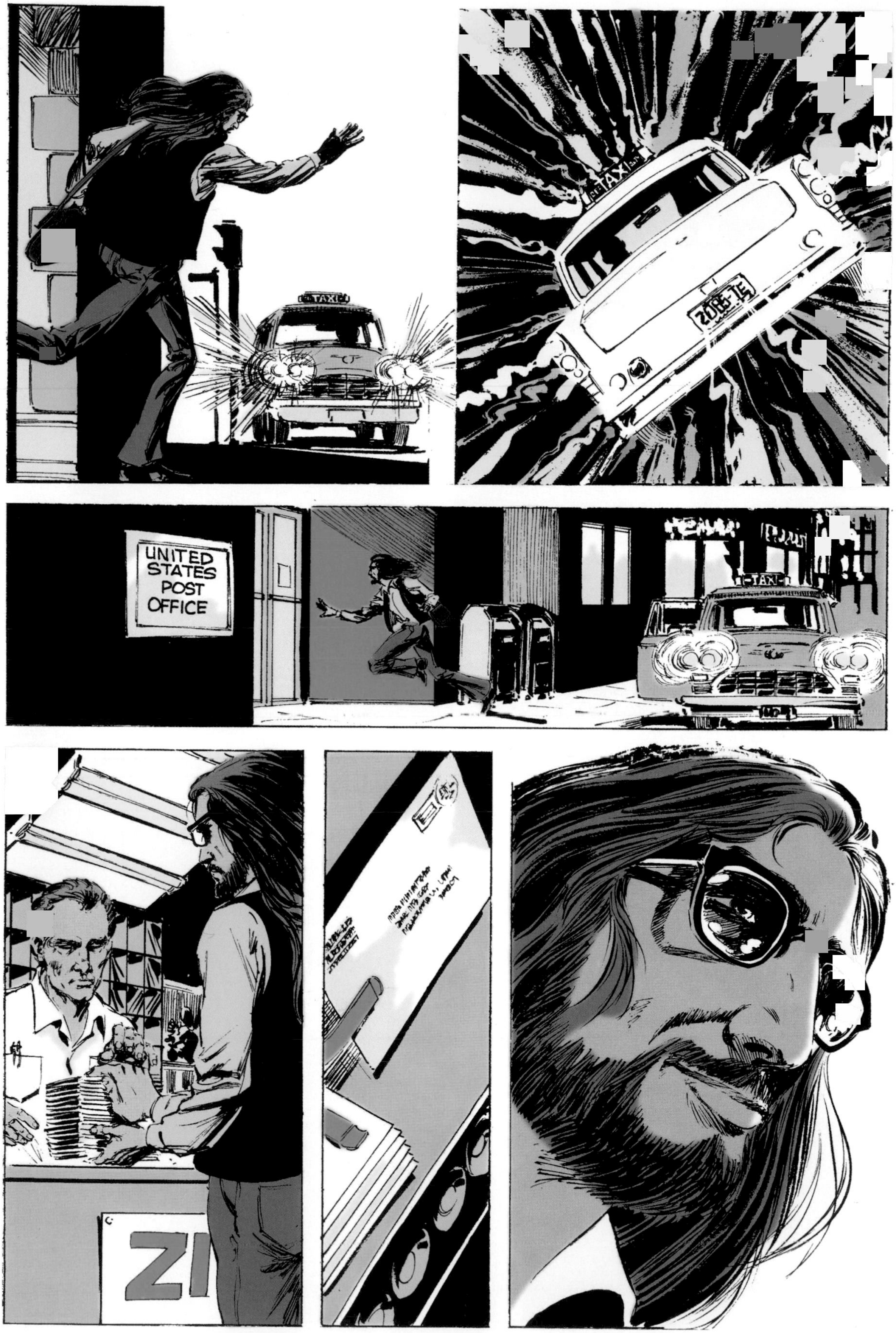
TAXI
UNITED STATES POST OFFICE
ZI

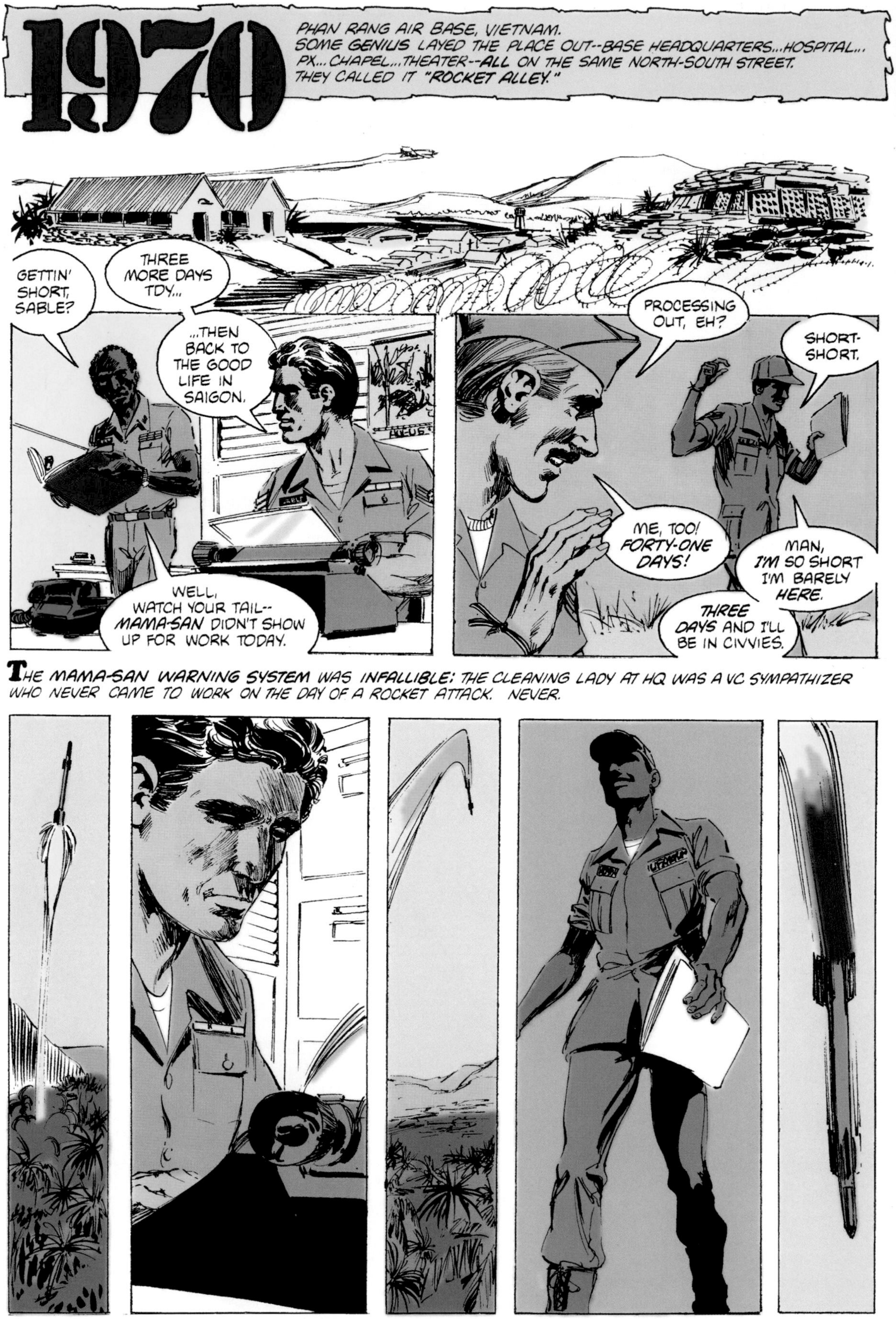
1970
PHAN RANG AIR BASE, VIETNAM.
SOME GENIUS LAYED THE PLACE OUT--BASE HEADQUARTERS...HOSPITAL... PX...CHAPEL...THEATER--ALL ON THE SAME NORTH-SOUTH STREET.
THEY CALLED IT "ROCKET ALLEY."
GETTIN' SHORT, SABLE?
THREE MORE DAYS TDY...
...THEN BACK TO THE GOOD LIFE IN SAIGON.
WELL, WATCH YOUR TAIL-- MAMA-SAN DIDN'T SHOW UP FOR WORK TODAY.
PROCESSING OUT, EH?
SHORT-SHORT.
ME, TOO! FORTY-ONE DAYS!
MAN, I'M SO SHORT I'M BARELY HERE.
THREE DAYS AND I'LL BE IN CIVVIES.
THE MAMA-SAN WARNING SYSTEM WAS INFALLIBLE: THE CLEANING LADY AT HQ WAS A VC SYMPATHIZER WHO NEVER CAME TO WORK ON THE DAY OF A ROCKET ATTACK. NEVER.

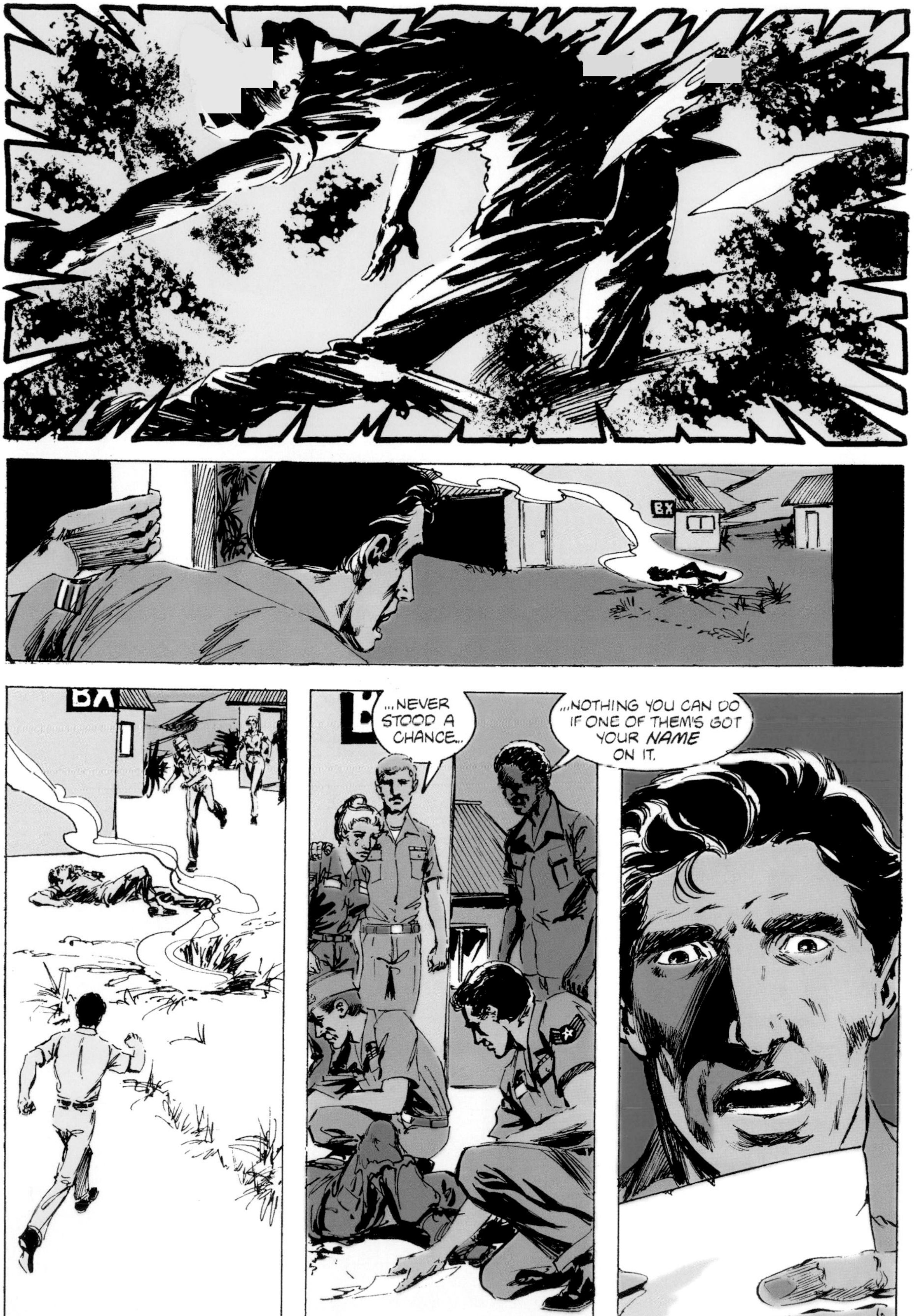
BX
BX
...NEVER STOOD A CHANCE...
...NOTHING YOU CAN DO IF ONE OF THEM'S GOT YOUR *NAME* ON IT.

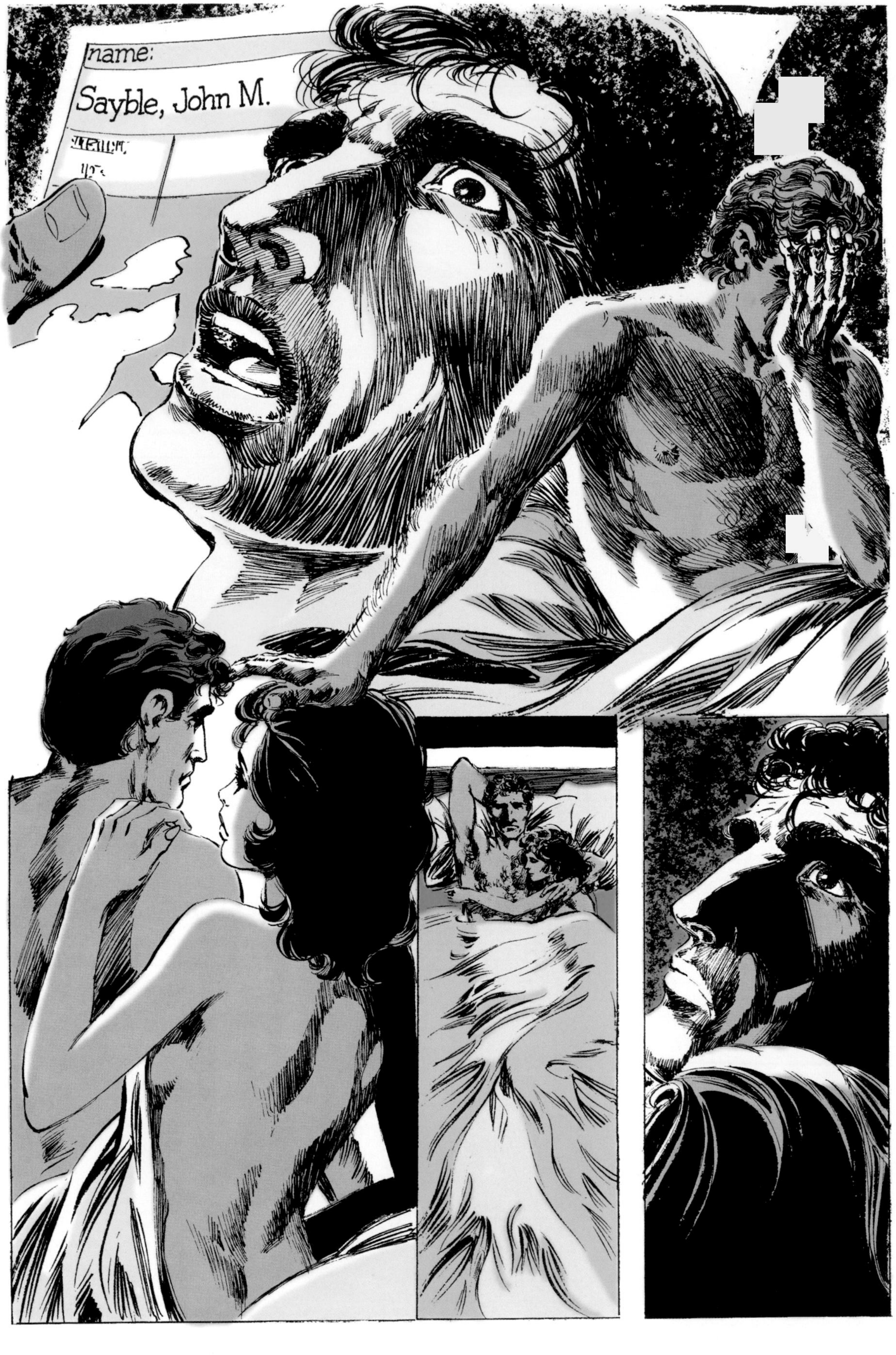
name:
Sayble, John M.

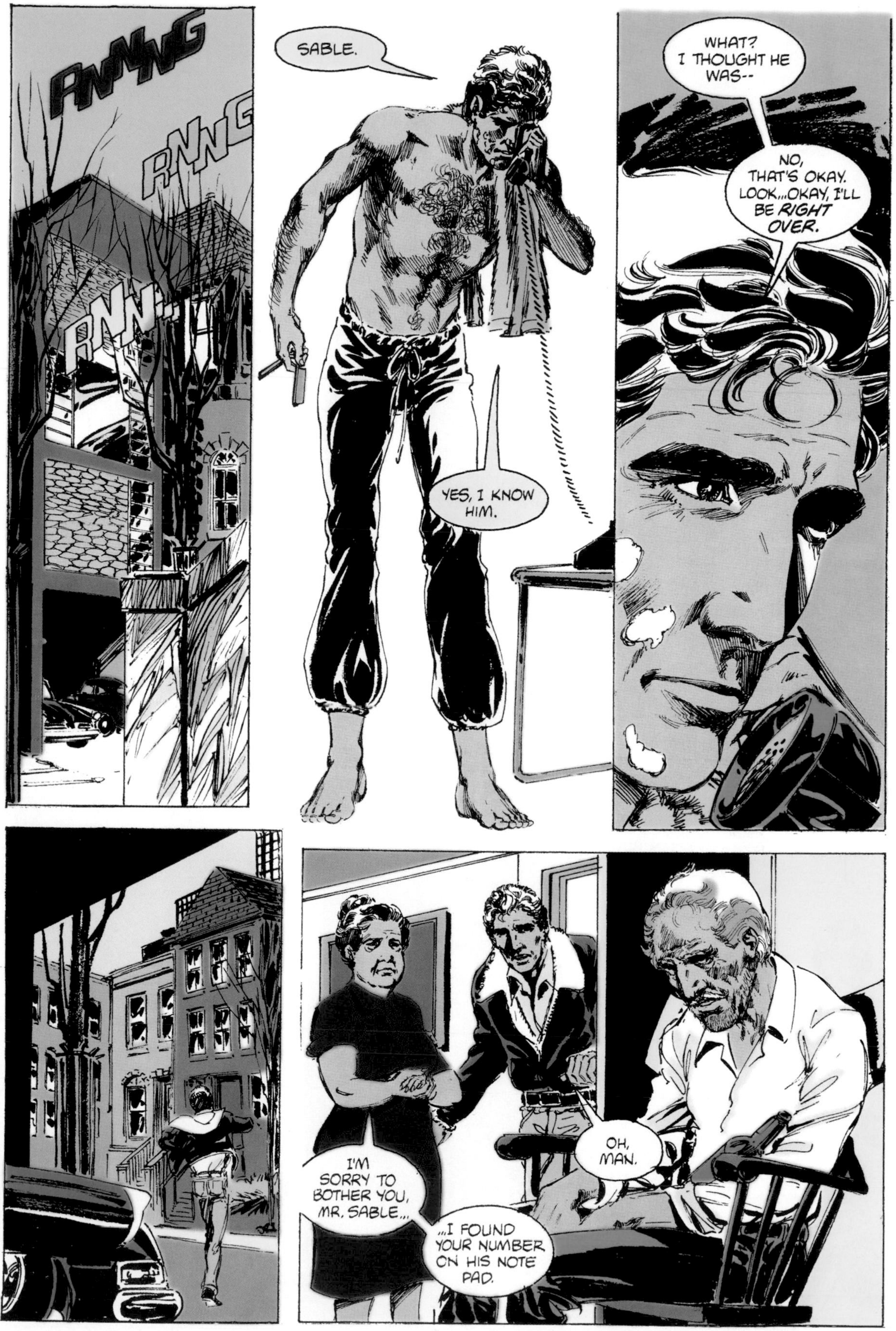
RNNNG
RNNNG
RNN...
SABLE.
YES, I KNOW HIM.
WHAT? I THOUGHT HE WAS--
NO, THAT'S OKAY. LOOK...OKAY, I'LL BE *RIGHT OVER*.
I'M SORRY TO BOTHER YOU, MR. SABLE...
...I FOUND YOUR NUMBER ON HIS NOTE PAD.
OH, MAN.

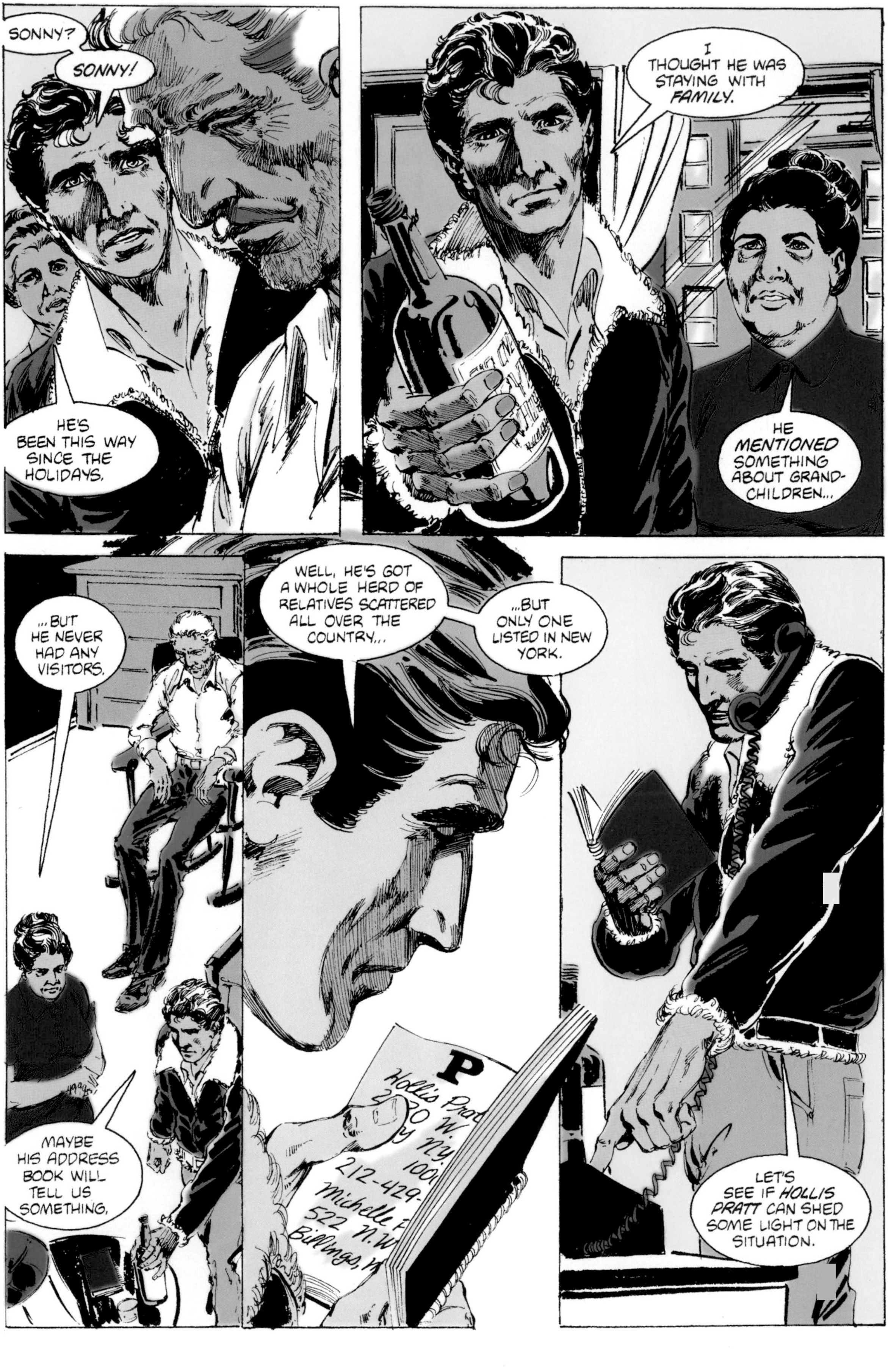
SONNY?
SONNY!
HE'S BEEN THIS WAY SINCE THE HOLIDAYS.
I THOUGHT HE WAS STAYING WITH FAMILY.
HE MENTIONED SOMETHING ABOUT GRAND-CHILDREN...
...BUT HE NEVER HAD ANY VISITORS.
MAYBE HIS ADDRESS BOOK WILL TELL US SOMETHING.
WELL, HE'S GOT A WHOLE HERD OF RELATIVES SCATTERED ALL OVER THE COUNTRY...
...BUT ONLY ONE LISTED IN NEW YORK.
P
Hollis Pratt
212-429-
Michelle
Billings,
LET'S SEE IF HOLLIS PRATT CAN SHED SOME LIGHT ON THE SITUATION.

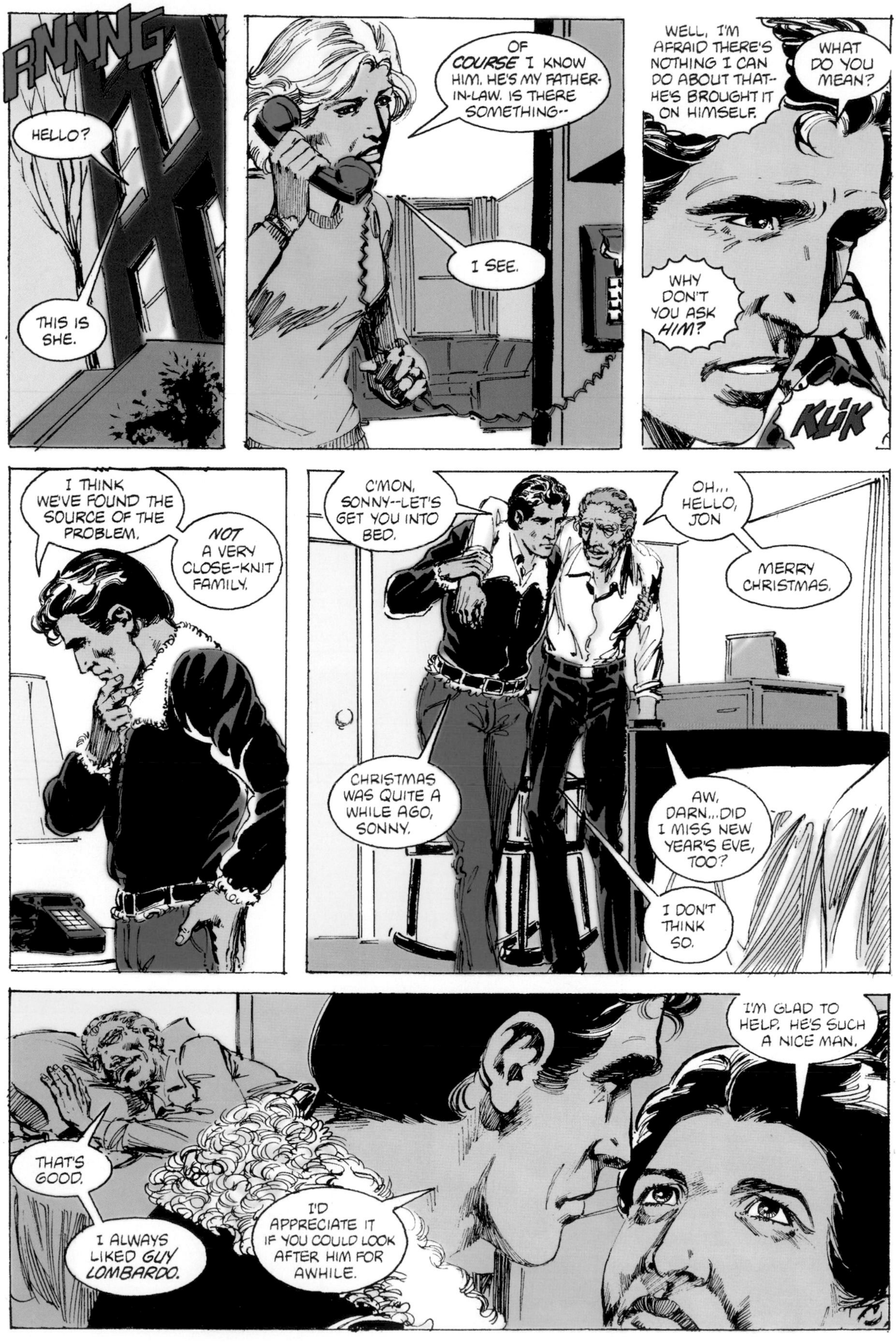
RNNNG
HELLO?
THIS IS SHE.
OF COURSE I KNOW HIM. HE'S MY FATHER-IN-LAW. IS THERE SOMETHING--
I SEE.
WELL, I'M AFRAID THERE'S NOTHING I CAN DO ABOUT THAT-- HE'S BROUGHT IT ON HIMSELF.
WHAT DO YOU MEAN?
WHY DON'T YOU ASK HIM?
KLIK
I THINK WE'VE FOUND THE SOURCE OF THE PROBLEM.
NOT A VERY CLOSE-KNIT FAMILY.
C'MON, SONNY--LET'S GET YOU INTO BED.
OH... HELLO, JON
MERRY CHRISTMAS.
CHRISTMAS WAS QUITE A WHILE AGO, SONNY.
AW, DARN... DID I MISS NEW YEAR'S EVE, TOO?
I DON'T THINK SO.
I'M GLAD TO HELP. HE'S SUCH A NICE MAN.
THAT'S GOOD.
I ALWAYS LIKED GUY LOMBARDO.
I'D APPRECIATE IT IF YOU COULD LOOK AFTER HIM FOR AWHILE.

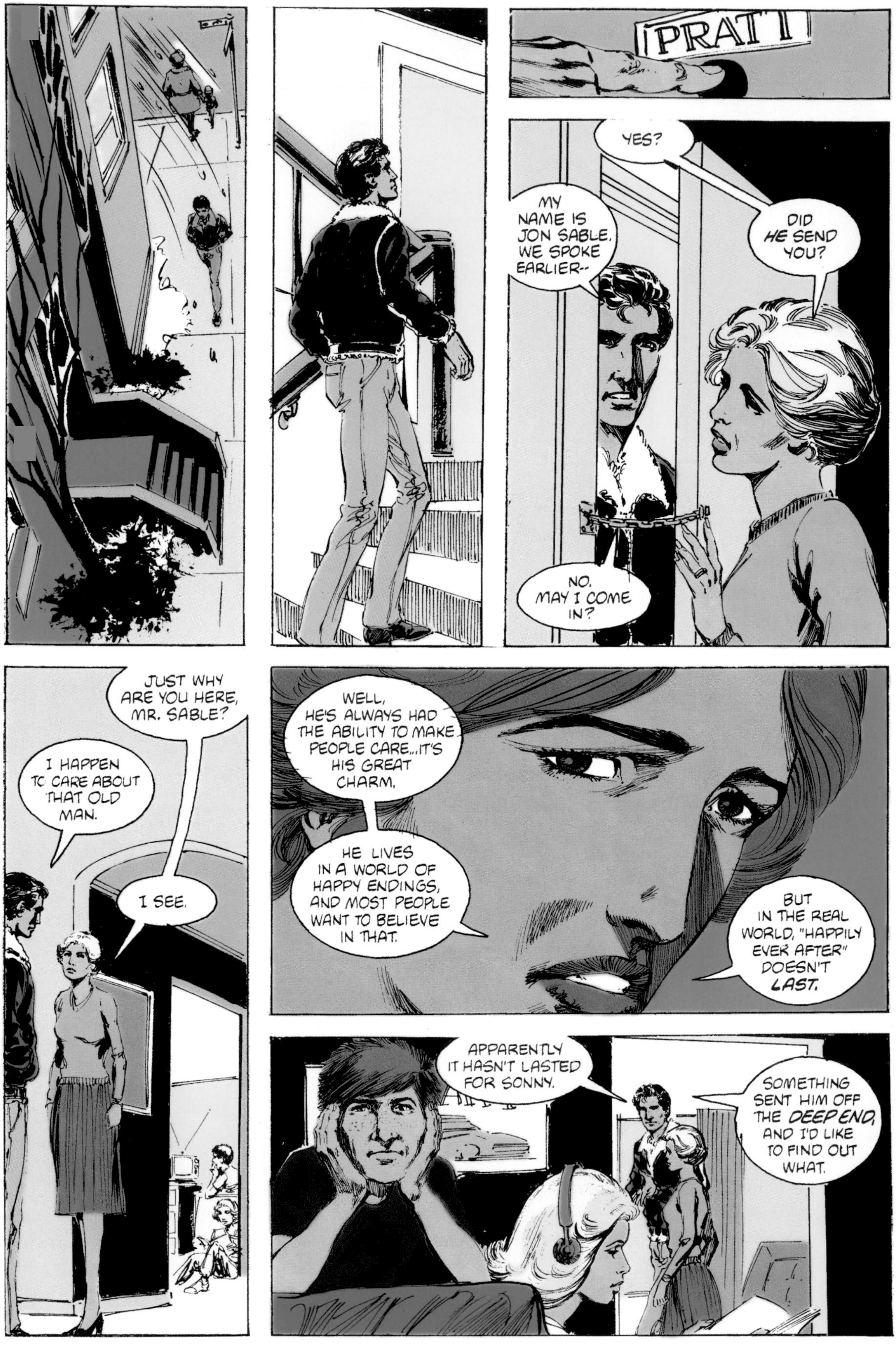
PRATT
YES?
MY NAME IS JON SABLE. WE SPOKE EARLIER--
DID HE SEND YOU?
NO. MAY I COME IN?
JUST WHY ARE YOU HERE, MR. SABLE?
I HAPPEN TO CARE ABOUT THAT OLD MAN.
I SEE.
WELL, HE'S ALWAYS HAD THE ABILITY TO MAKE PEOPLE CARE...IT'S HIS GREAT CHARM.
HE LIVES IN A WORLD OF HAPPY ENDINGS, AND MOST PEOPLE WANT TO BELIEVE IN THAT.
BUT IN THE REAL WORLD, "HAPPILY EVER AFTER" DOESN'T LAST.
APPARENTLY IT HASN'T LASTED FOR SONNY.
SOMETHING SENT HIM OFF THE DEEP END, AND I'D LIKE TO FIND OUT WHAT.

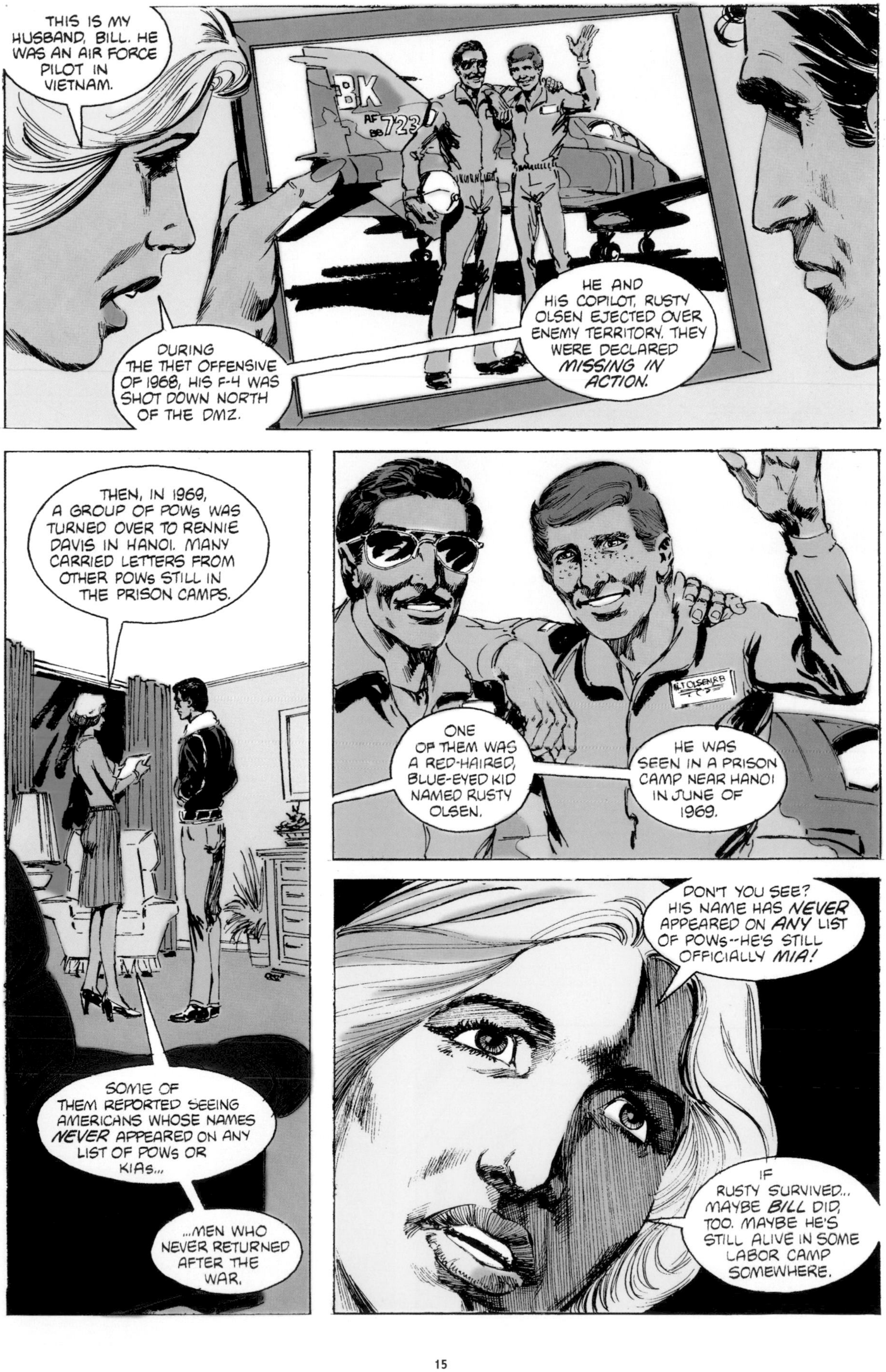

THIS IS MY HUSBAND, BILL. HE WAS AN AIR FORCE PILOT IN VIETNAM.
BK
AF 723
DURING THE THET OFFENSIVE OF 1968, HIS F-4 WAS SHOT DOWN NORTH OF THE DMZ.
HE AND HIS COPILOT, RUSTY OLSEN EJECTED OVER ENEMY TERRITORY. THEY WERE DECLARED *MISSING IN ACTION.*
THEN, IN 1969, A GROUP OF POWs WAS TURNED OVER TO RENNIE DAVIS IN HANOI. MANY CARRIED LETTERS FROM OTHER POWs STILL IN THE PRISON CAMPS.
SOME OF THEM REPORTED SEEING AMERICANS WHOSE NAMES *NEVER* APPEARED ON ANY LIST OF POWs OR KIAs...
...MEN WHO NEVER RETURNED AFTER THE WAR.
ONE OF THEM WAS A RED-HAIRED, BLUE-EYED KID NAMED RUSTY OLSEN.
HE WAS SEEN IN A PRISON CAMP NEAR HANOI IN JUNE OF 1969.
DON'T YOU SEE? HIS NAME HAS *NEVER* APPEARED ON *ANY* LIST OF POWs--HE'S STILL OFFICIALLY *MIA!*
IF RUSTY SURVIVED... MAYBE *BILL* DID, TOO. MAYBE HE'S STILL ALIVE IN SOME LABOR CAMP SOMEWHERE.

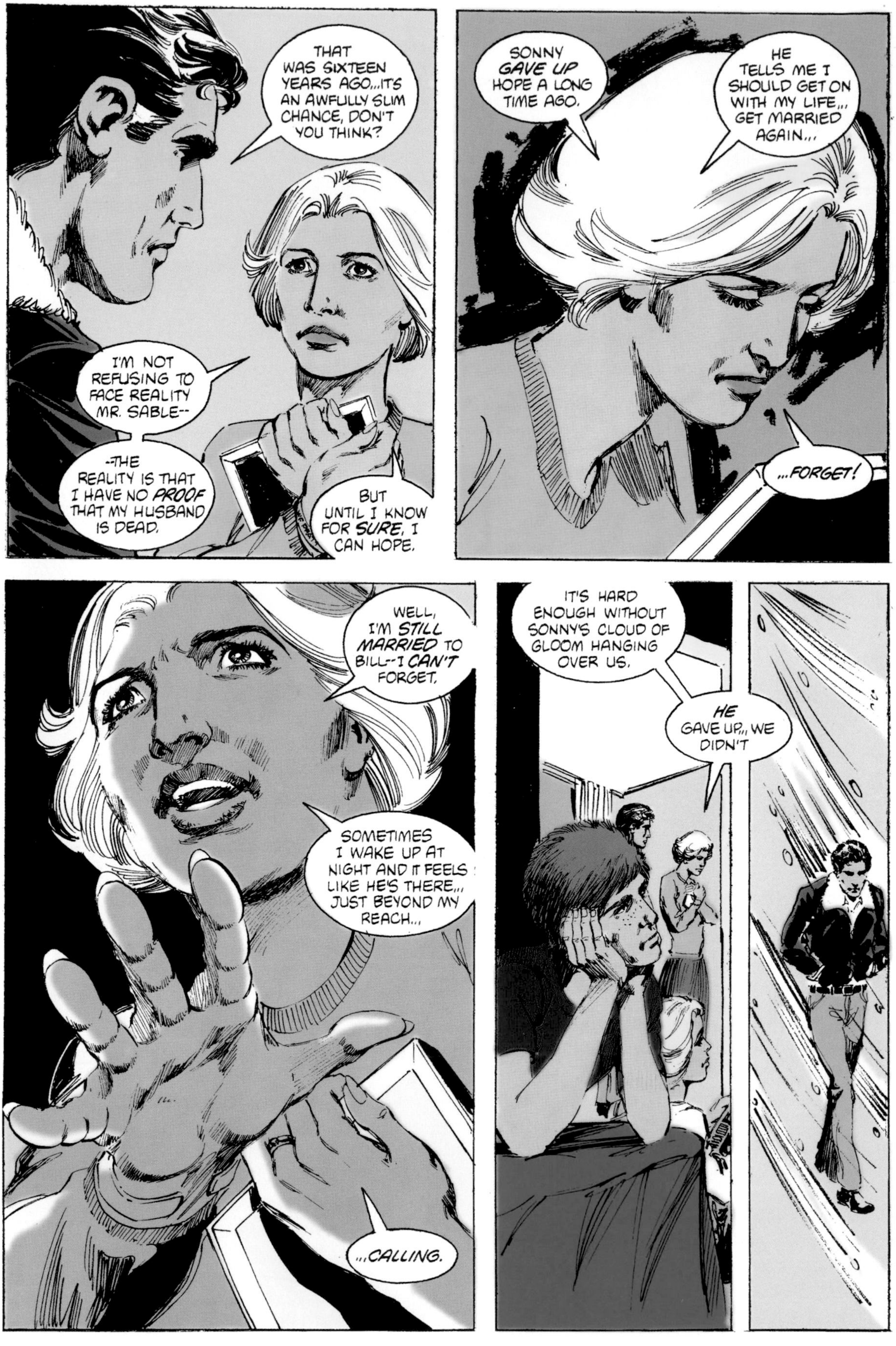
THAT WAS SIXTEEN YEARS AGO... IT'S AN AWFULLY SLIM CHANCE, DON'T YOU THINK?
I'M NOT REFUSING TO FACE REALITY MR. SABLE--
--THE REALITY IS THAT I HAVE NO PROOF THAT MY HUSBAND IS DEAD.
BUT UNTIL I KNOW FOR SURE, I CAN HOPE.
SONNY GAVE UP HOPE A LONG TIME AGO.
HE TELLS ME I SHOULD GET ON WITH MY LIFE... GET MARRIED AGAIN...
...FORGET!
WELL, I'M STILL MARRIED TO BILL--I CAN'T FORGET.
SOMETIMES I WAKE UP AT NIGHT AND IT FEELS LIKE HE'S THERE... JUST BEYOND MY REACH...
...CALLING.
IT'S HARD ENOUGH WITHOUT SONNY'S CLOUD OF GLOOM HANGING OVER US.
HE GAVE UP... WE DIDN'T

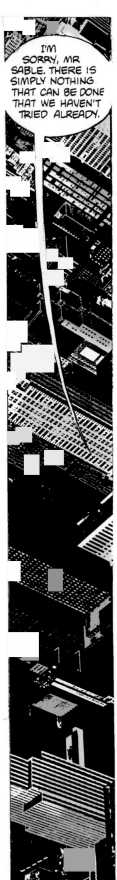

I'M SORRY, MR SABLE. THERE IS SIMPLY NOTHING THAT CAN BE DONE THAT WE HAVEN'T TRIED ALREADY.

THE STATE DEPARTMENT IS WORKING WITH ALL THE *MIA* GROUPS TO SECURE WHATEVER INFORMATION WE CAN...

...BUT HANOI *INSISTS* THAT THEY KNOW NOTHING ABOUT AMERICANS REMAINING IN PRISON CAMPS.

WHAT ABOUT GUYS LIKE LIEUTENANT RUSSELL B. OLSEN?

HE WAS NEVER EVEN *REPORTED CAPTURED,* BUT THERE'S *EVIDENCE* HE *WAS THERE*--!

WAS... YES, BUT SOME MEN *DIE* IN POW CAMPS, MR. SABLE.

IT IS CERTAINLY *POSSIBLE* THAT SOME OF OUR MEN REMAIN IN NORTH VIETNAM... PERHAPS BY *CHOICE*-- DESERTERS, TURNCOATS.... MAYBE *BRAINWASHED.*

BUT THE *OPERATIVE* WORD HERE IS "EVIDENCE."

IF THERE WAS *CONCRETE EVIDENCE* THAT *ANY* POWs REMAIN IN VIETNAM, I *ASSURE* YOU WE WOULD USE *EVERY MEANS* TO SECURE THEIR RELEASE.

IF SOMEONE WOULD BRING US JUST *ONE SHRED OF PROOF.*

MAYBE SOMEONE WILL.

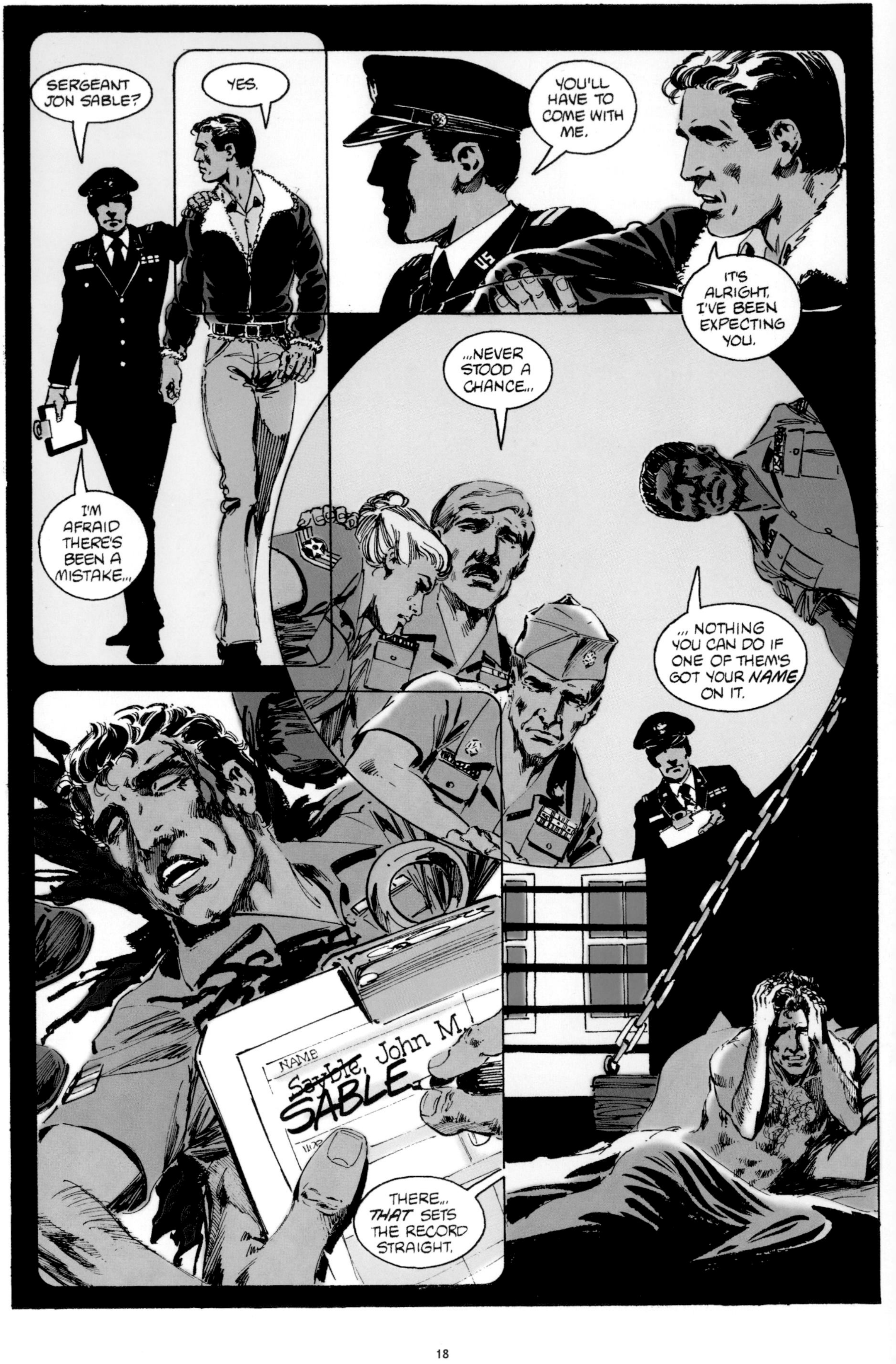
SERGEANT JON SABLE?
YES.
I'M AFRAID THERE'S BEEN A MISTAKE...
YOU'LL HAVE TO COME WITH ME.
IT'S ALRIGHT, I'VE BEEN EXPECTING YOU.
...NEVER STOOD A CHANCE...
... NOTHING YOU CAN DO IF ONE OF THEM'S GOT YOUR NAME ON IT.
NAME
Sayble, John M.
SABLE
THERE... THAT SETS THE RECORD STRAIGHT.

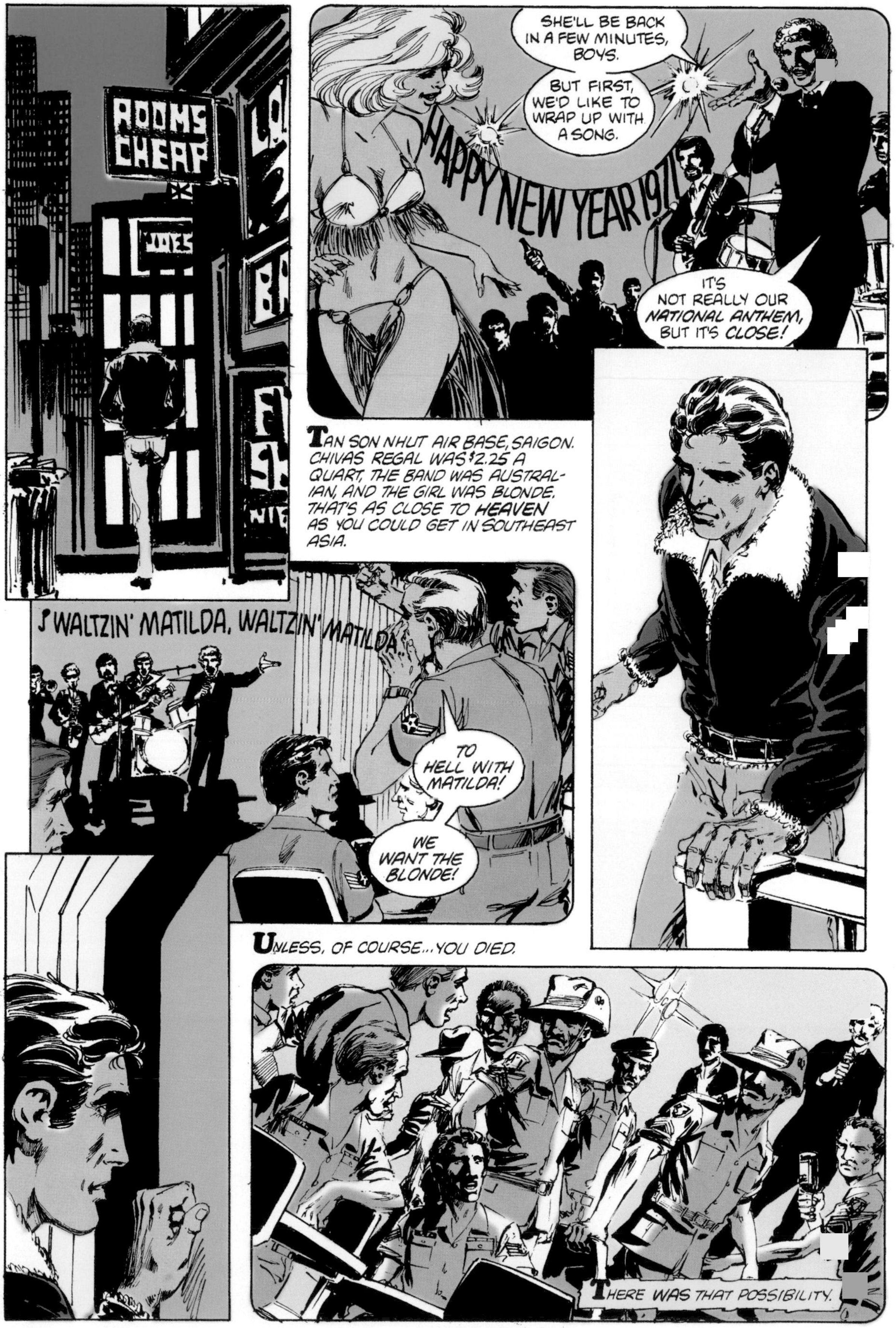
ROOMS CHEAP
JOE'S
SHE'LL BE BACK IN A FEW MINUTES, BOYS.
BUT FIRST, WE'D LIKE TO WRAP UP WITH A SONG.
HAPPY NEW YEAR 1971
IT'S NOT REALLY OUR NATIONAL ANTHEM, BUT IT'S CLOSE!
TAN SON NHUT AIR BASE, SAIGON. CHIVAS REGAL WAS $2.25 A QUART, THE BAND WAS AUSTRALIAN, AND THE GIRL WAS BLONDE. THAT'S AS CLOSE TO HEAVEN AS YOU COULD GET IN SOUTHEAST ASIA.
♪ WALTZIN' MATILDA, WALTZIN' MATILDA...
TO HELL WITH MATILDA!
WE WANT THE BLONDE!
UNLESS, OF COURSE... YOU DIED.
THERE WAS THAT POSSIBILITY.

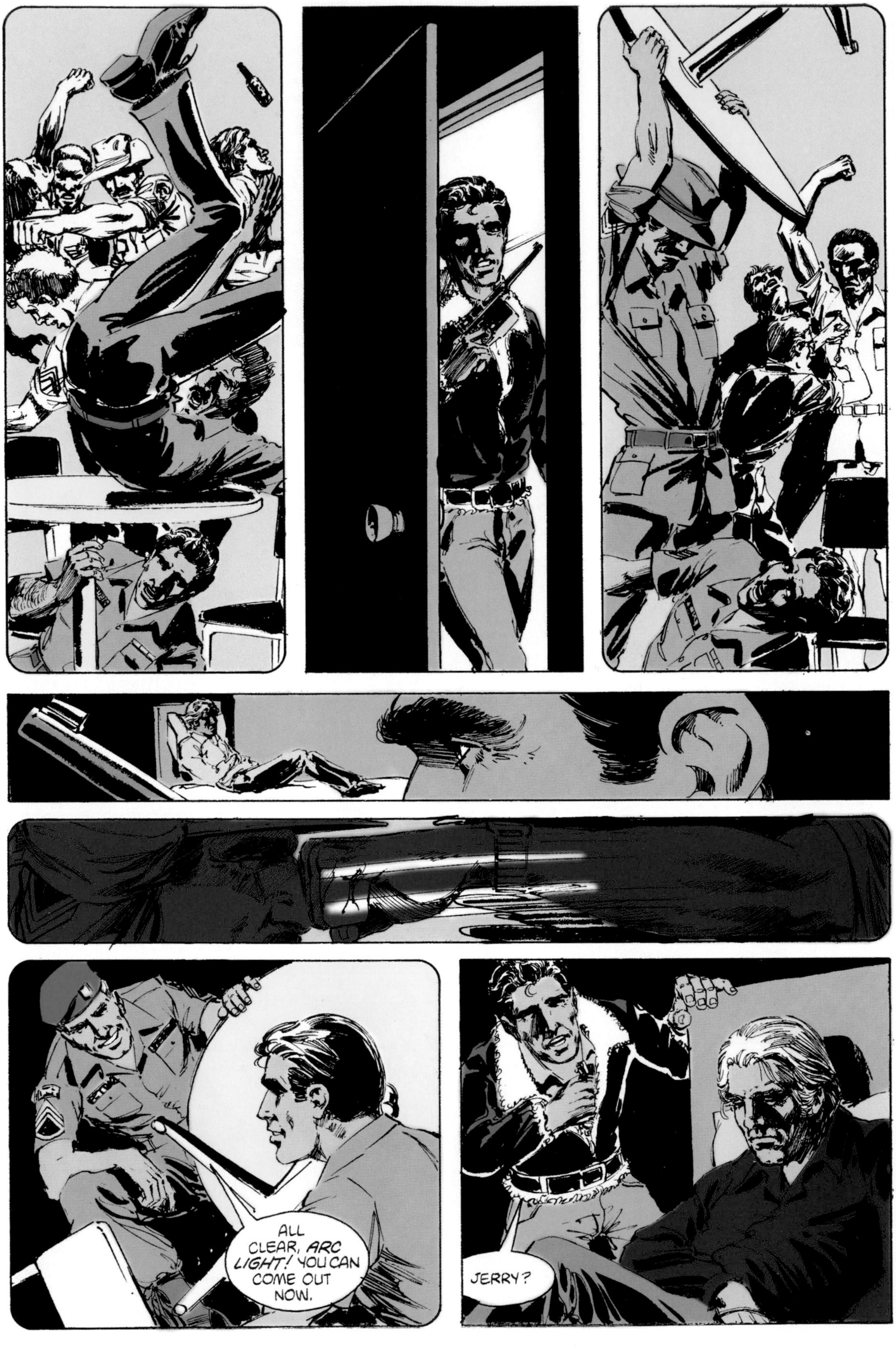
ALL CLEAR, ARC LIGHT! YOU CAN COME OUT NOW.
JERRY?

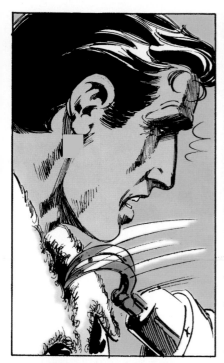

JERRY! FOR GOD'S SAKE, IT'S ME!

JON SABLE!

ARC LIGHT? WHAT THE HELL?

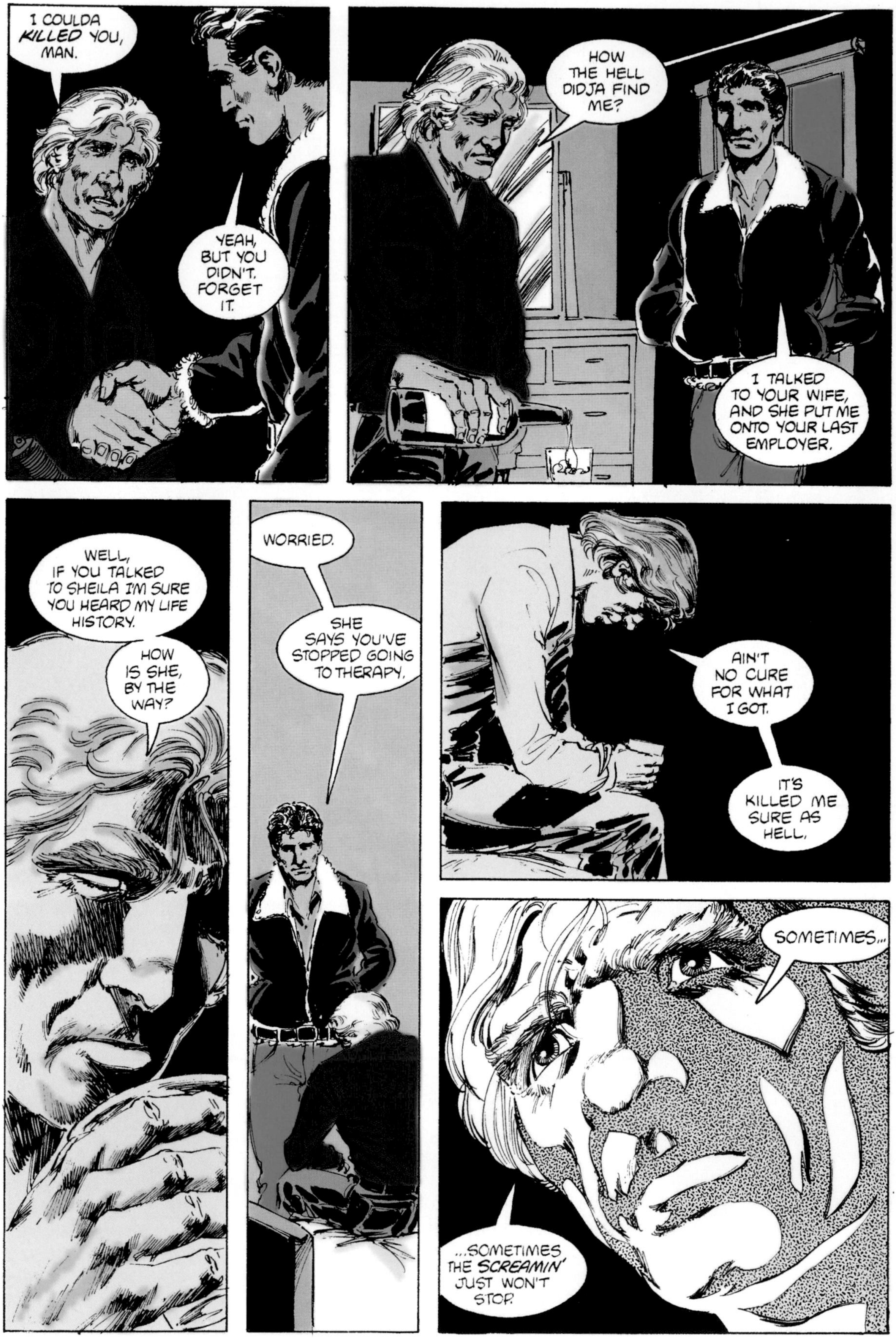
I COULDA KILLED YOU, MAN.
YEAH, BUT YOU DIDN'T. FORGET IT.
HOW THE HELL DIDJA FIND ME?
I TALKED TO YOUR WIFE, AND SHE PUT ME ONTO YOUR LAST EMPLOYER.
WELL, IF YOU TALKED TO SHEILA I'M SURE YOU HEARD MY LIFE HISTORY.
HOW IS SHE, BY THE WAY?
WORRIED.
SHE SAYS YOU'VE STOPPED GOING TO THERAPY.
AIN'T NO CURE FOR WHAT I GOT.
IT'S KILLED ME SURE AS HELL.
SOMETIMES...
...SOMETIMES THE SCREAMIN' JUST WON'T STOP.

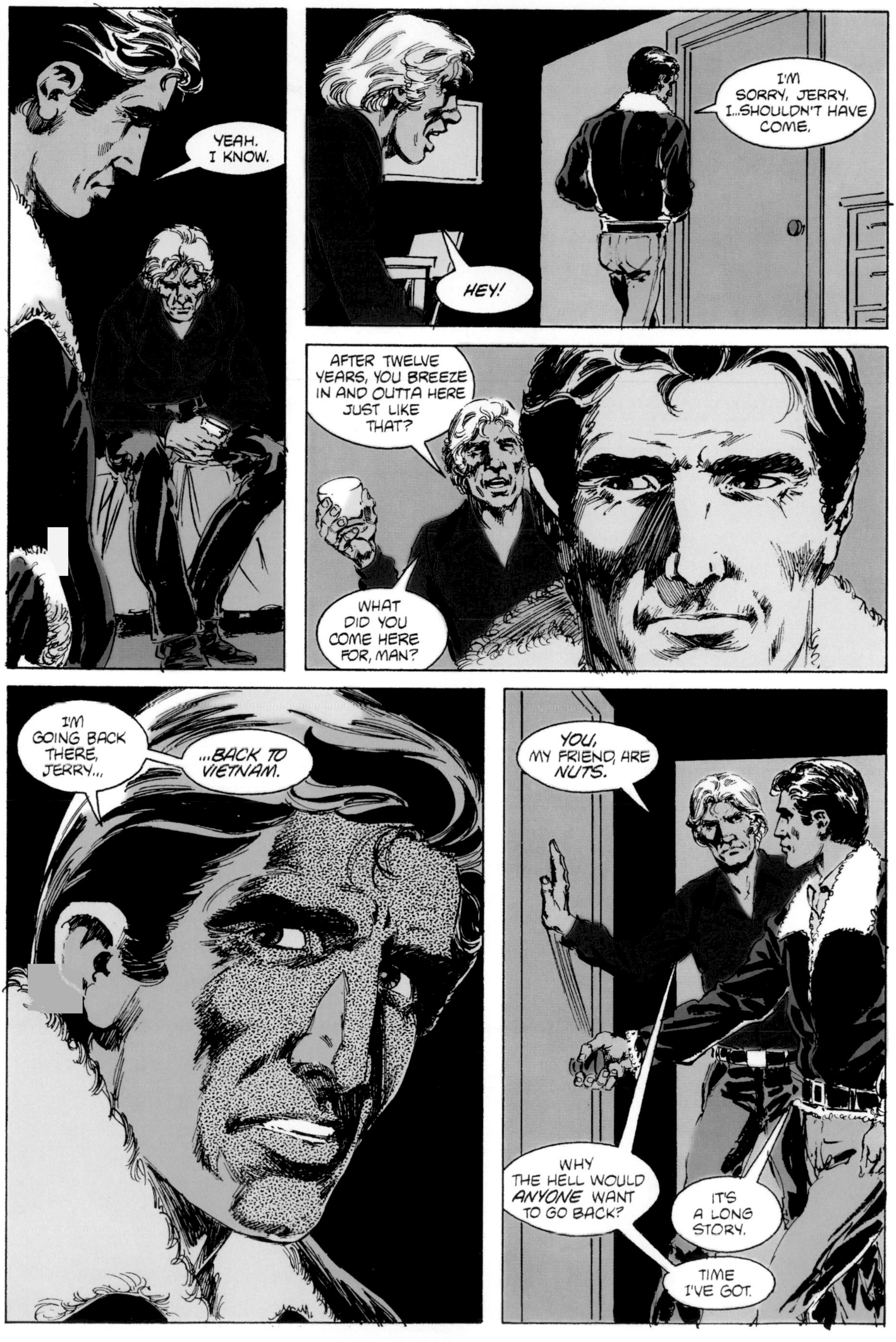

YEAH. I KNOW.
HEY!
I'M SORRY, JERRY. I...SHOULDN'T HAVE COME.
AFTER TWELVE YEARS, YOU BREEZE IN AND OUTTA HERE JUST LIKE THAT?
WHAT DID YOU COME HERE FOR, MAN?
I'M GOING BACK THERE, JERRY...
...BACK TO VIETNAM.
YOU, MY FRIEND, ARE NUTS.
WHY THE HELL WOULD ANYONE WANT TO GO BACK?
IT'S A LONG STORY.
TIME I'VE GOT.

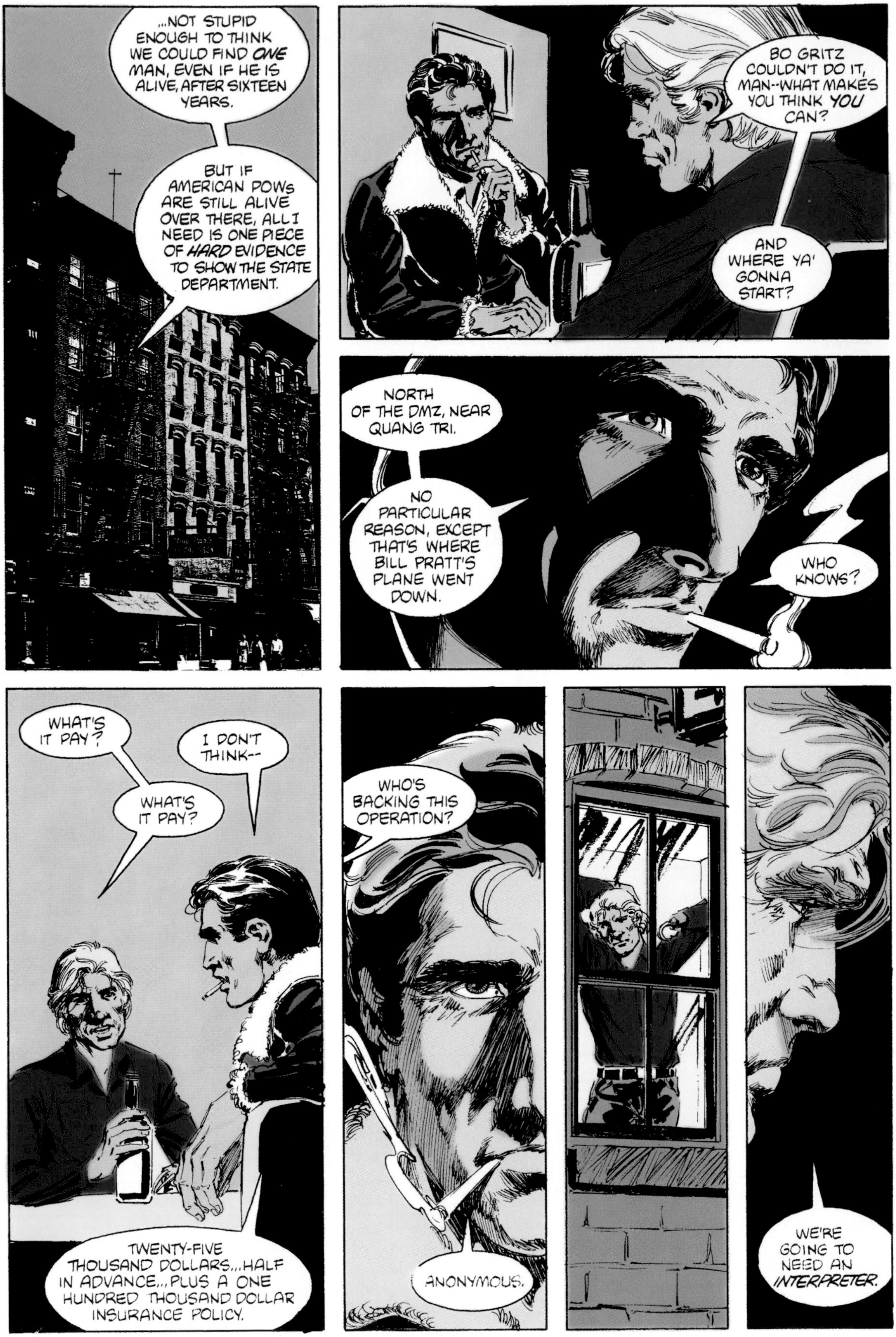
...NOT STUPID ENOUGH TO THINK WE COULD FIND ONE MAN, EVEN IF HE IS ALIVE, AFTER SIXTEEN YEARS.
BUT IF AMERICAN POWs ARE STILL ALIVE OVER THERE, ALL I NEED IS ONE PIECE OF HARD EVIDENCE TO SHOW THE STATE DEPARTMENT.
BO GRITZ COULDN'T DO IT, MAN--WHAT MAKES YOU THINK YOU CAN?
AND WHERE YA' GONNA START?
NORTH OF THE DMZ, NEAR QUANG TRI.
NO PARTICULAR REASON, EXCEPT THAT'S WHERE BILL PRATT'S PLANE WENT DOWN.
WHO KNOWS?
WHAT'S IT PAY?
I DON'T THINK--
WHAT'S IT PAY?
TWENTY-FIVE THOUSAND DOLLARS... HALF IN ADVANCE... PLUS A ONE HUNDRED THOUSAND DOLLAR INSURANCE POLICY.
WHO'S BACKING THIS OPERATION?
ANONYMOUS.
WE'RE GOING TO NEED AN INTERPRETER.

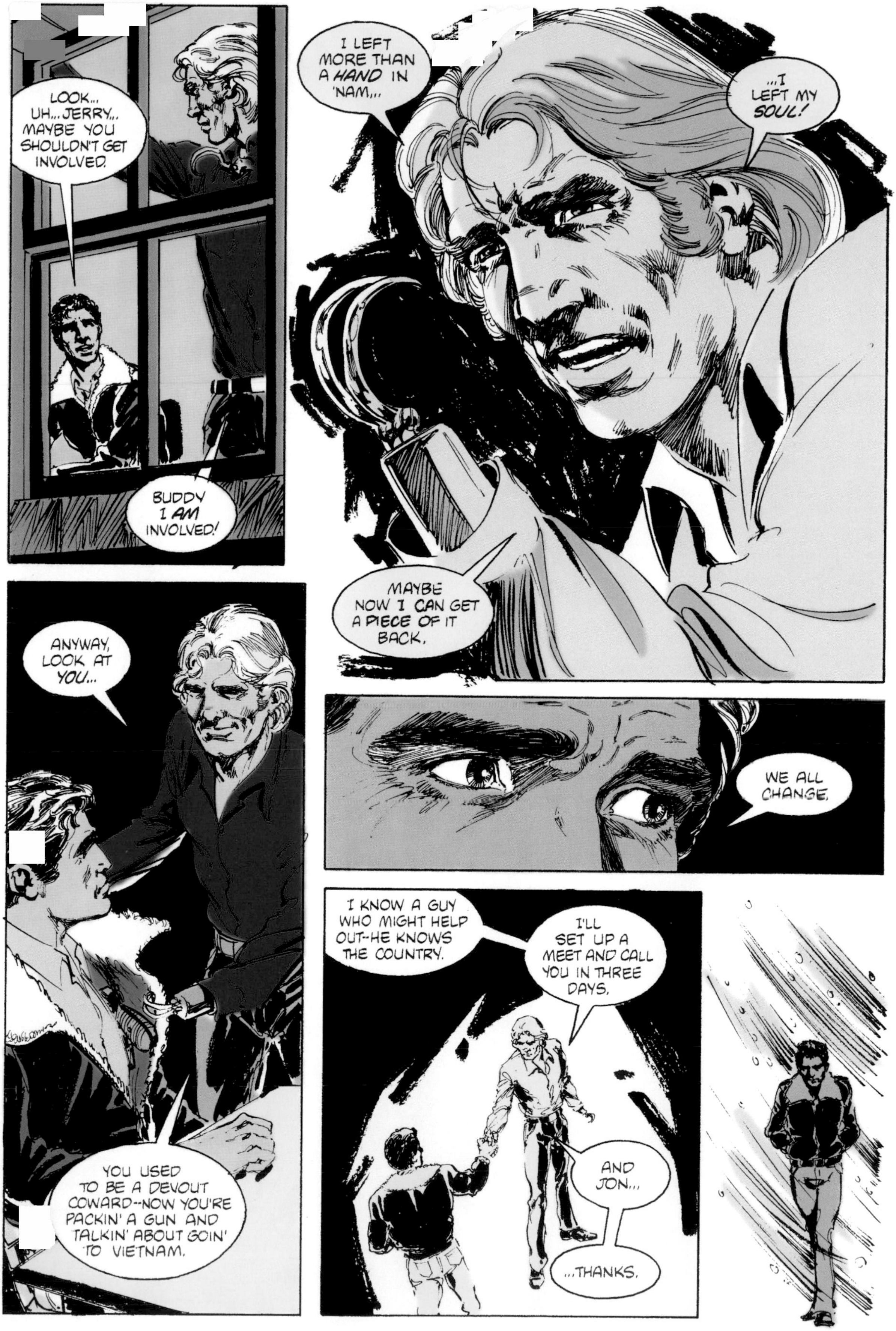
LOOK... UH... JERRY... MAYBE YOU SHOULDN'T GET INVOLVED.
BUDDY I AM INVOLVED!
I LEFT MORE THAN A HAND IN 'NAM...
...I LEFT MY SOUL!
MAYBE NOW I CAN GET A PIECE OF IT BACK.
ANYWAY, LOOK AT YOU...
YOU USED TO BE A DEVOUT COWARD--NOW YOU'RE PACKIN' A GUN AND TALKIN' ABOUT GOIN' TO VIETNAM.
WE ALL CHANGE.
I KNOW A GUY WHO MIGHT HELP OUT--HE KNOWS THE COUNTRY.
I'LL SET UP A MEET AND CALL YOU IN THREE DAYS.
AND JON...
...THANKS.

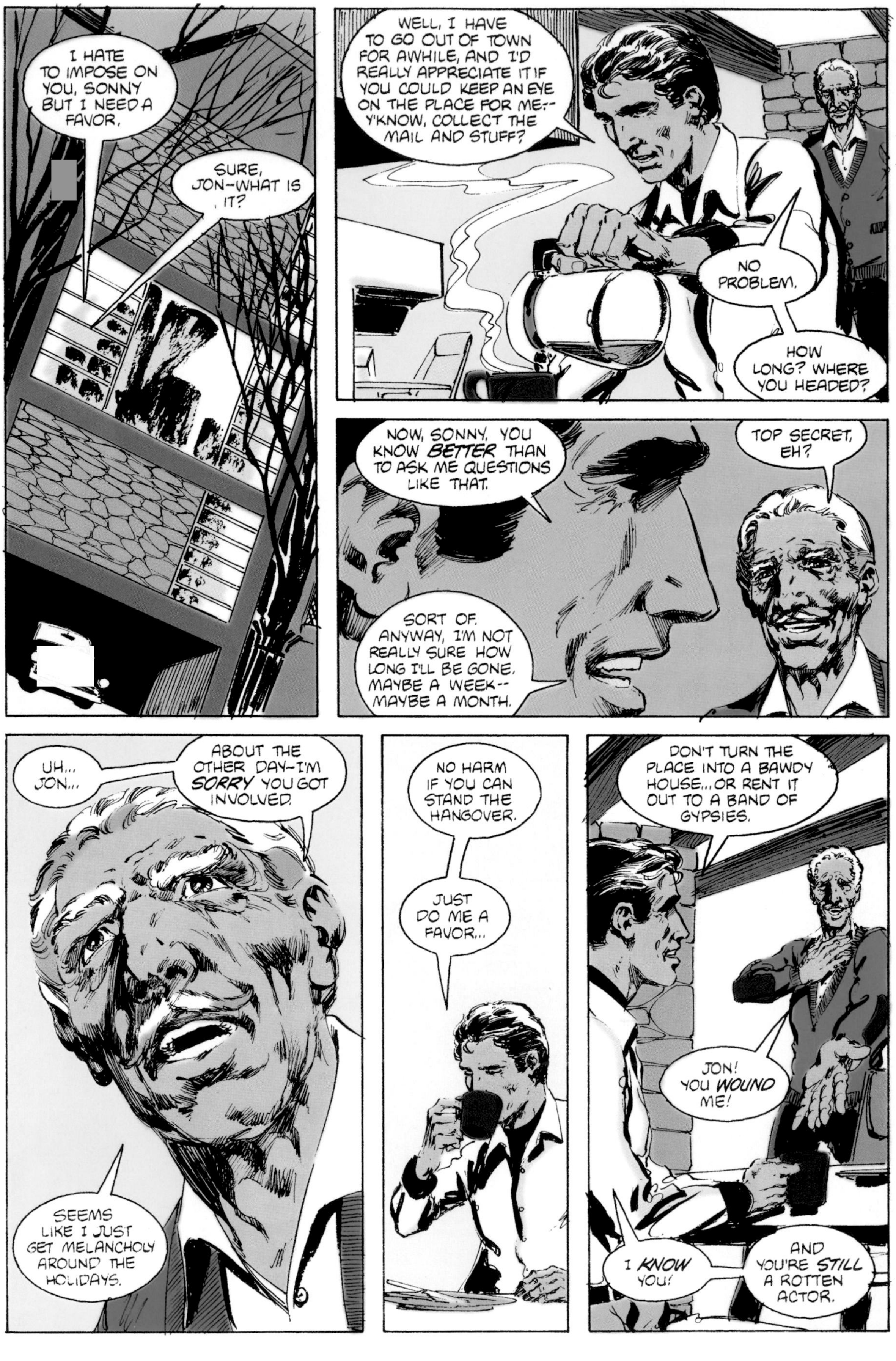
I HATE TO IMPOSE ON YOU, SONNY BUT I NEED A FAVOR.
SURE, JON--WHAT IS IT?
WELL, I HAVE TO GO OUT OF TOWN FOR AWHILE, AND I'D REALLY APPRECIATE IT IF YOU COULD KEEP AN EYE ON THE PLACE FOR ME:-- Y'KNOW, COLLECT THE MAIL AND STUFF?
NO PROBLEM.
HOW LONG? WHERE YOU HEADED?
NOW, SONNY, YOU KNOW BETTER THAN TO ASK ME QUESTIONS LIKE THAT.
TOP SECRET, EH?
SORT OF. ANYWAY, I'M NOT REALLY SURE HOW LONG I'LL BE GONE. MAYBE A WEEK-- MAYBE A MONTH.
UH... JON...
ABOUT THE OTHER DAY--I'M SORRY YOU GOT INVOLVED.
SEEMS LIKE I JUST GET MELANCHOLY AROUND THE HOLIDAYS.
NO HARM IF YOU CAN STAND THE HANGOVER.
JUST DO ME A FAVOR...
DON'T TURN THE PLACE INTO A BAWDY HOUSE...OR RENT IT OUT TO A BAND OF GYPSIES.
JON! YOU WOUND ME!
I KNOW YOU!
AND YOU'RE STILL A ROTTEN ACTOR.

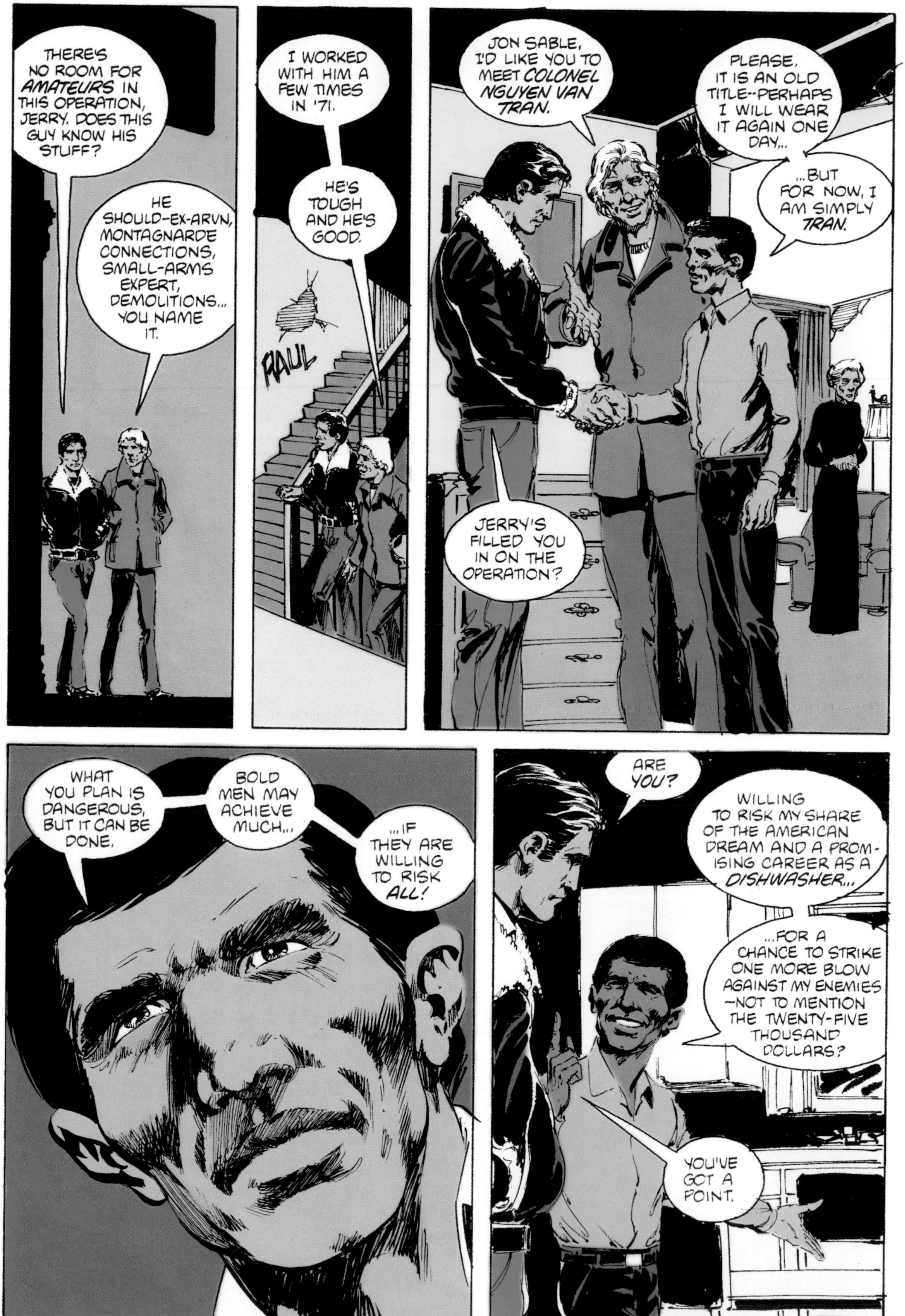
THERE'S NO ROOM FOR AMATEURS IN THIS OPERATION, JERRY. DOES THIS GUY KNOW HIS STUFF?
HE SHOULD--EX-ARVN, MONTAGNARDE CONNECTIONS, SMALL-ARMS EXPERT, DEMOLITIONS... YOU NAME IT.
I WORKED WITH HIM A FEW TIMES IN '71.
HE'S TOUGH AND HE'S GOOD.
RAUL
JON SABLE, I'D LIKE YOU TO MEET COLONEL NGUYEN VAN TRAN.
PLEASE. IT IS AN OLD TITLE--PERHAPS I WILL WEAR IT AGAIN ONE DAY...
...BUT FOR NOW, I AM SIMPLY TRAN.
JERRY'S FILLED YOU IN ON THE OPERATION?
WHAT YOU PLAN IS DANGEROUS, BUT IT CAN BE DONE.
BOLD MEN MAY ACHIEVE MUCH...
...IF THEY ARE WILLING TO RISK ALL!
ARE YOU?
WILLING TO RISK MY SHARE OF THE AMERICAN DREAM AND A PROMISING CAREER AS A DISHWASHER...
...FOR A CHANCE TO STRIKE ONE MORE BLOW AGAINST MY ENEMIES --NOT TO MENTION THE TWENTY-FIVE THOUSAND DOLLARS?
YOU'VE GOT A POINT.

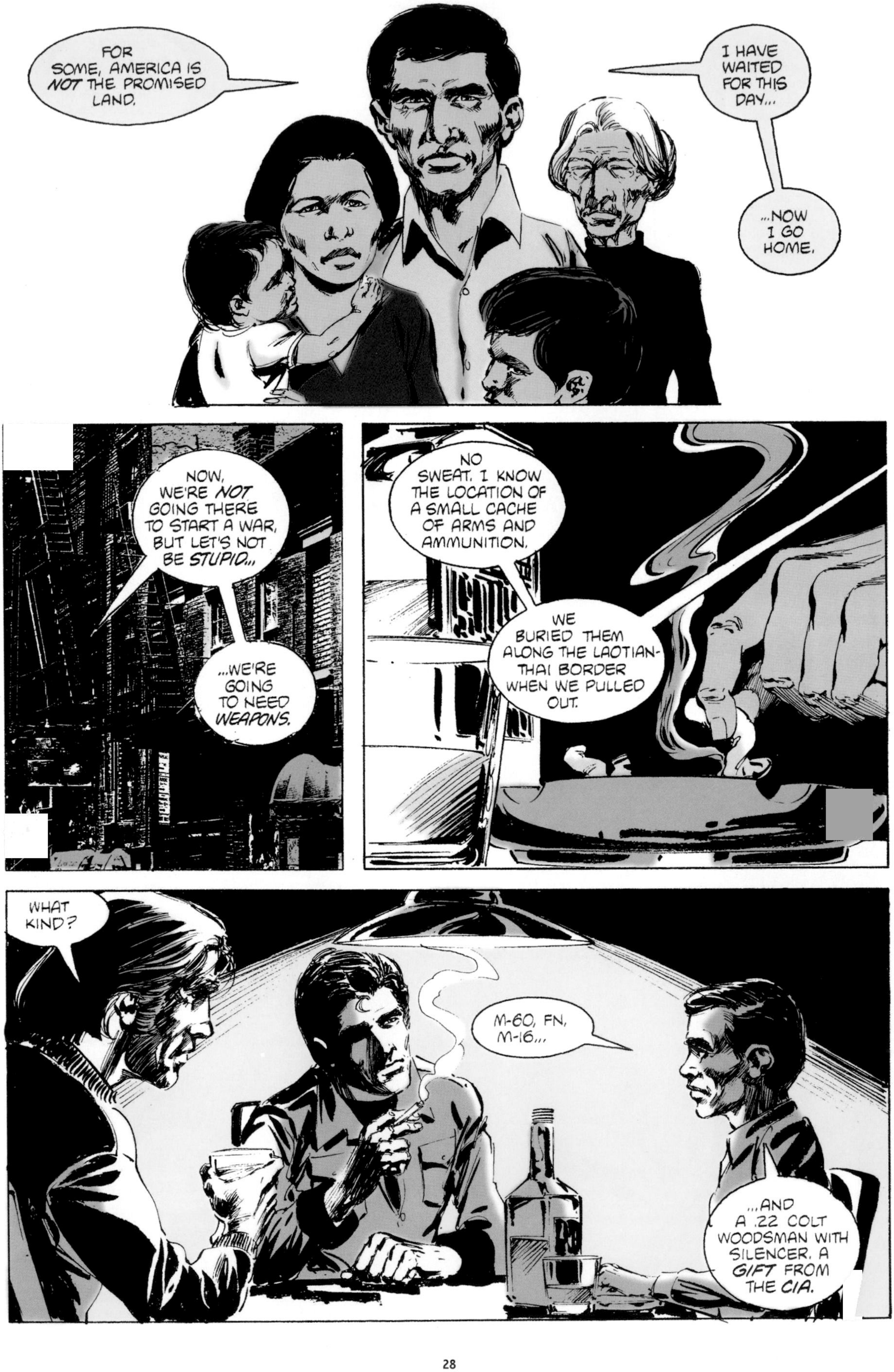
FOR SOME, AMERICA IS NOT THE PROMISED LAND.
I HAVE WAITED FOR THIS DAY...
...NOW I GO HOME.
NOW, WE'RE NOT GOING THERE TO START A WAR, BUT LET'S NOT BE STUPID...
...WE'RE GOING TO NEED WEAPONS.
NO SWEAT. I KNOW THE LOCATION OF A SMALL CACHE OF ARMS AND AMMUNITION.
WE BURIED THEM ALONG THE LAOTIAN-THAI BORDER WHEN WE PULLED OUT.
WHAT KIND?
M-60, FN, M-16...
...AND A .22 COLT WOODSMAN WITH SILENCER. A GIFT FROM THE CIA.

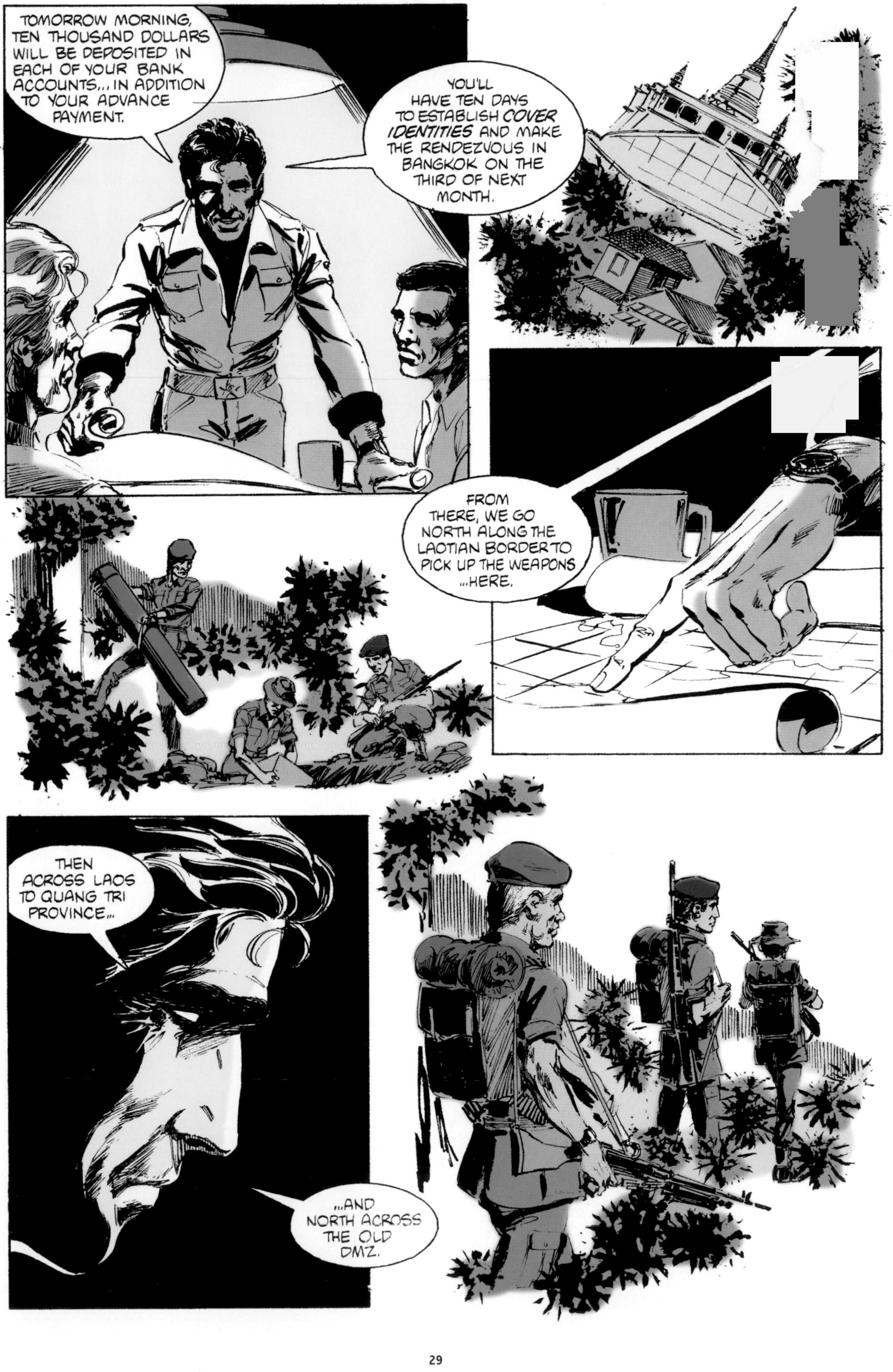
TOMORROW MORNING, TEN THOUSAND DOLLARS WILL BE DEPOSITED IN EACH OF YOUR BANK ACCOUNTS... IN ADDITION TO YOUR ADVANCE PAYMENT.
YOU'LL HAVE TEN DAYS TO ESTABLISH *COVER IDENTITIES* AND MAKE THE RENDEZVOUS IN BANGKOK ON THE THIRD OF NEXT MONTH.
FROM THERE, WE GO NORTH ALONG THE LAOTIAN BORDER TO PICK UP THE WEAPONS ...HERE.
THEN ACROSS LAOS TO QUANG TRI PROVINCE...
...AND NORTH ACROSS THE OLD DMZ.

JUST FOR THE SAKE OF ARGUMENT... NOT THAT IT'S LIKELY TO COME UP...

...HOW DO WE GET *OUT?*

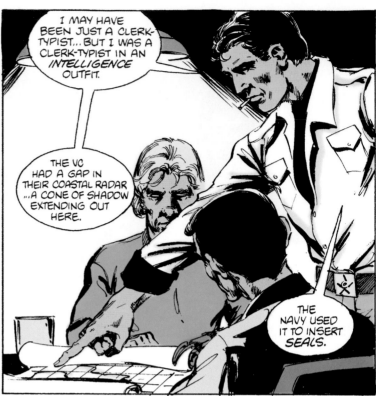

I MAY HAVE BEEN JUST A CLERK-TYPIST... BUT I WAS A CLERK-TYPIST IN AN *INTELLIGENCE* OUTFIT.

THE VC HAD A GAP IN THEIR COASTAL RADAR ...A CONE OF SHADOW EXTENDING OUT HERE.

THE NAVY USED IT TO INSERT *SEALS.*

OUR PICK-UP IS A FISHING BOAT OUT OF HONG KONG.

IT WILL BE WAITING A MILE OFF THE COAST, EVERY THIRD NIGHT, FROM 2200 TO 0100, BEGINNING ON THE FIFTEENTH.

ALL FOR ONE AND ONE FOR ALL?

EVERY MAN FOR HIMSELF.

LA CHAIM.

WHAT HAPPENS IF THEY'VE *FILLED* THAT GAP?

YEAH, *WHAT?*

THEN WE MIGHT AS WELL KEEP SWIMMING.

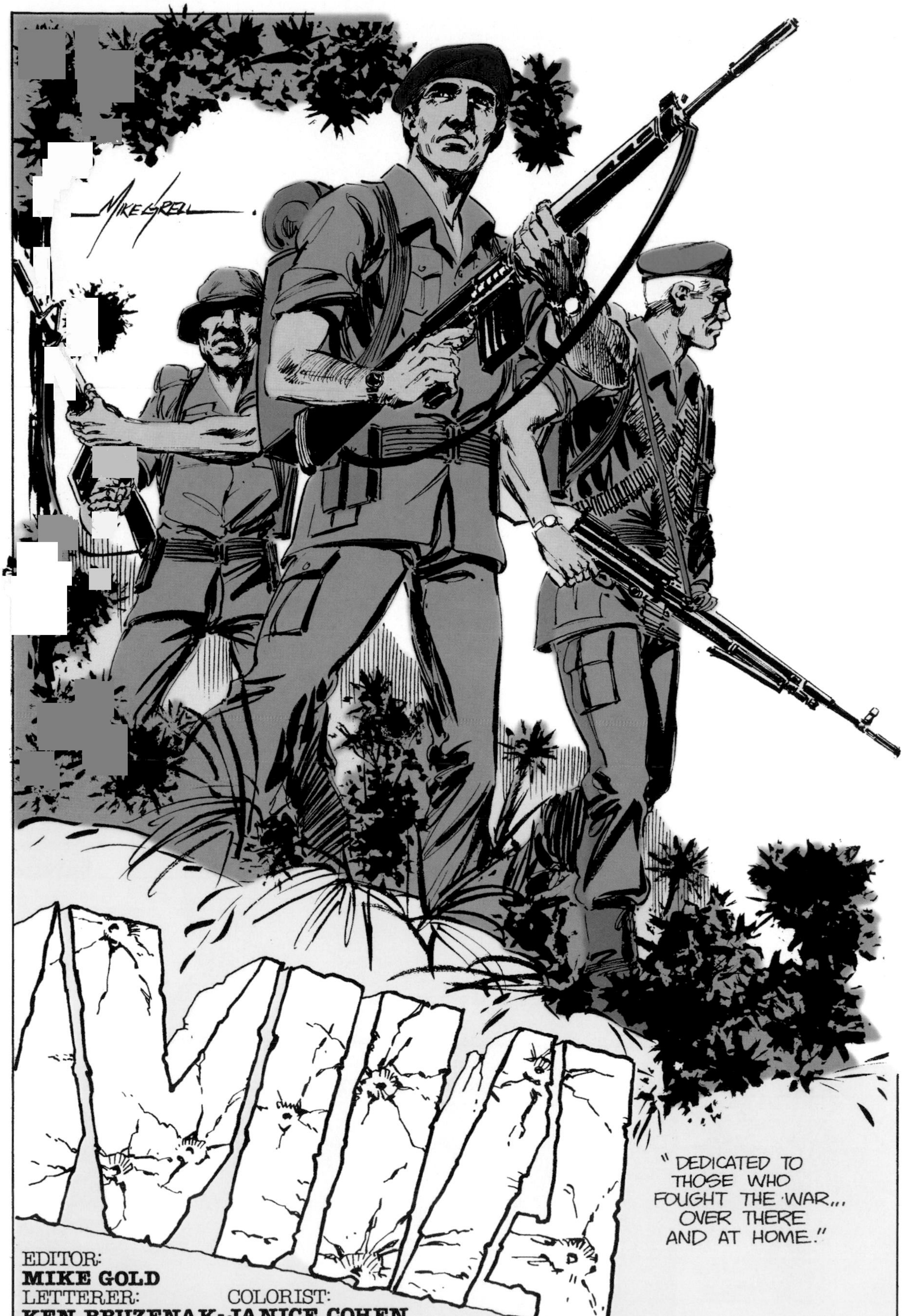
"DEDICATED TO THOSE WHO FOUGHT THE WAR... OVER THERE AND AT HOME."
EDITOR:
MIKE GOLD
LETTERER: COLORIST:
KEN BRUZENAK-JANICE COHEN

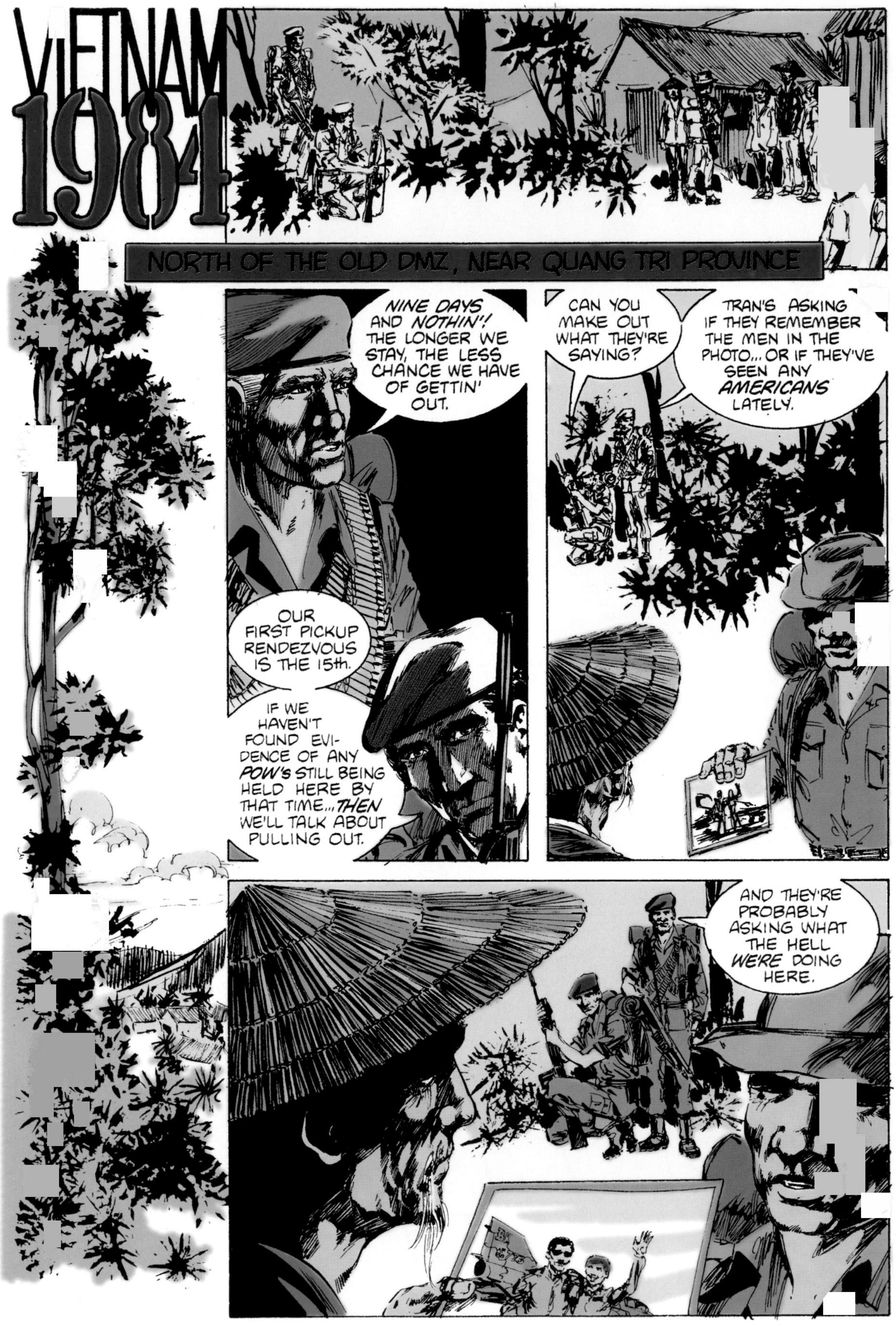

VIETNAM 1984
NORTH OF THE OLD DMZ, NEAR QUANG TRI PROVINCE
NINE DAYS AND NOTHIN'! THE LONGER WE STAY, THE LESS CHANCE WE HAVE OF GETTIN' OUT.
OUR FIRST PICKUP RENDEZVOUS IS THE 15th.
IF WE HAVEN'T FOUND EVI-DENCE OF ANY POW's STILL BEING HELD HERE BY THAT TIME... THEN WE'LL TALK ABOUT PULLING OUT.
CAN YOU MAKE OUT WHAT THEY'RE SAYING?
TRAN'S ASKING IF THEY REMEMBER THE MEN IN THE PHOTO... OR IF THEY'VE SEEN ANY AMERICANS LATELY.
AND THEY'RE PROBABLY ASKING WHAT THE HELL WE'RE DOING HERE.

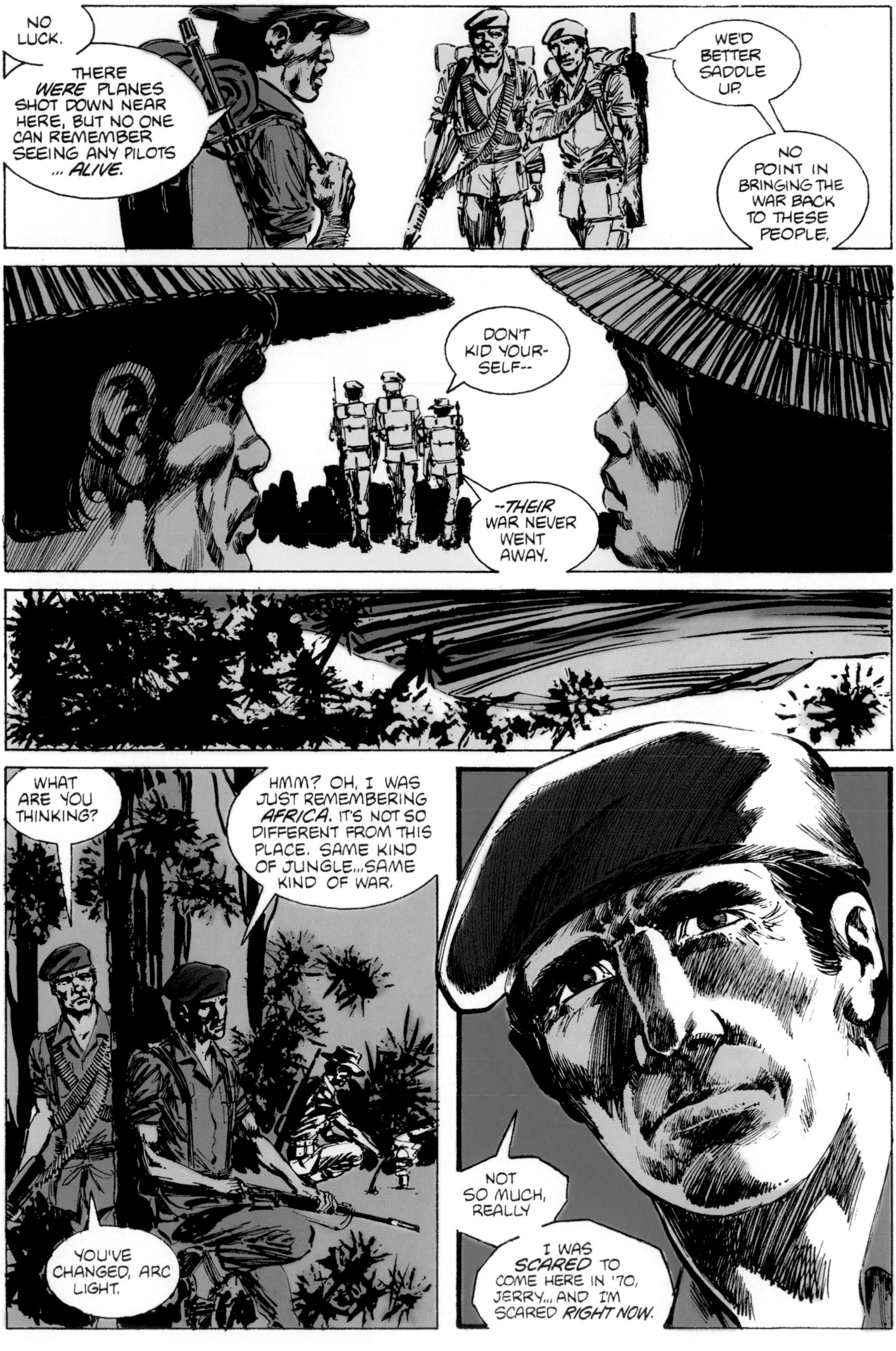

NO LUCK.
THERE *WERE* PLANES SHOT DOWN NEAR HERE, BUT NO ONE CAN REMEMBER SEEING ANY PILOTS ... *ALIVE*.
WE'D BETTER SADDLE UP.
NO POINT IN BRINGING THE WAR BACK TO THESE PEOPLE.
DON'T KID YOURSELF--
--*THEIR* WAR NEVER WENT AWAY.
WHAT ARE YOU THINKING?
HMM? OH, I WAS JUST REMEMBERING *AFRICA*. IT'S NOT SO DIFFERENT FROM THIS PLACE. SAME KIND OF JUNGLE...SAME KIND OF WAR.
YOU'VE CHANGED, ARC LIGHT.
NOT SO MUCH, REALLY
I WAS *SCARED* TO COME HERE IN '70, JERRY... AND I'M SCARED *RIGHT NOW*.

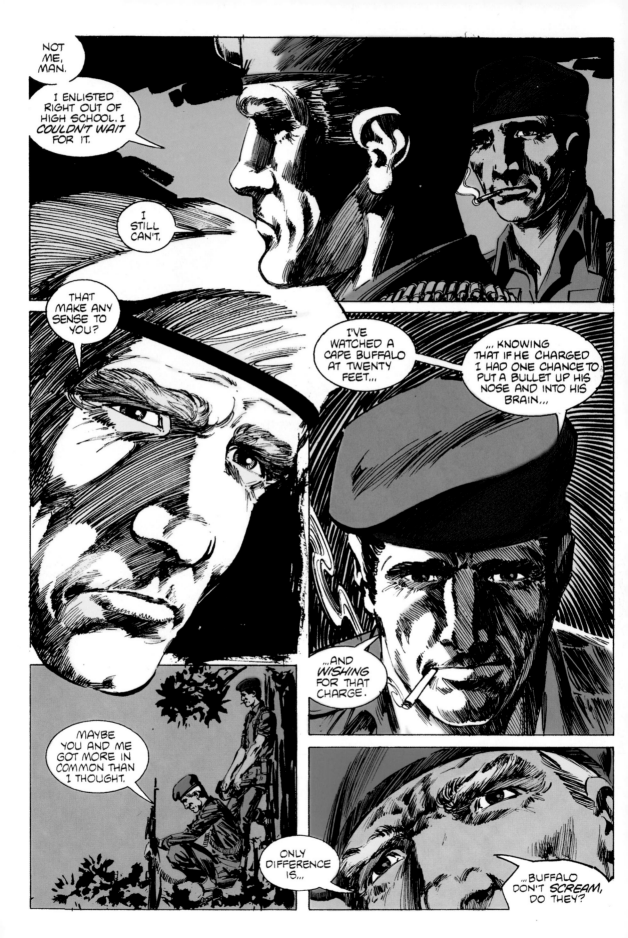

NOT ME, MAN.

I ENLISTED RIGHT OUT OF HIGH SCHOOL. I *COULDN'T WAIT* FOR IT.

I STILL CAN'T.

THAT MAKE ANY SENSE TO YOU?

I'VE WATCHED A CAPE BUFFALO AT TWENTY FEET...

... KNOWING THAT IF HE CHARGED I HAD ONE CHANCE TO PUT A BULLET UP HIS NOSE AND INTO HIS BRAIN...

...AND *WISHING* FOR THAT CHARGE.

MAYBE YOU AND ME GOT MORE IN COMMON THAN I THOUGHT.

ONLY DIFFERENCE IS...

...BUFFALO DON'T *SCREAM*, DO THEY?

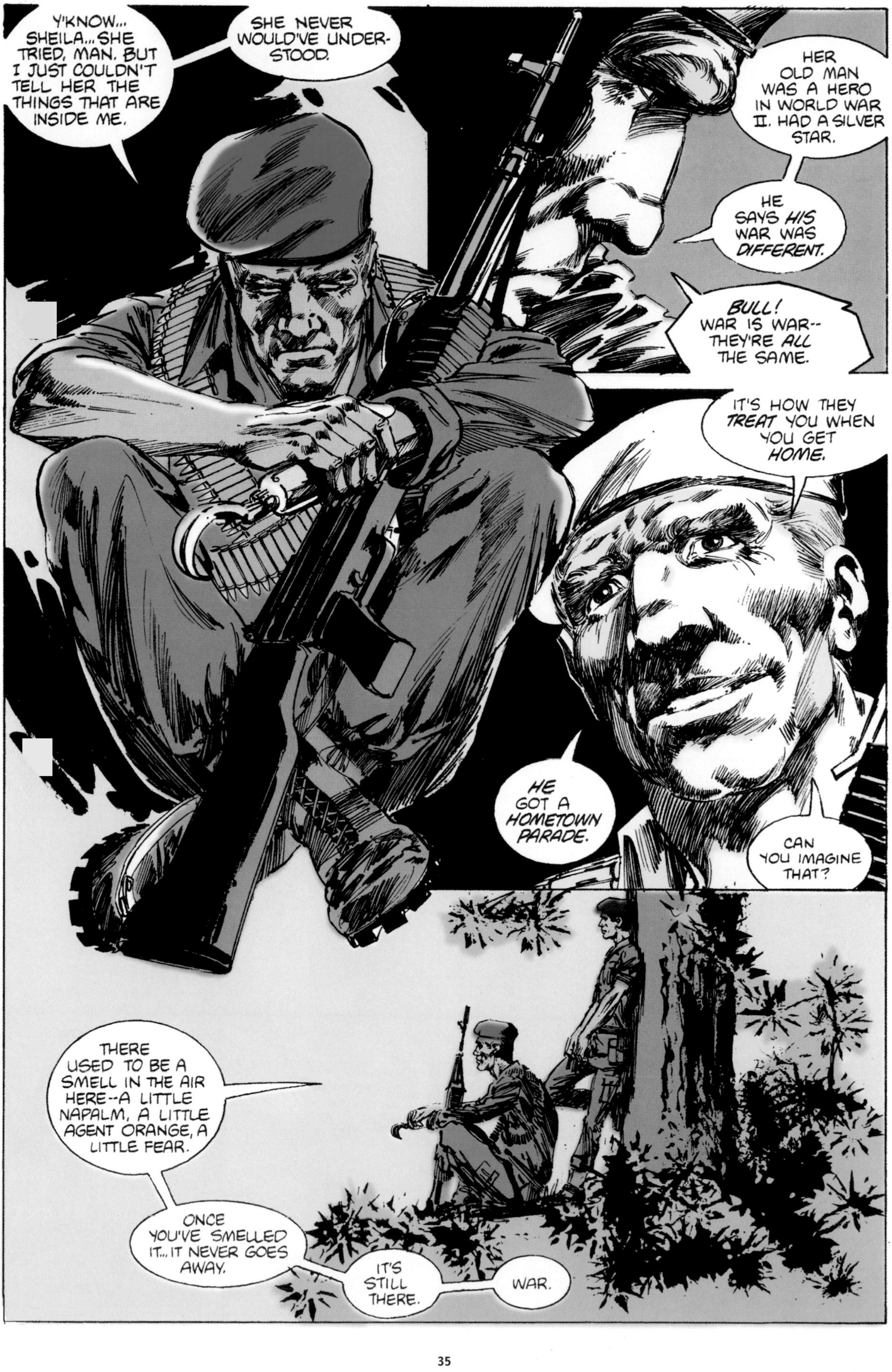
Y'KNOW... SHEILA... SHE TRIED, MAN. BUT I JUST COULDN'T TELL HER THE THINGS THAT ARE INSIDE ME.
SHE NEVER WOULD'VE UNDER-STOOD.
HER OLD MAN WAS A HERO IN WORLD WAR II. HAD A SILVER STAR.
HE SAYS HIS WAR WAS DIFFERENT.
BULL! WAR IS WAR-- THEY'RE ALL THE SAME.
IT'S HOW THEY TREAT YOU WHEN YOU GET HOME.
HE GOT A HOMETOWN PARADE.
CAN YOU IMAGINE THAT?
THERE USED TO BE A SMELL IN THE AIR HERE--A LITTLE NAPALM, A LITTLE AGENT ORANGE, A LITTLE FEAR.
ONCE YOU'VE SMELLED IT... IT NEVER GOES AWAY.
IT'S STILL THERE.
WAR.

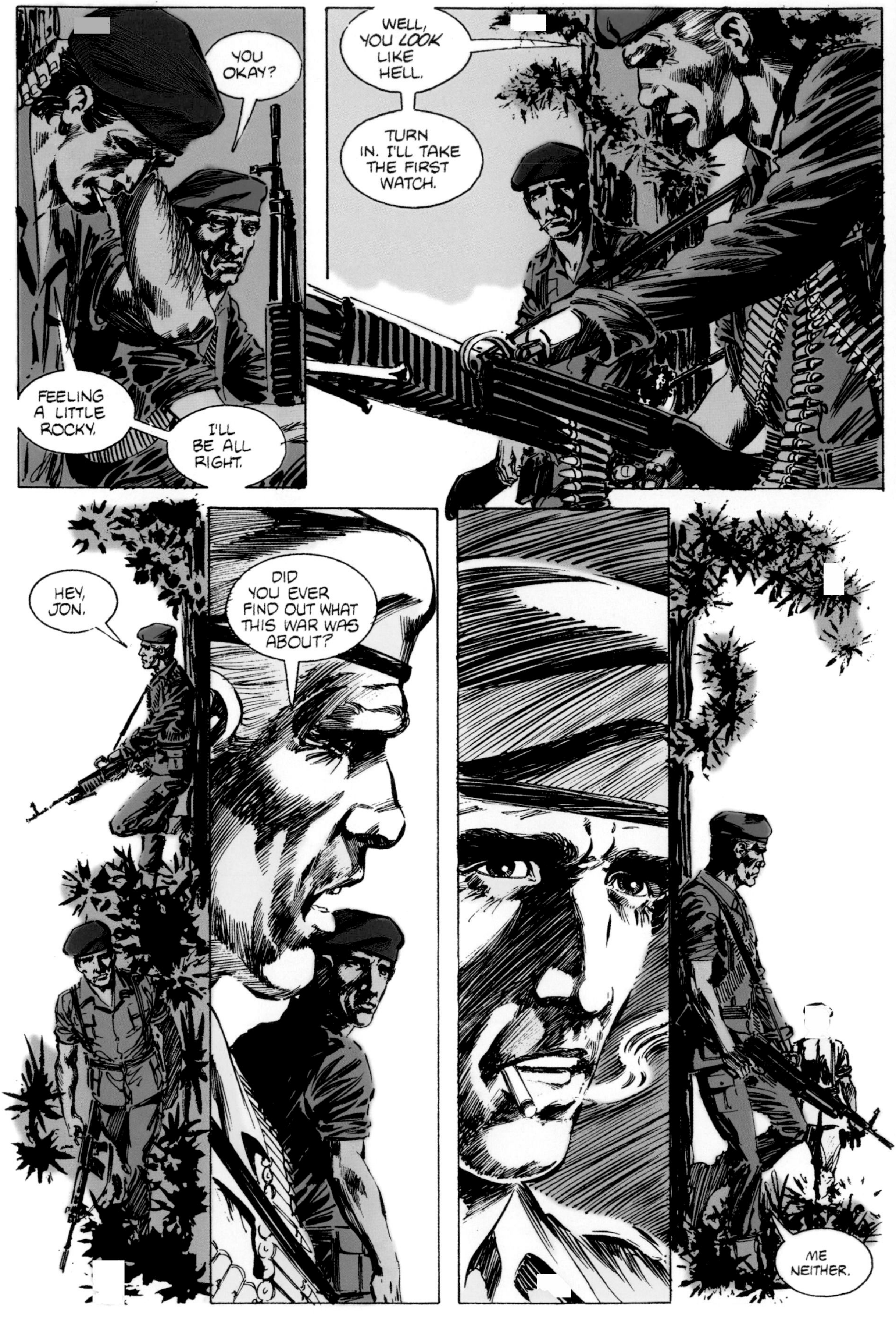

YOU OKAY?
FEELING A LITTLE ROCKY.
I'LL BE ALL RIGHT.
WELL, YOU LOOK LIKE HELL.
TURN IN. I'LL TAKE THE FIRST WATCH.
HEY, JON.
DID YOU EVER FIND OUT WHAT THIS WAR WAS ABOUT?
ME NEITHER.

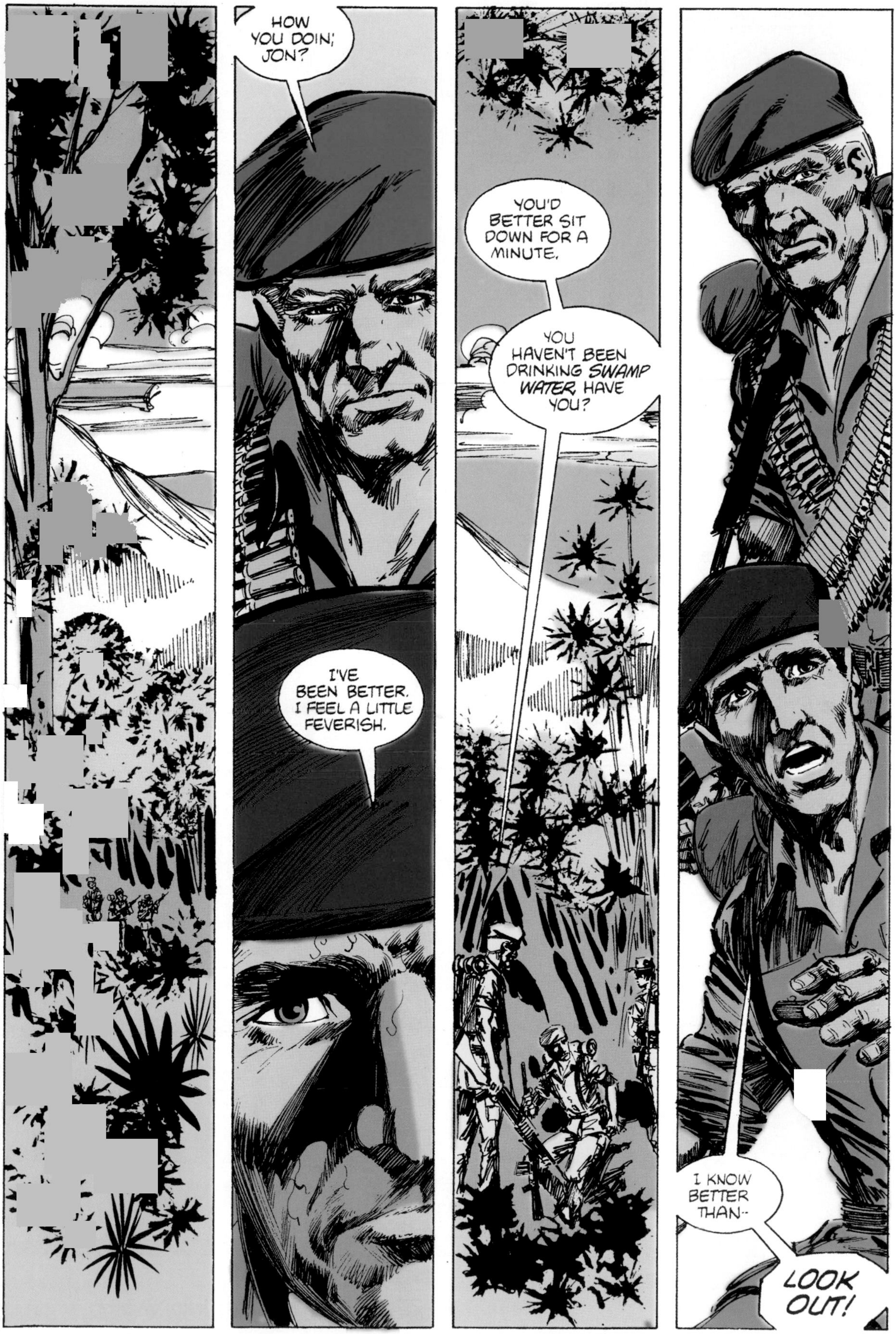
HOW YOU DOIN', JON?
I'VE BEEN BETTER. I FEEL A LITTLE FEVERISH.
YOU'D BETTER SIT DOWN FOR A MINUTE.
YOU HAVEN'T BEEN DRINKING *SWAMP WATER*, HAVE YOU?
I KNOW BETTER THAN--
LOOK OUT!

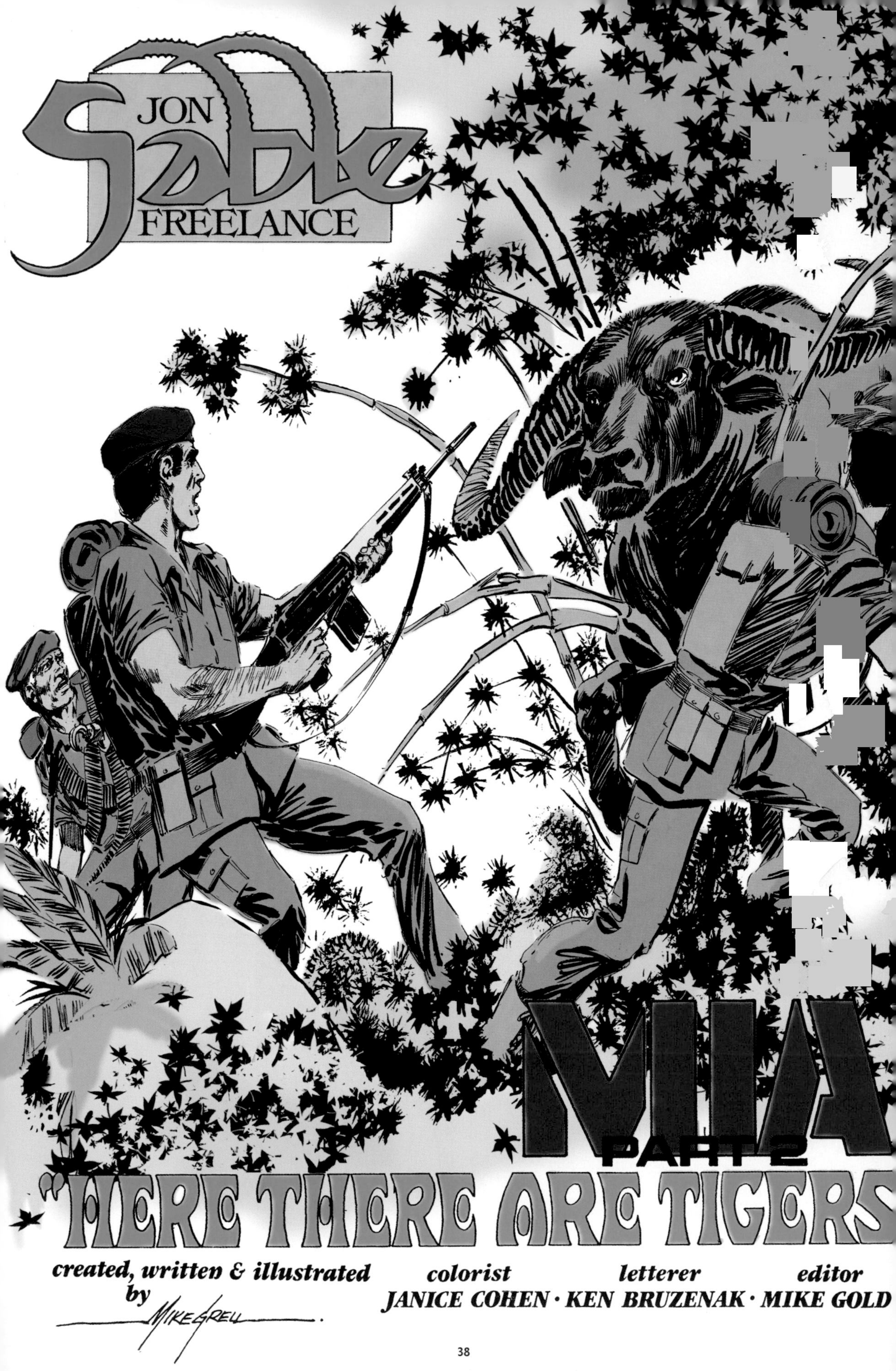
JON SABLE FREELANCE
MIA
PART 2
"HERE THERE ARE TIGERS
created, written & illustrated by MIKE GRELL
colorist JANICE COHEN · letterer KEN BRUZENAK · editor MIKE GOLD

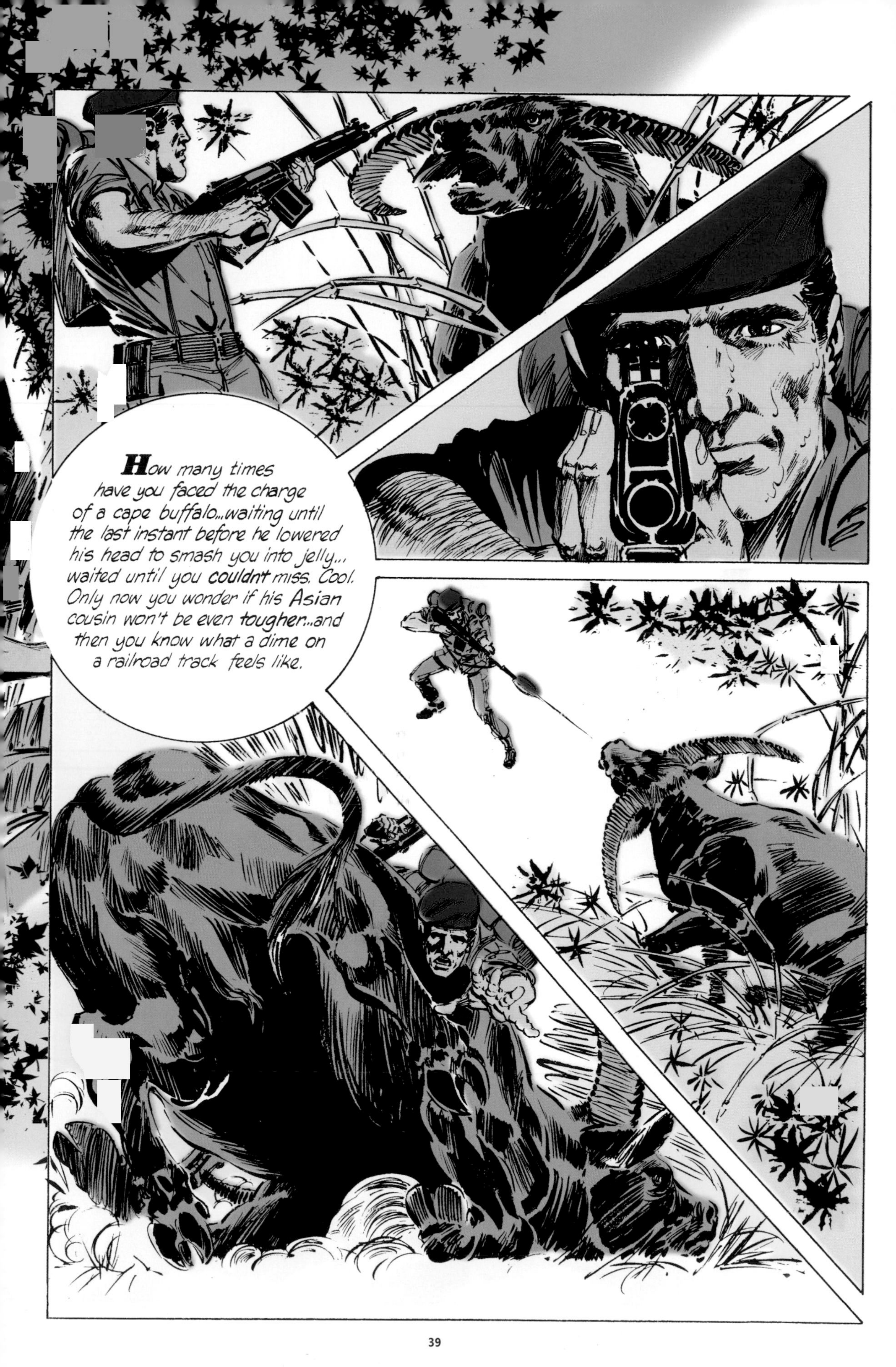
How many times have you faced the charge of a cape buffalo...waiting until the last instant before he lowered his head to smash you into jelly... waited until you couldn't miss. Cool. Only now you wonder if his Asian cousin won't be even tougher...and then you know what a dime on a railroad track feels like.

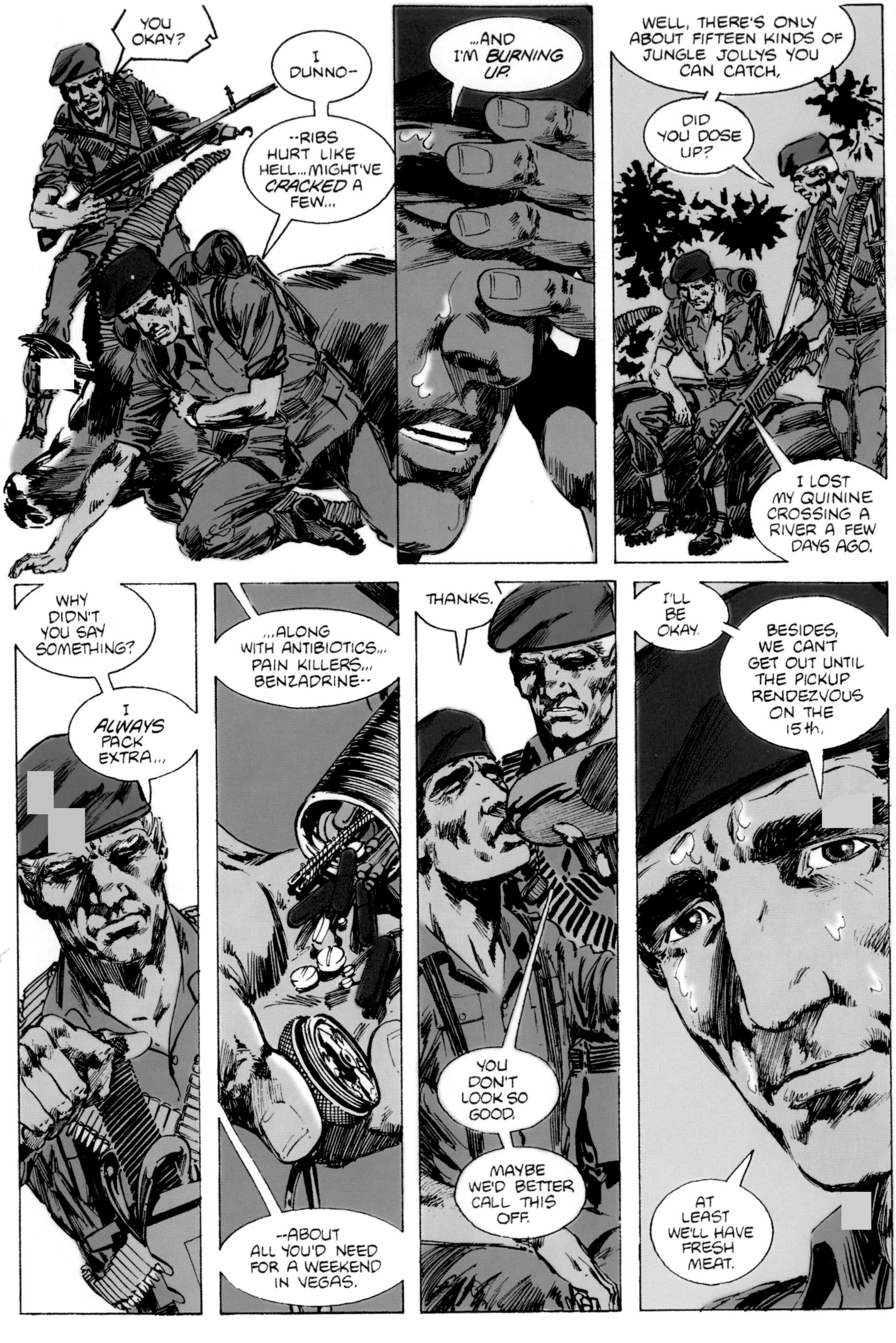
YOU OKAY?
I DUNNO--
--RIBS HURT LIKE HELL...MIGHT'VE CRACKED A FEW...
...AND I'M BURNING UP.
WELL, THERE'S ONLY ABOUT FIFTEEN KINDS OF JUNGLE JOLLYS YOU CAN CATCH.
DID YOU DOSE UP?
I LOST MY QUININE CROSSING A RIVER A FEW DAYS AGO.
WHY DIDN'T YOU SAY SOMETHING?
I ALWAYS PACK EXTRA...
...ALONG WITH ANTIBIOTICS... PAIN KILLERS... BENZADRINE--
--ABOUT ALL YOU'D NEED FOR A WEEKEND IN VEGAS.
THANKS.
YOU DON'T LOOK SO GOOD.
MAYBE WE'D BETTER CALL THIS OFF.
I'LL BE OKAY.
BESIDES, WE CAN'T GET OUT UNTIL THE PICKUP RENDEZVOUS ON THE 15th.
AT LEAST WE'LL HAVE FRESH MEAT.

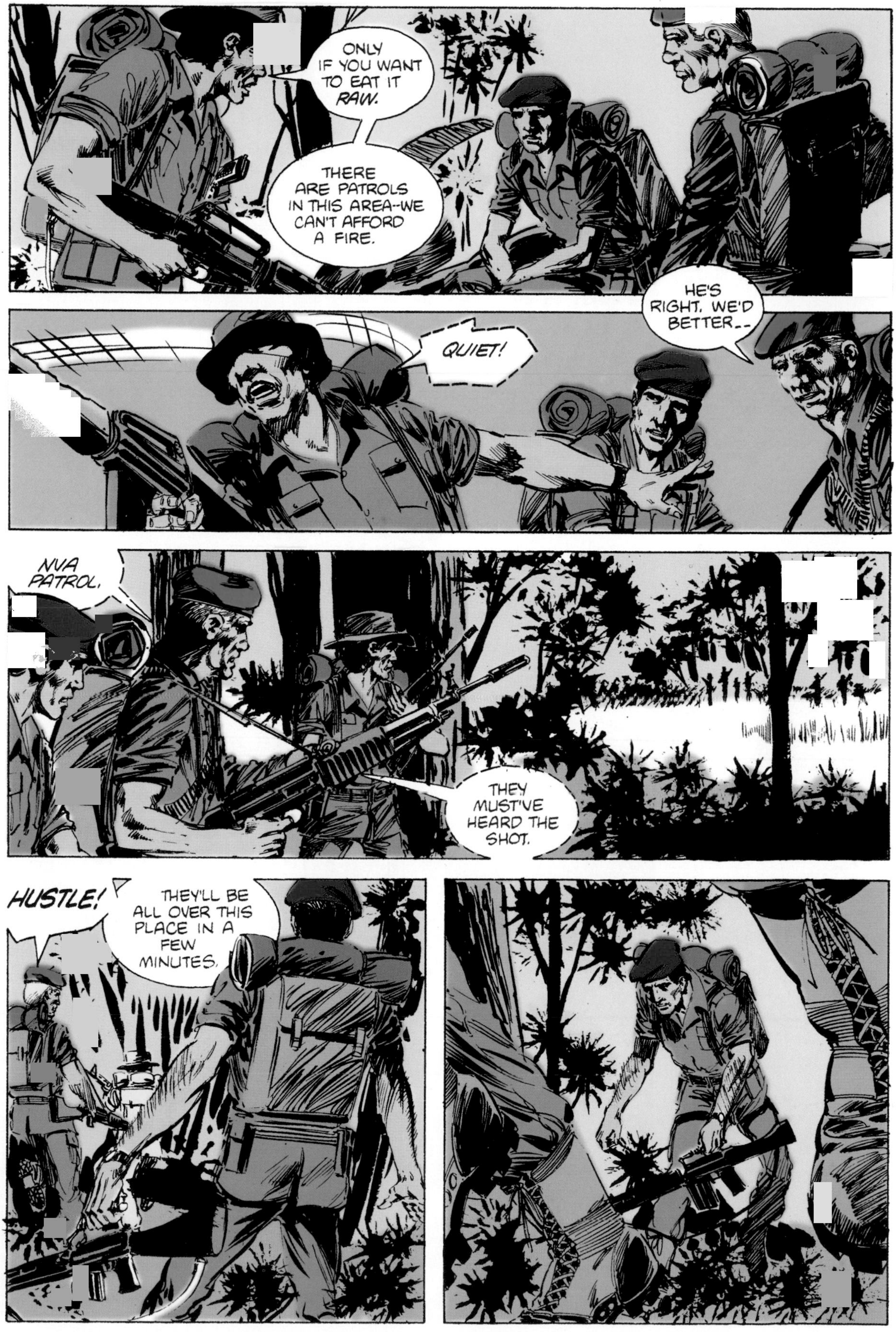

ONLY IF YOU WANT TO EAT IT RAW.
THERE ARE PATROLS IN THIS AREA--WE CAN'T AFFORD A FIRE.
HE'S RIGHT. WE'D BETTER--
QUIET!
NVA PATROL.
THEY MUST'VE HEARD THE SHOT.
HUSTLE!
THEY'LL BE ALL OVER THIS PLACE IN A FEW MINUTES.

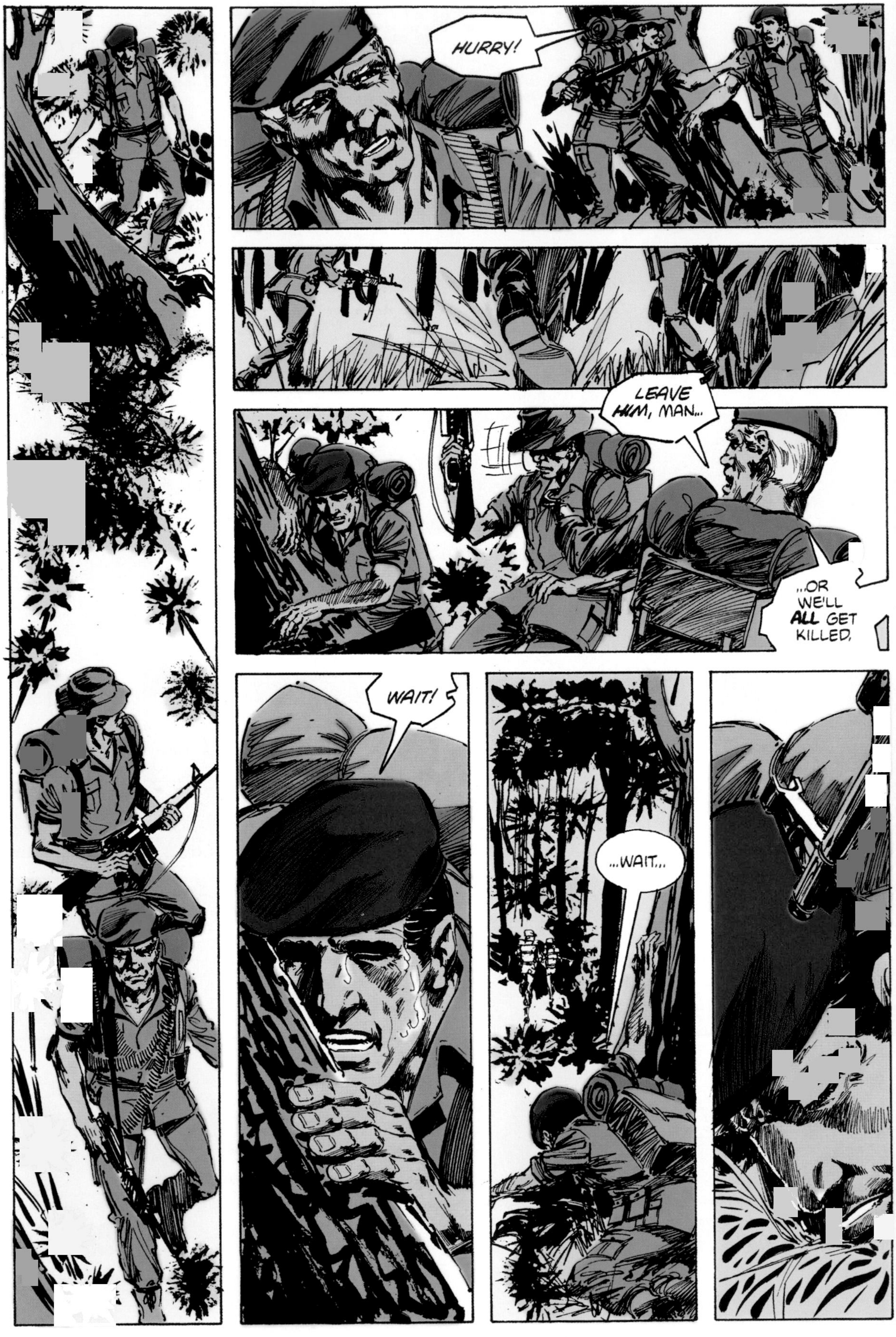
HURRY!
LEAVE HIM, MAN...
...OR WE'LL ALL GET KILLED.
WAIT!
...WAIT...

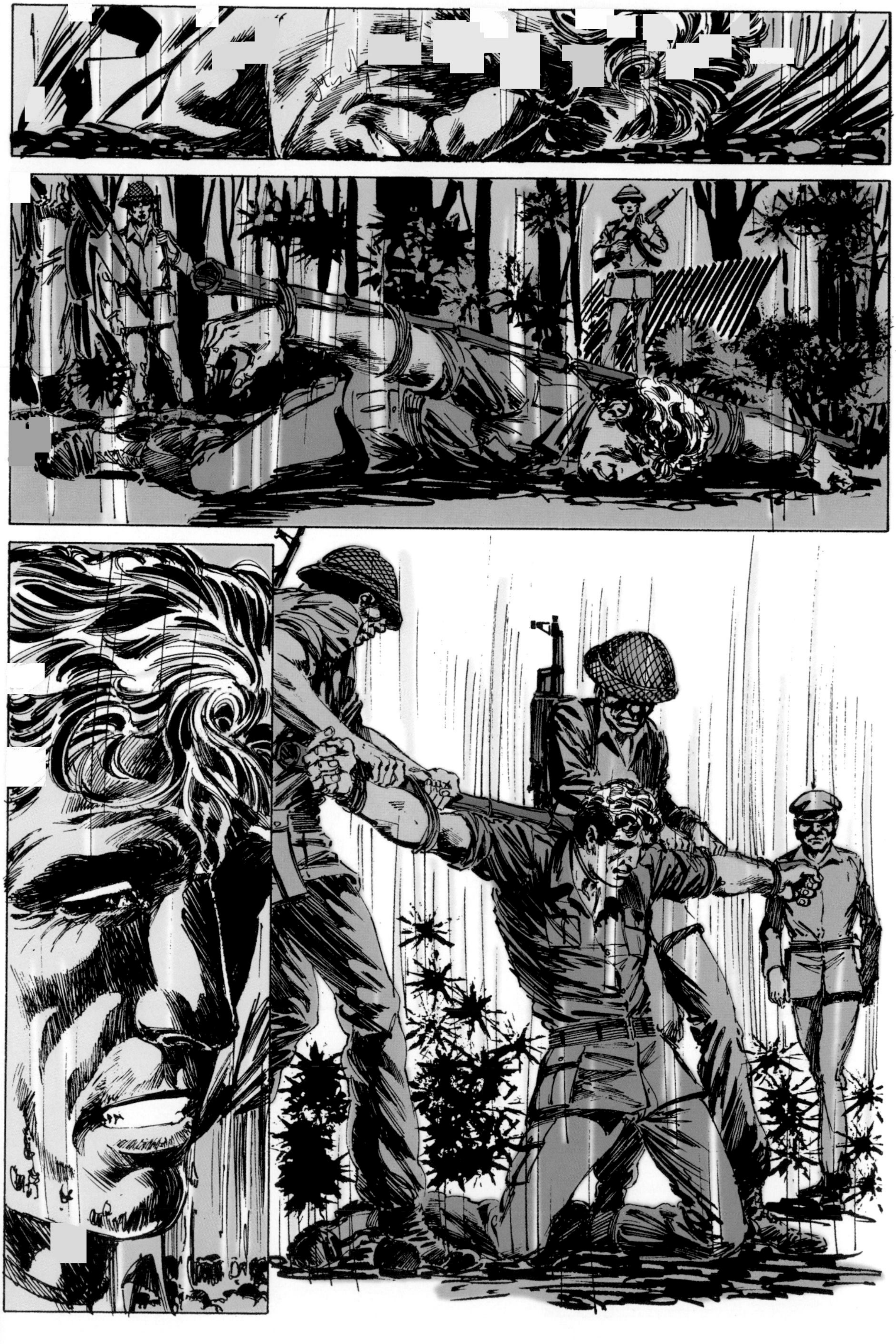

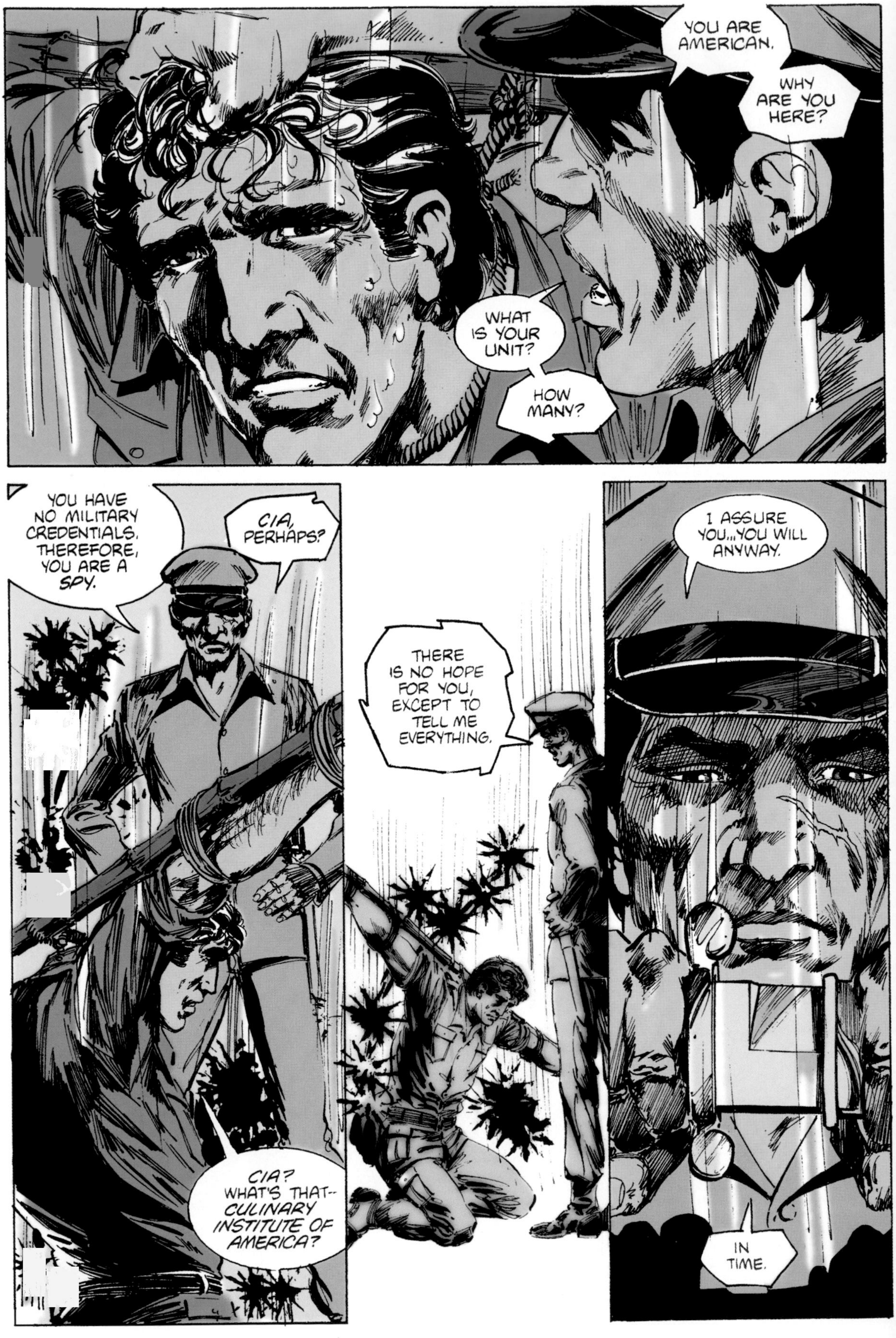
YOU ARE AMERICAN.
WHY ARE YOU HERE?
WHAT IS YOUR UNIT?
HOW MANY?
YOU HAVE NO MILITARY CREDENTIALS. THEREFORE, YOU ARE A *SPY*.
CIA, PERHAPS?
CIA? WHAT'S THAT-- *CULINARY INSTITUTE OF AMERICA?*
THERE IS NO HOPE FOR YOU, EXCEPT TO TELL ME EVERYTHING.
I ASSURE YOU... YOU WILL ANYWAY.
IN TIME.

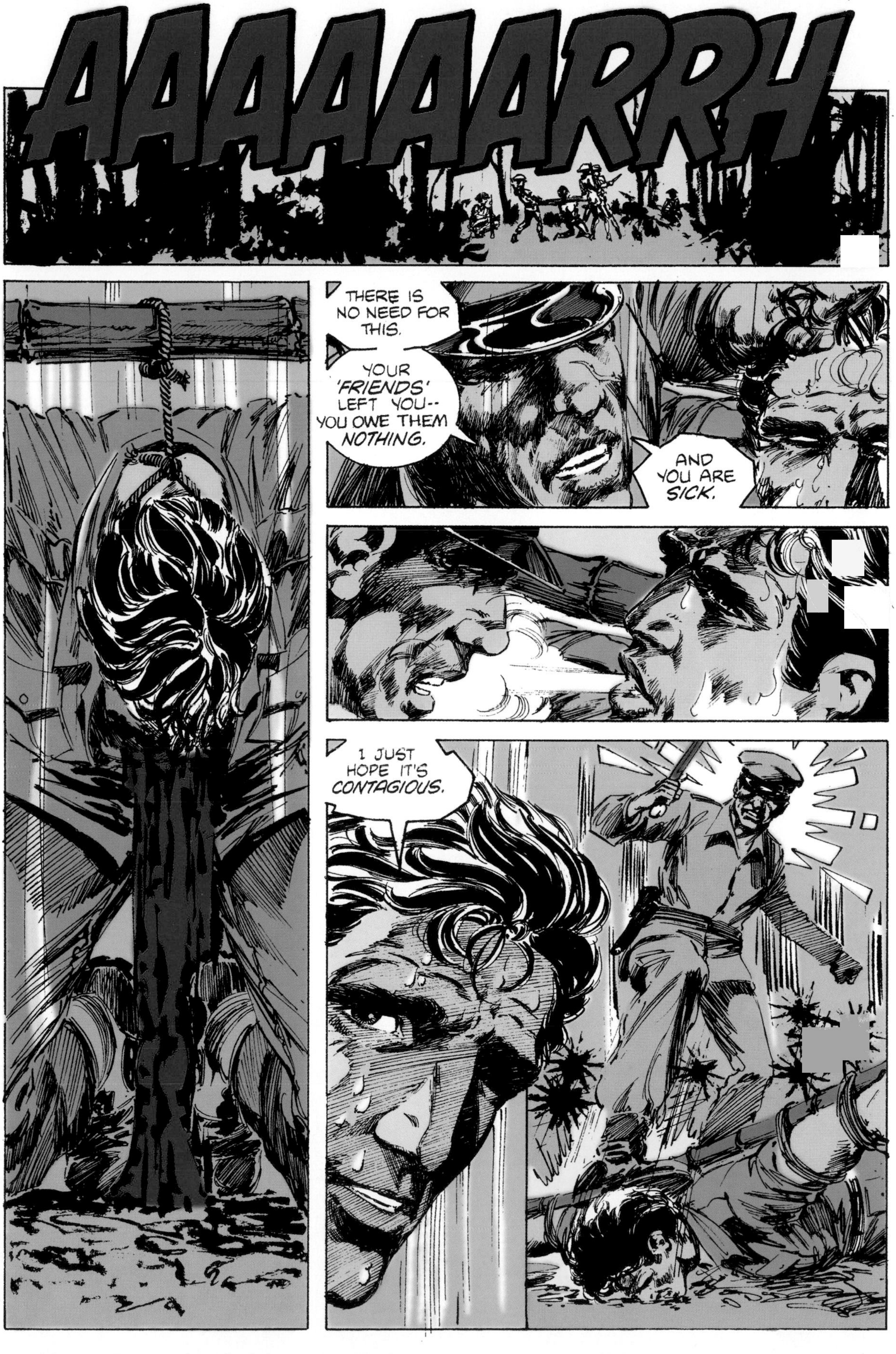
AAAAAARRH
THERE IS NO NEED FOR THIS.
YOUR 'FRIENDS' LEFT YOU-- YOU OWE THEM NOTHING.
AND YOU ARE SICK.
I JUST HOPE IT'S CONTAGIOUS.

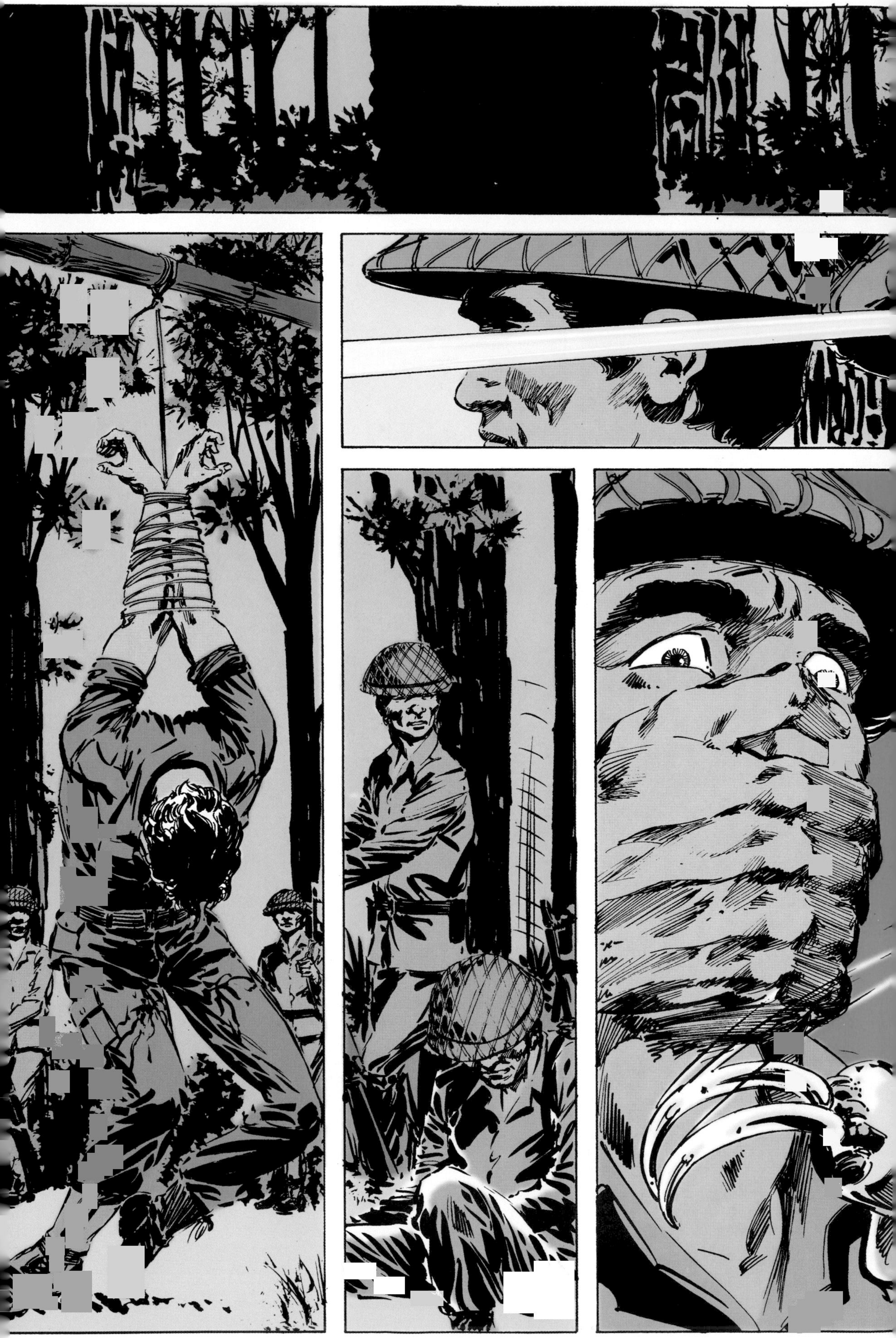

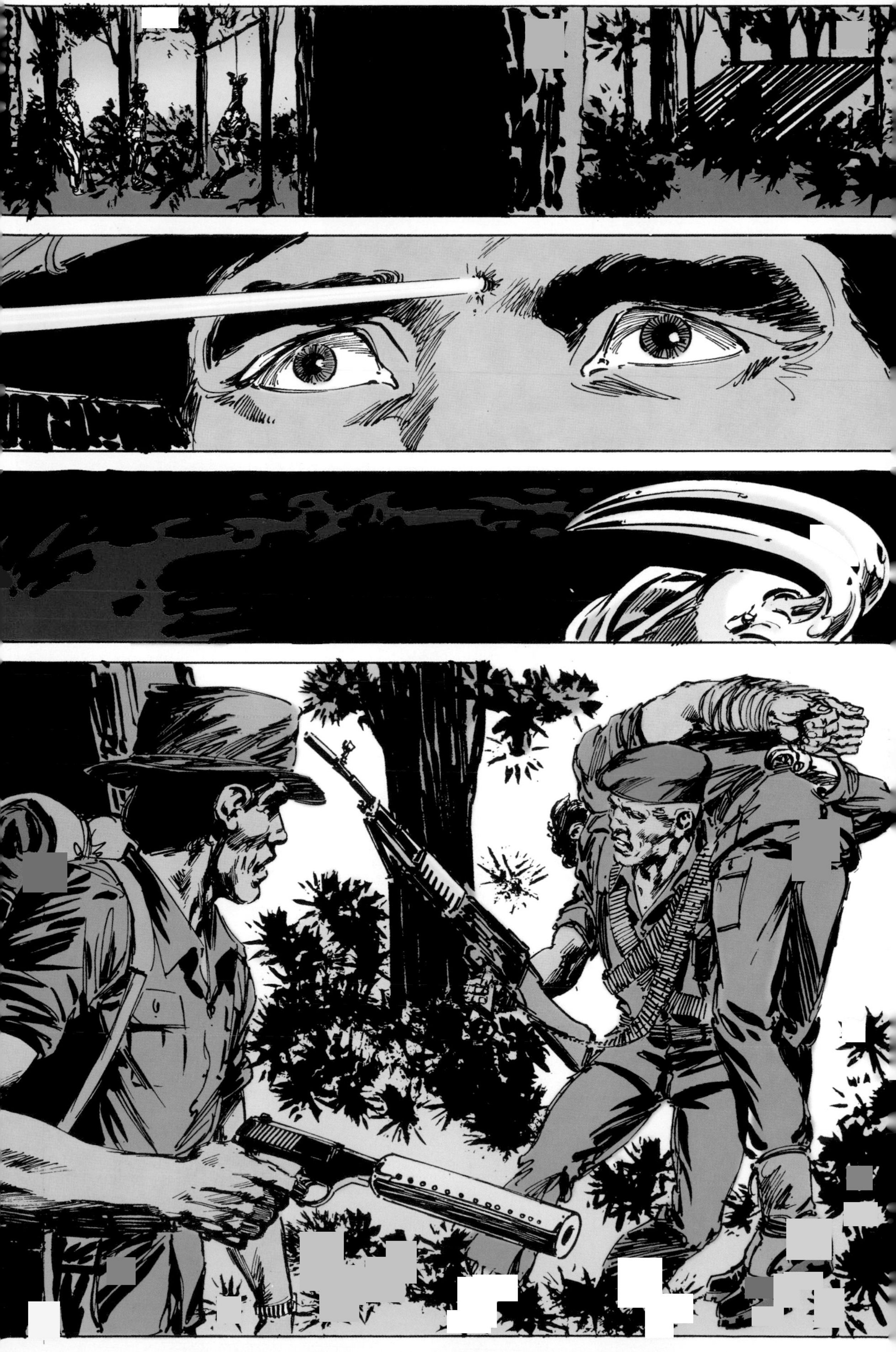

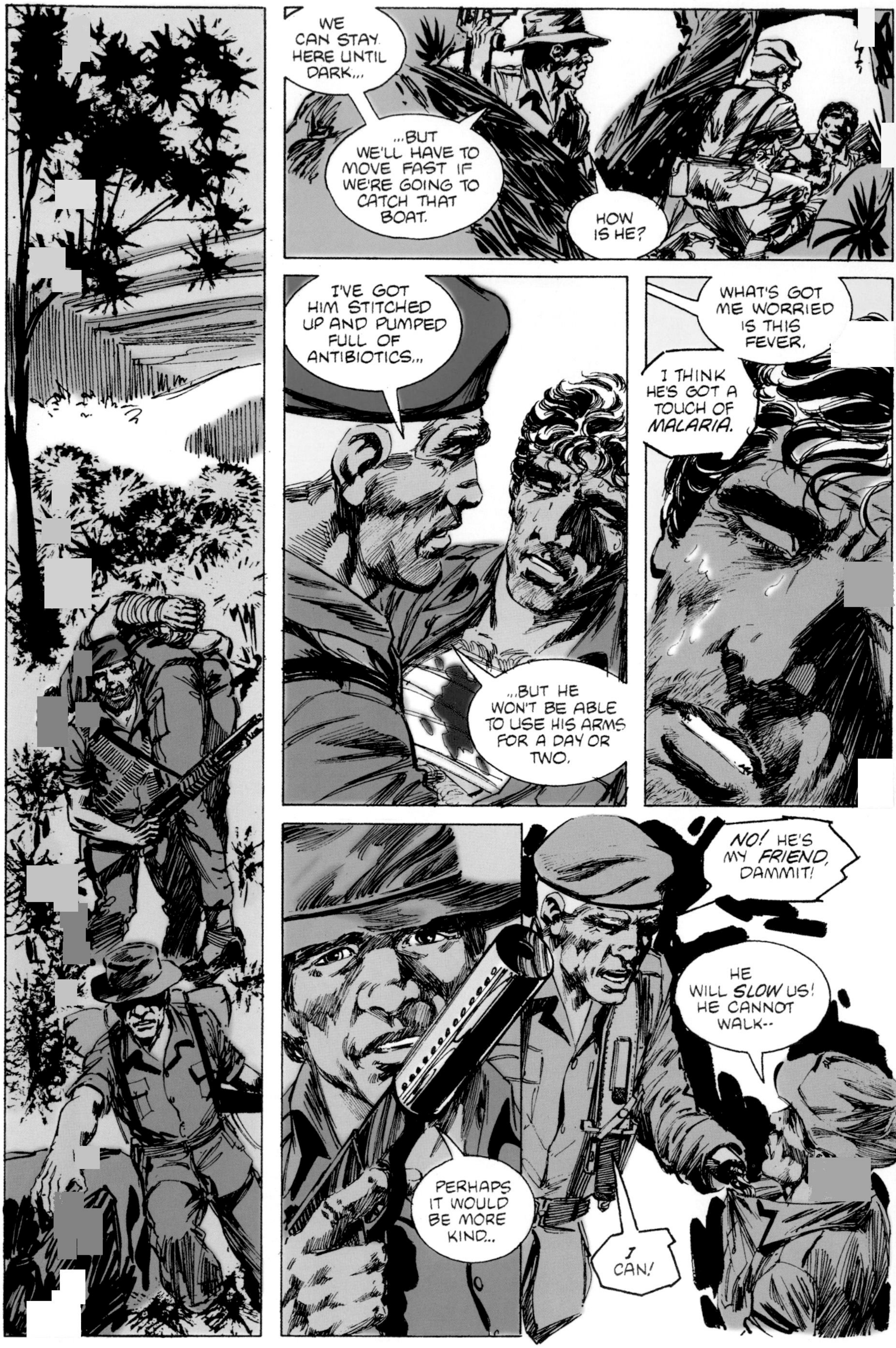
WE CAN STAY. HERE UNTIL DARK...
...BUT WE'LL HAVE TO MOVE FAST IF WE'RE GOING TO CATCH THAT BOAT.
HOW IS HE?
I'VE GOT HIM STITCHED UP AND PUMPED FULL OF ANTIBIOTICS...
...BUT HE WON'T BE ABLE TO USE HIS ARMS FOR A DAY OR TWO.
WHAT'S GOT ME WORRIED IS THIS FEVER.
I THINK HE'S GOT A TOUCH OF MALARIA.
PERHAPS IT WOULD BE MORE KIND...
NO! HE'S MY FRIEND, DAMMIT!
HE WILL SLOW US! HE CANNOT WALK--
I CAN!

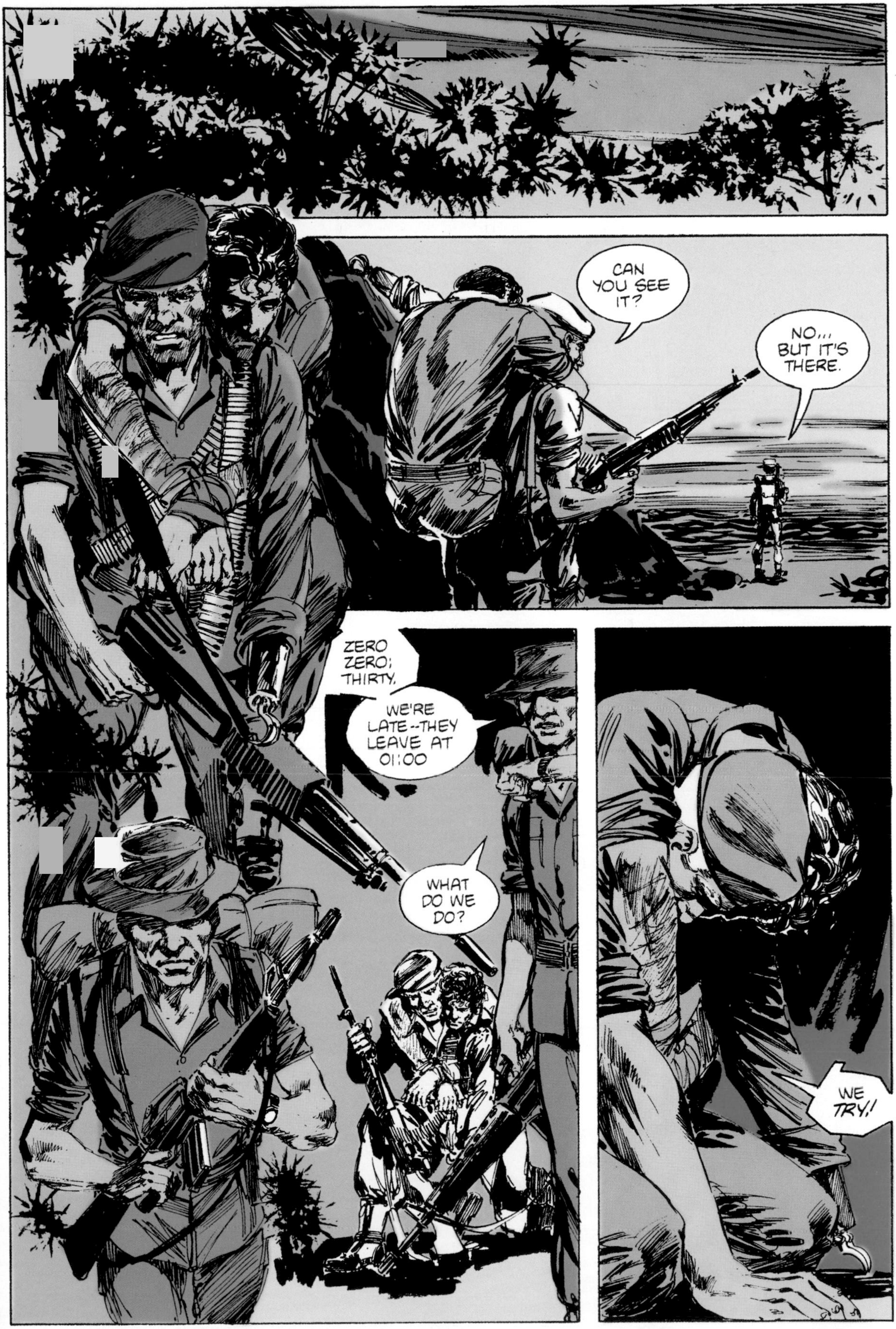
CAN YOU SEE IT?
NO... BUT IT'S THERE.
ZERO ZERO; THIRTY.
WE'RE LATE--THEY LEAVE AT 01:00
WHAT DO WE DO?
WE TRY!

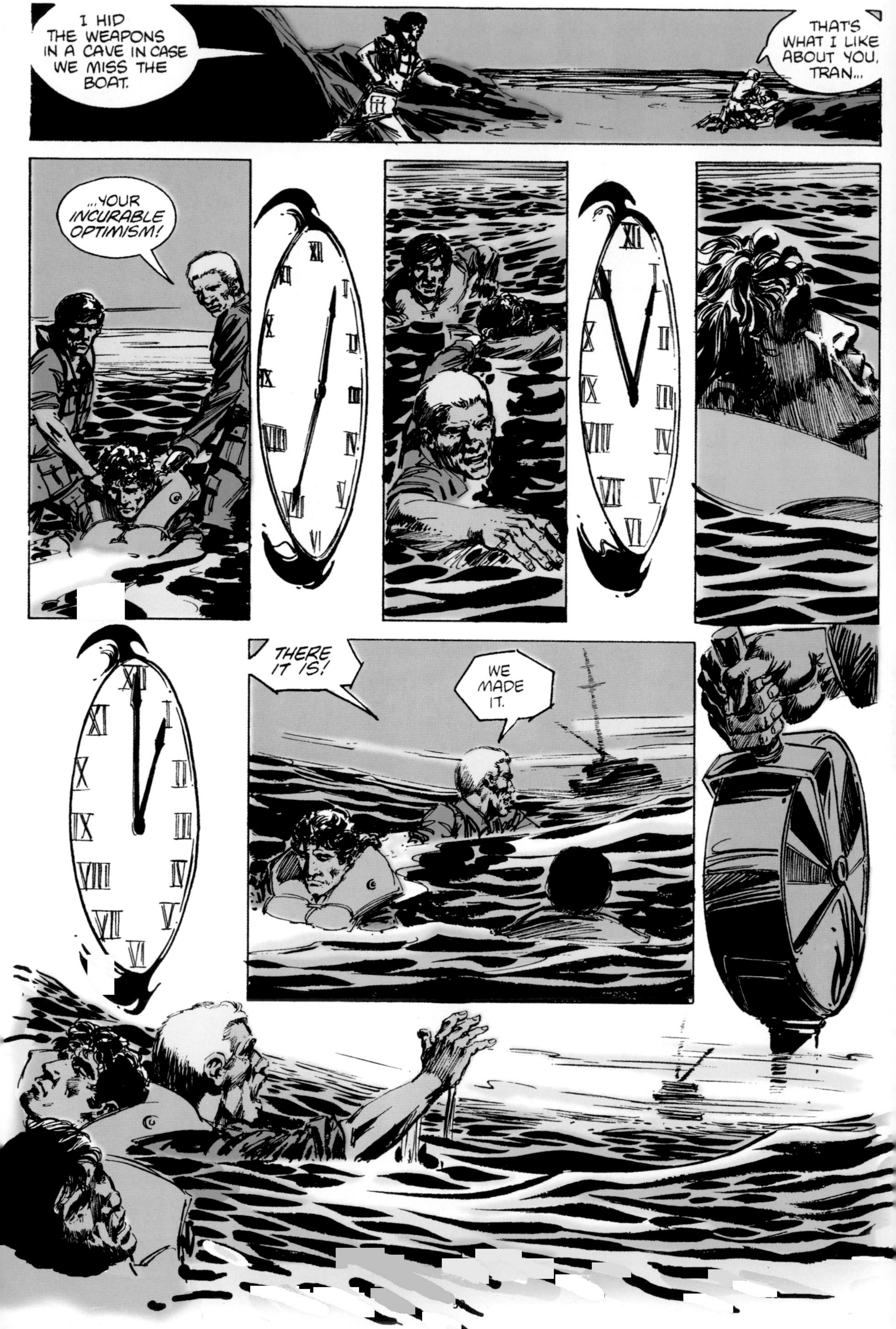
I HID THE WEAPONS IN A CAVE IN CASE WE MISS THE BOAT.
THAT'S WHAT I LIKE ABOUT YOU, TRAN...
...YOUR INCURABLE OPTIMISM!
THERE IT IS!
WE MADE IT.

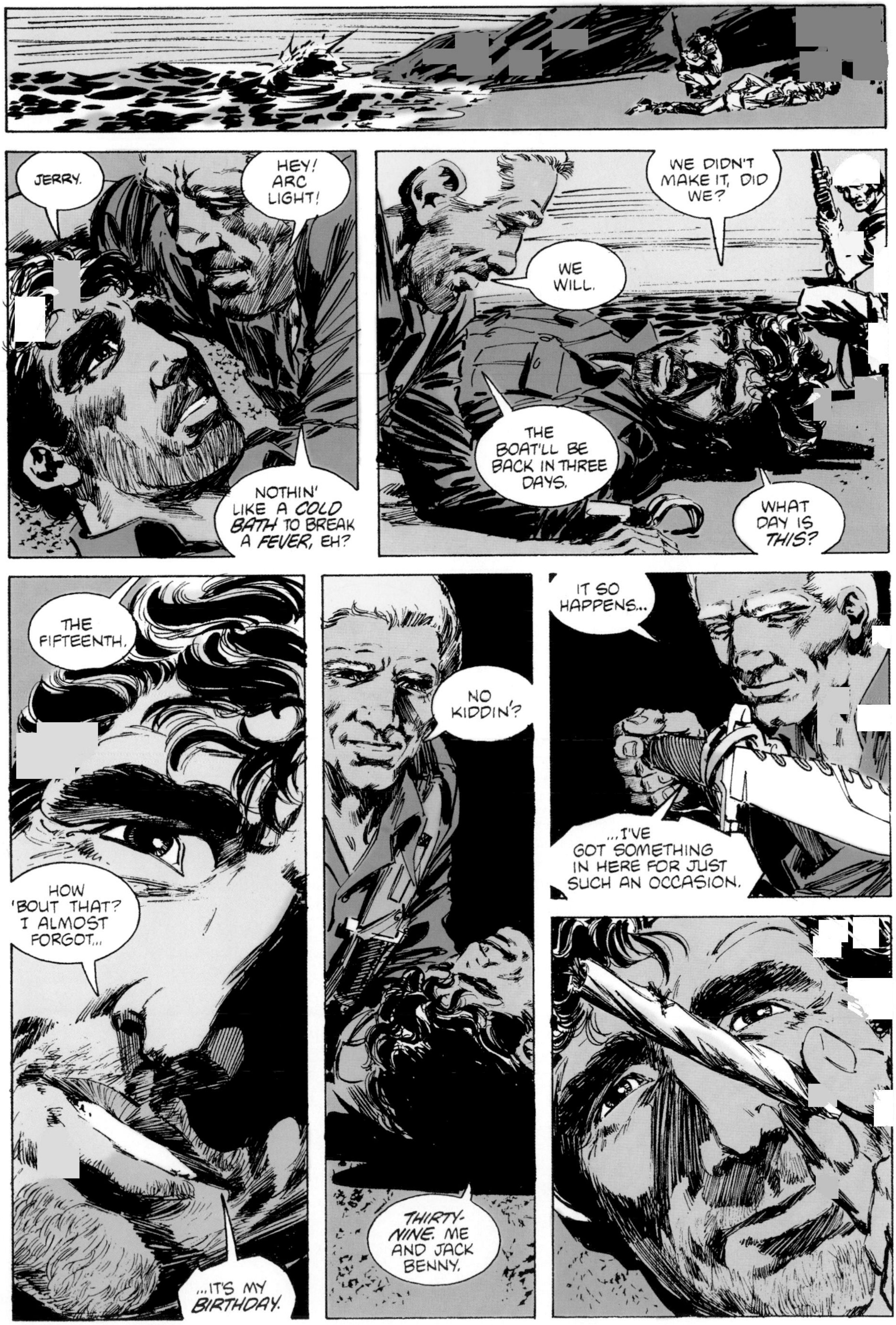
JERRY.
HEY! ARC LIGHT!
NOTHIN' LIKE A COLD BATH TO BREAK A FEVER, EH?
WE DIDN'T MAKE IT, DID WE?
WE WILL.
THE BOAT'LL BE BACK IN THREE DAYS.
WHAT DAY IS THIS?
THE FIFTEENTH.
HOW 'BOUT THAT? I ALMOST FORGOT...
...IT'S MY BIRTHDAY.
NO KIDDIN'?
THIRTY-NINE. ME AND JACK BENNY.
IT SO HAPPENS...
...I'VE GOT SOMETHING IN HERE FOR JUST SUCH AN OCCASION.

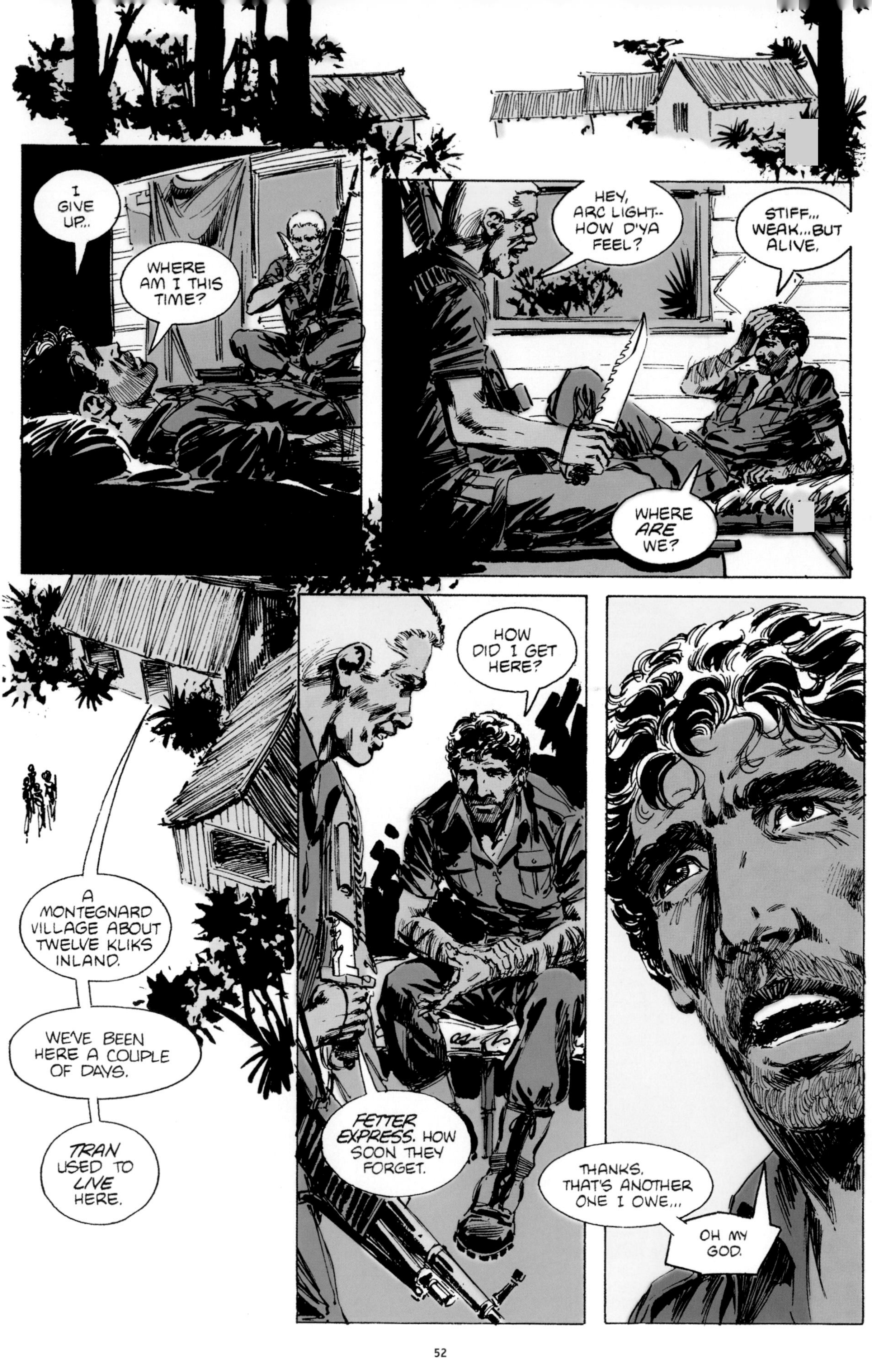
I GIVE UP...
WHERE AM I THIS TIME?
HEY, ARC LIGHT-- HOW D'YA FEEL?
STIFF... WEAK...BUT ALIVE.
WHERE ARE WE?
A MONTEGNARD VILLAGE ABOUT TWELVE KLIKS INLAND.
WE'VE BEEN HERE A COUPLE OF DAYS.
TRAN USED TO LIVE HERE.
HOW DID I GET HERE?
FETTER EXPRESS. HOW SOON THEY FORGET.
THANKS. THAT'S ANOTHER ONE I OWE...
OH MY GOD.

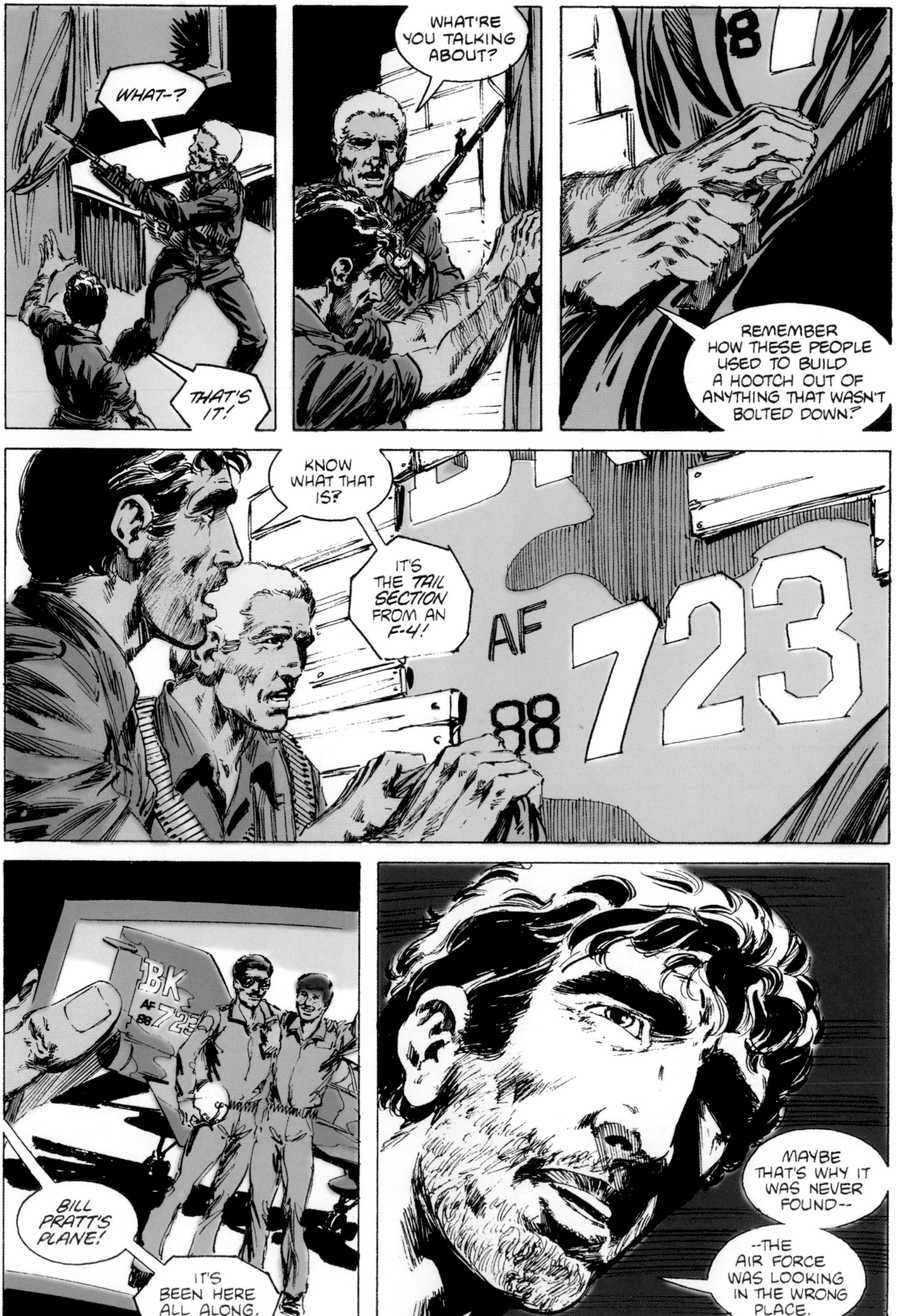
WHAT-?
THAT'S IT!
WHAT'RE YOU TALKING ABOUT?
8
REMEMBER HOW THESE PEOPLE USED TO BUILD A HOOTCH OUT OF ANYTHING THAT WASN'T BOLTED DOWN?
KNOW WHAT THAT IS?
IT'S THE TAIL SECTION FROM AN F-4!
AF
88
723
BK
AF
88
723
BILL PRATT'S PLANE!
IT'S BEEN HERE ALL ALONG.
MAYBE THAT'S WHY IT WAS NEVER FOUND--
--THE AIR FORCE WAS LOOKING IN THE WRONG PLACE.

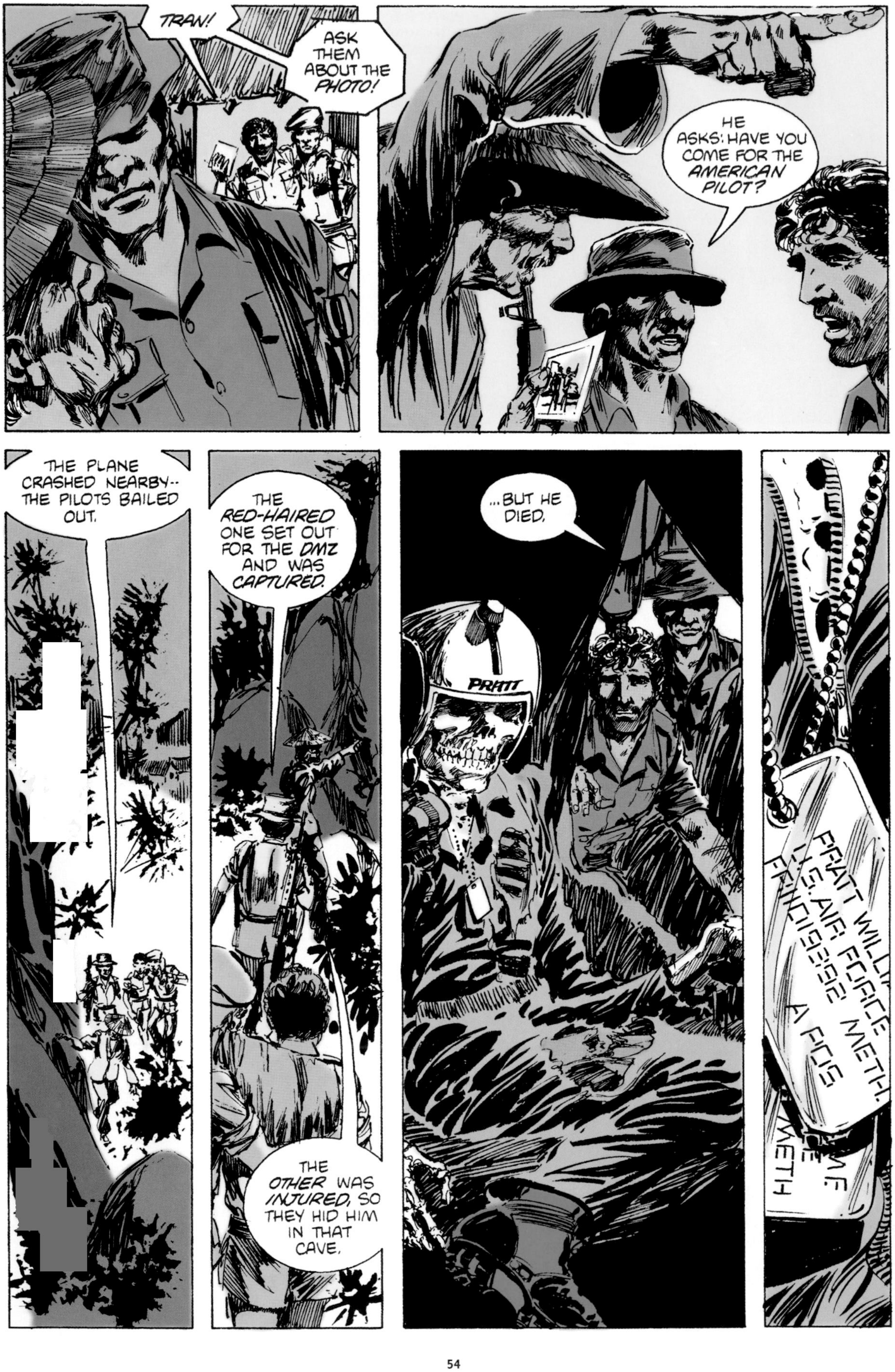
TRAN!
ASK THEM ABOUT THE PHOTO!
HE ASKS: HAVE YOU COME FOR THE AMERICAN PILOT?
THE PLANE CRASHED NEARBY-- THE PILOTS BAILED OUT.
THE RED-HAIRED ONE SET OUT FOR THE DMZ AND WAS CAPTURED.
THE OTHER WAS INJURED, SO THEY HID HIM IN THAT CAVE.
...BUT HE DIED.
PRATT
PRATT WILLI
U.S. AIR FORCE METH.

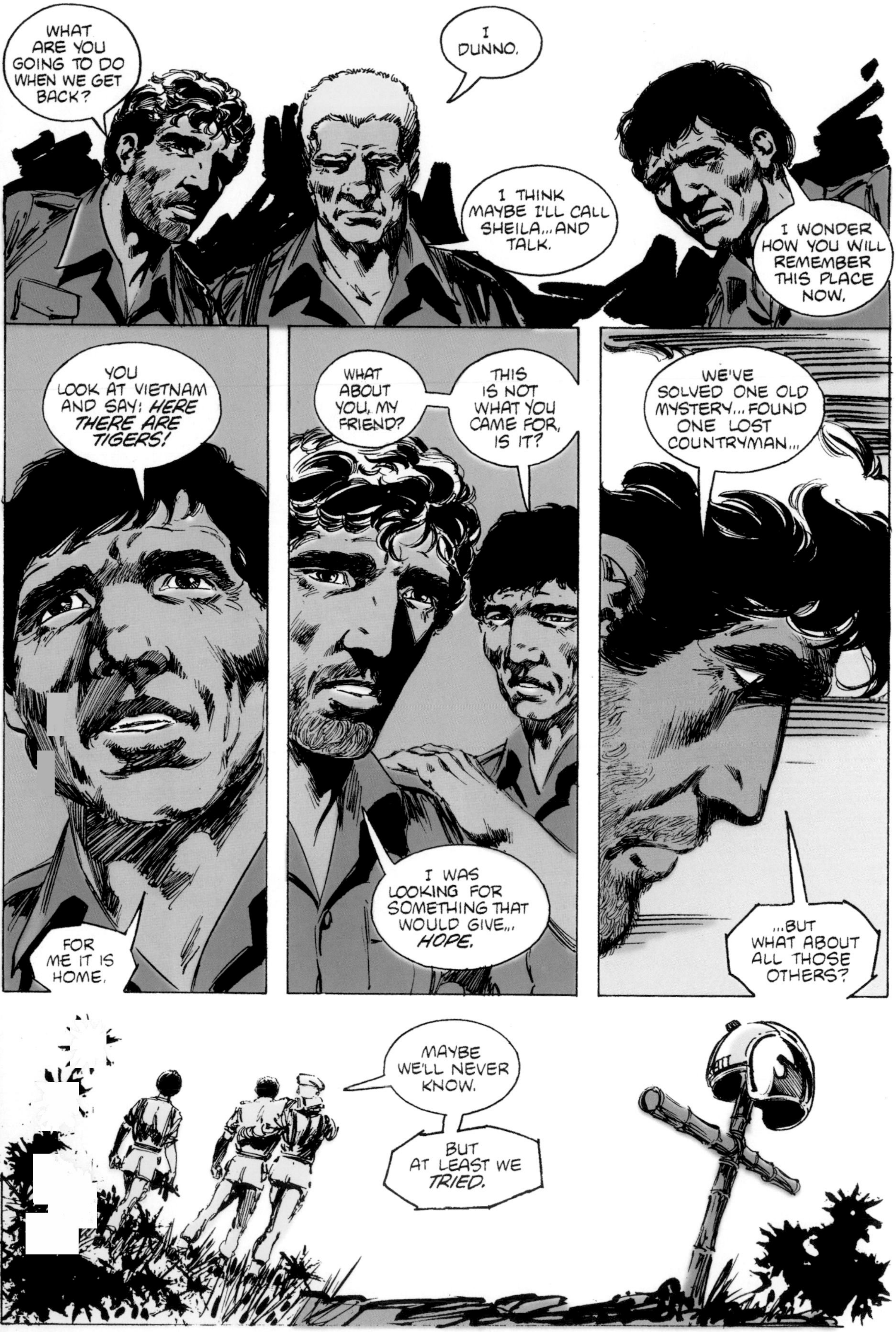
WHAT ARE YOU GOING TO DO WHEN WE GET BACK?
I DUNNO.
I THINK MAYBE I'LL CALL SHEILA... AND TALK.
I WONDER HOW YOU WILL REMEMBER THIS PLACE NOW.
YOU LOOK AT VIETNAM AND SAY: *HERE THERE ARE TIGERS!*
FOR ME IT IS HOME.
WHAT ABOUT YOU, MY FRIEND?
THIS IS NOT WHAT YOU CAME FOR, IS IT?
I WAS LOOKING FOR SOMETHING THAT WOULD GIVE... *HOPE.*
WE'VE SOLVED ONE OLD MYSTERY... FOUND ONE LOST COUNTRYMAN...
...BUT WHAT ABOUT ALL THOSE OTHERS?
MAYBE WE'LL NEVER KNOW.
BUT AT LEAST WE *TRIED.*

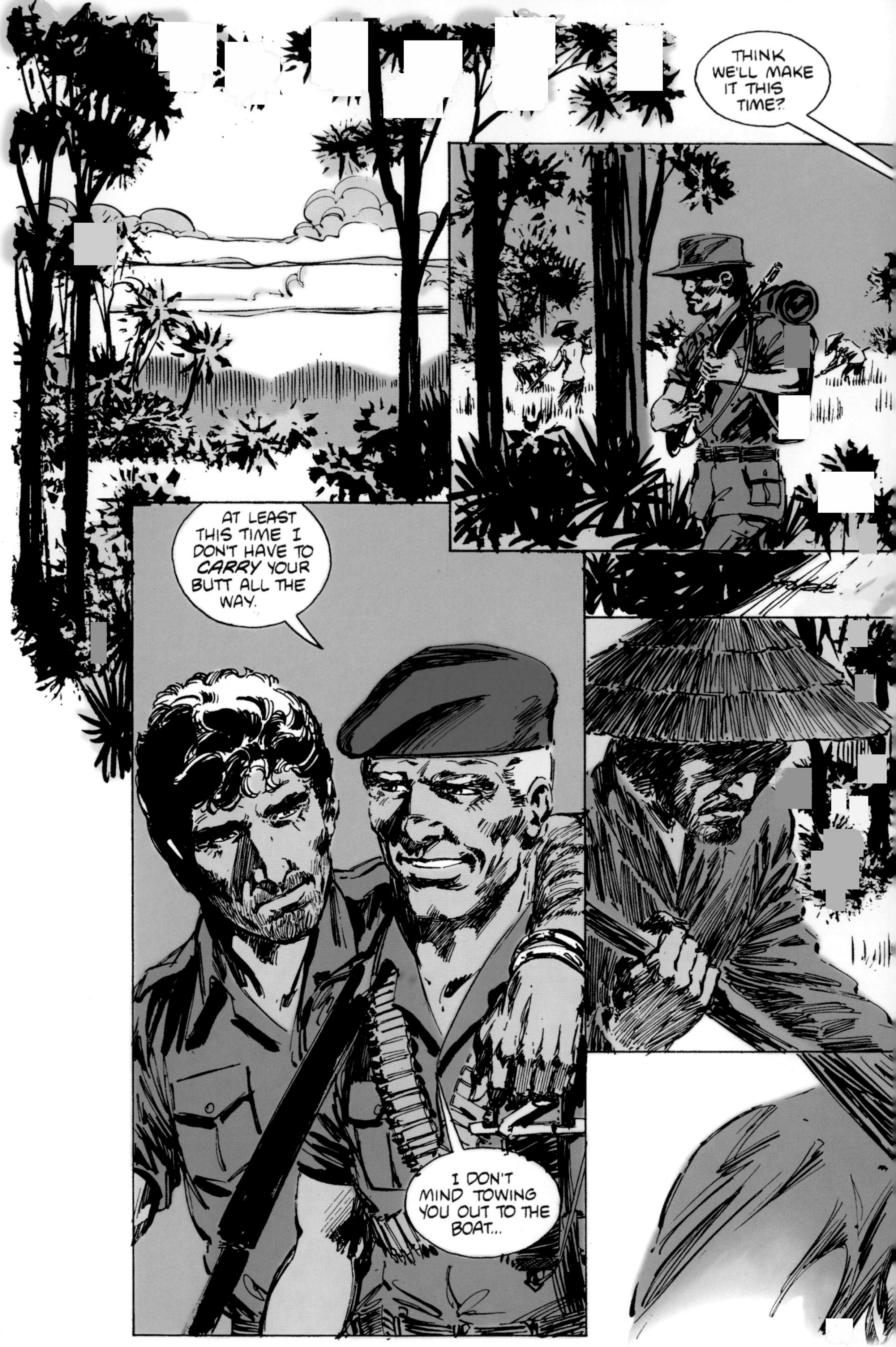
THINK WE'LL MAKE IT THIS TIME?
AT LEAST THIS TIME I DON'T HAVE TO CARRY YOUR BUTT ALL THE WAY.
I DON'T MIND TOWING YOU OUT TO THE BOAT...

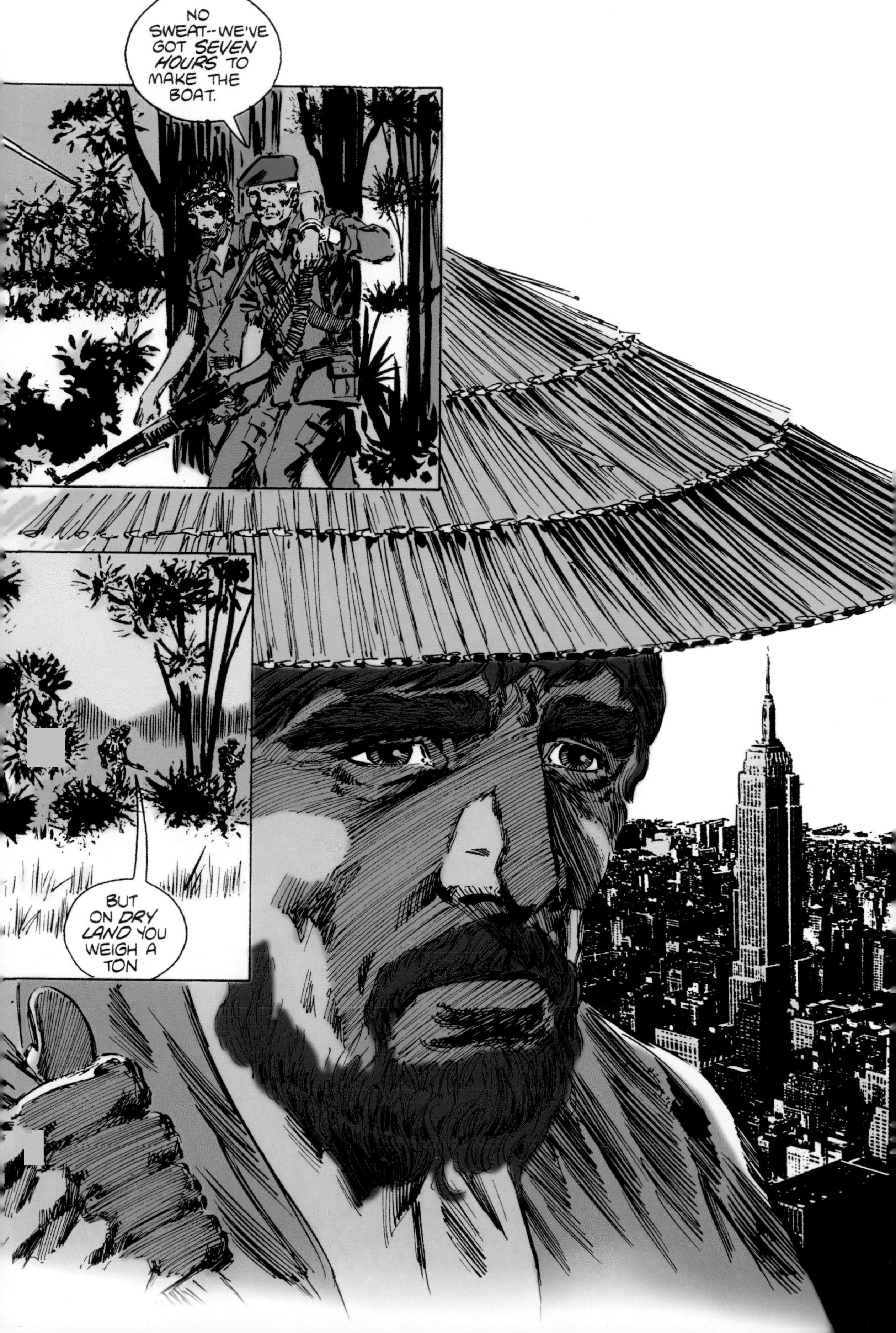
NO SWEAT--WE'VE GOT SEVEN HOURS TO MAKE THE BOAT.
BUT ON DRY LAND YOU WEIGH A TON

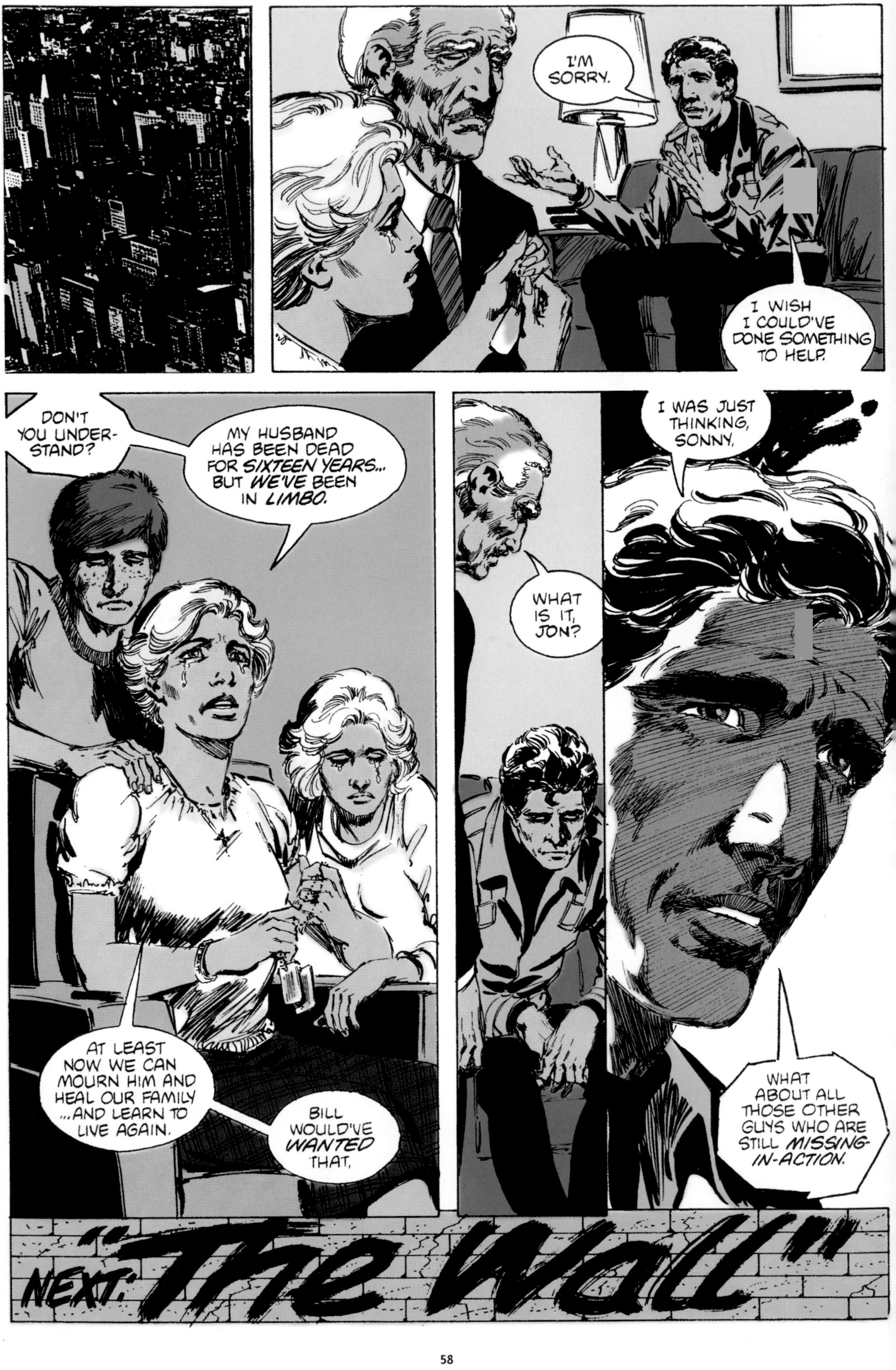
I'M SORRY.
I WISH I COULD'VE DONE SOMETHING TO HELP.
DON'T YOU UNDER-STAND?
MY HUSBAND HAS BEEN DEAD FOR SIXTEEN YEARS... BUT WE'VE BEEN IN LIMBO.
AT LEAST NOW WE CAN MOURN HIM AND HEAL OUR FAMILY ...AND LEARN TO LIVE AGAIN.
BILL WOULD'VE WANTED THAT.
I WAS JUST THINKING, SONNY.
WHAT IS IT, JON?
WHAT ABOUT ALL THOSE OTHER GUYS WHO ARE STILL MISSING-IN-ACTION.
NEXT: "The Wall"

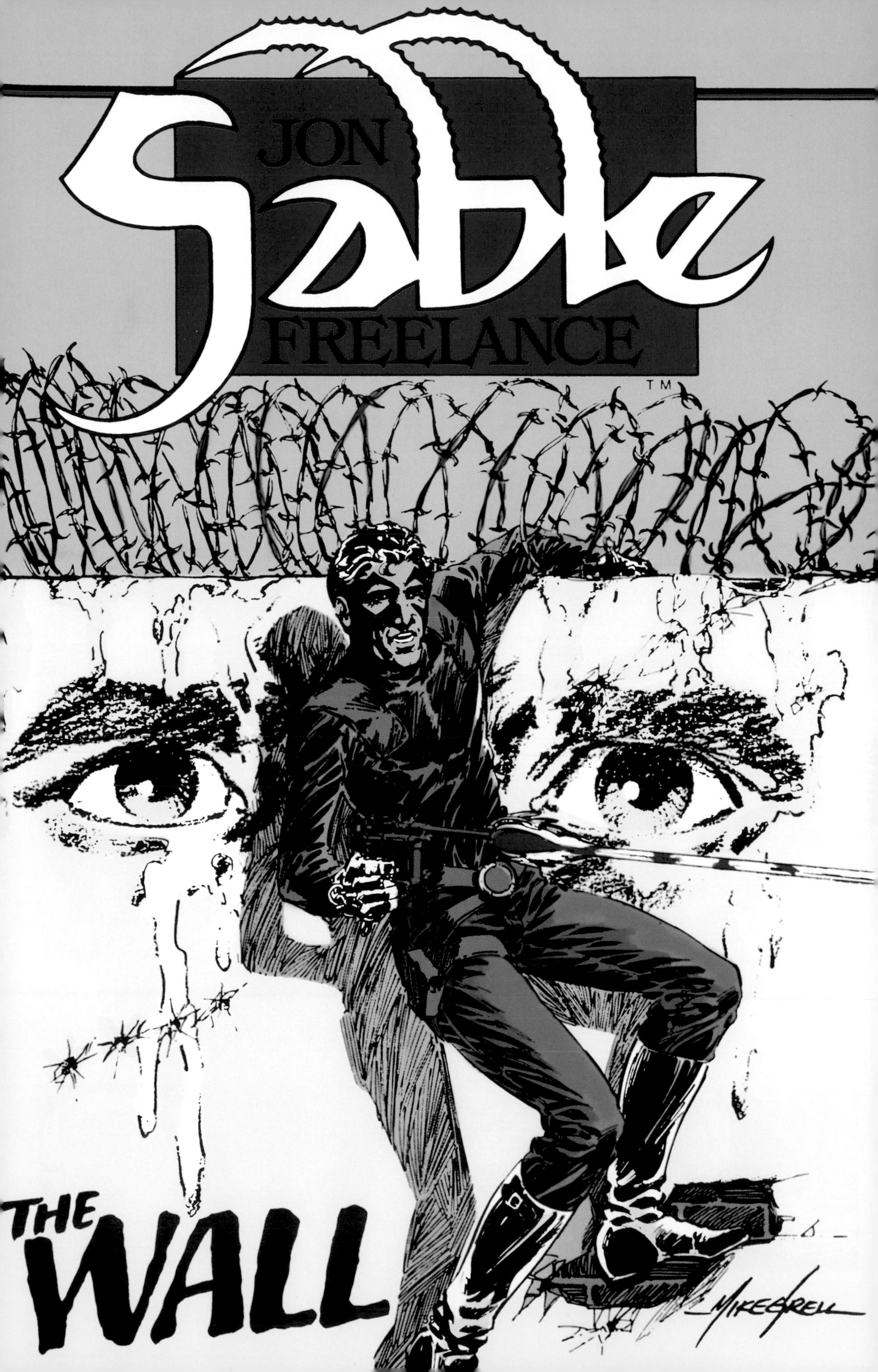
JON
Sable
FREELANCE
TM
THE
WALL
MIKE GRELL

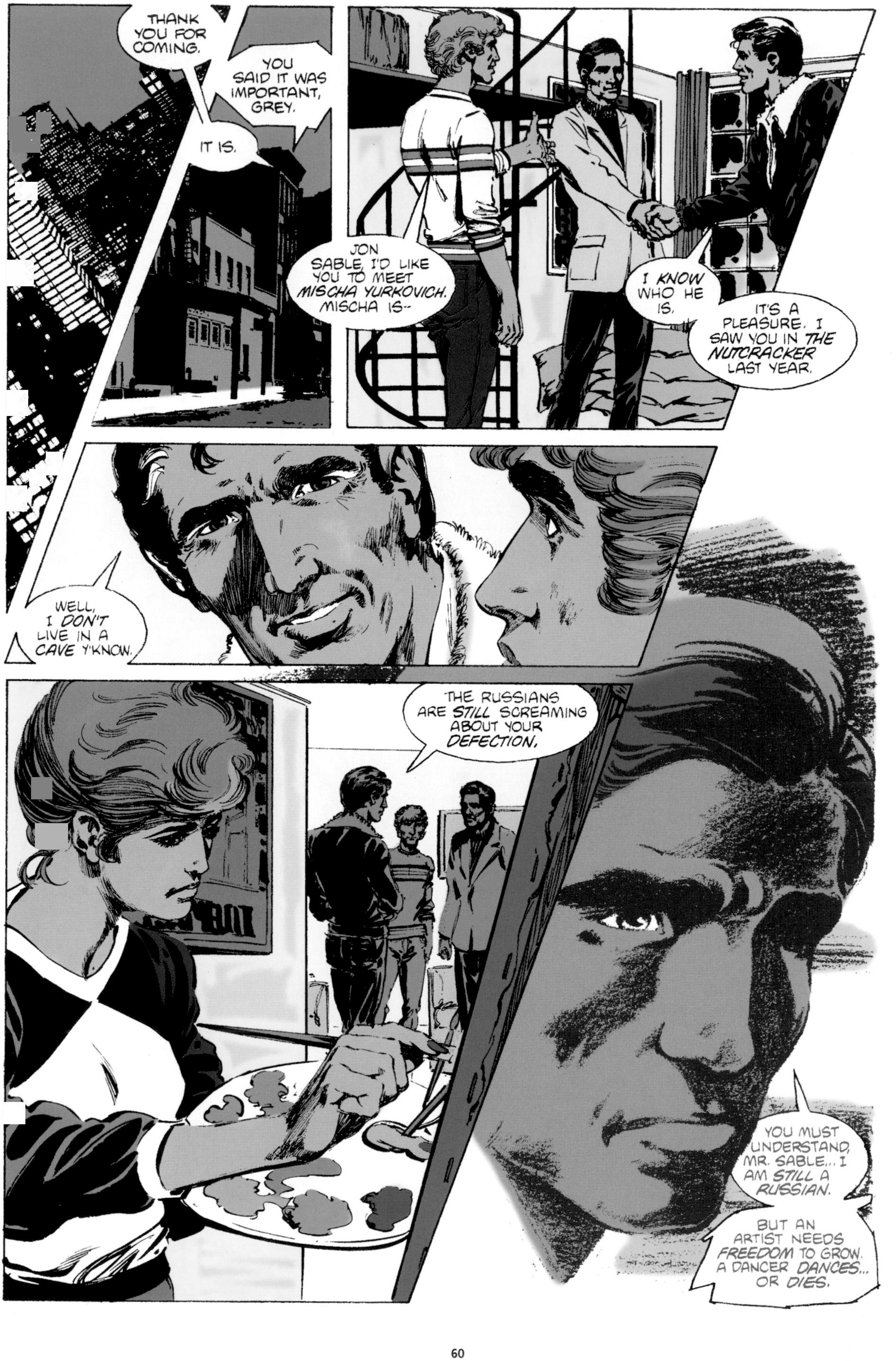
THANK YOU FOR COMING.
YOU SAID IT WAS IMPORTANT, GREY.
IT IS.
JON SABLE, I'D LIKE YOU TO MEET MISCHA YURKOVICH. MISCHA IS--
I KNOW WHO HE IS.
IT'S A PLEASURE. I SAW YOU IN THE NUTCRACKER LAST YEAR.
WELL, I DON'T LIVE IN A CAVE Y'KNOW.
THE RUSSIANS ARE STILL SCREAMING ABOUT YOUR DEFECTION.
YOU MUST UNDERSTAND, MR. SABLE... I AM STILL A RUSSIAN.
BUT AN ARTIST NEEDS FREEDOM TO GROW. A DANCER DANCES... OR DIES.

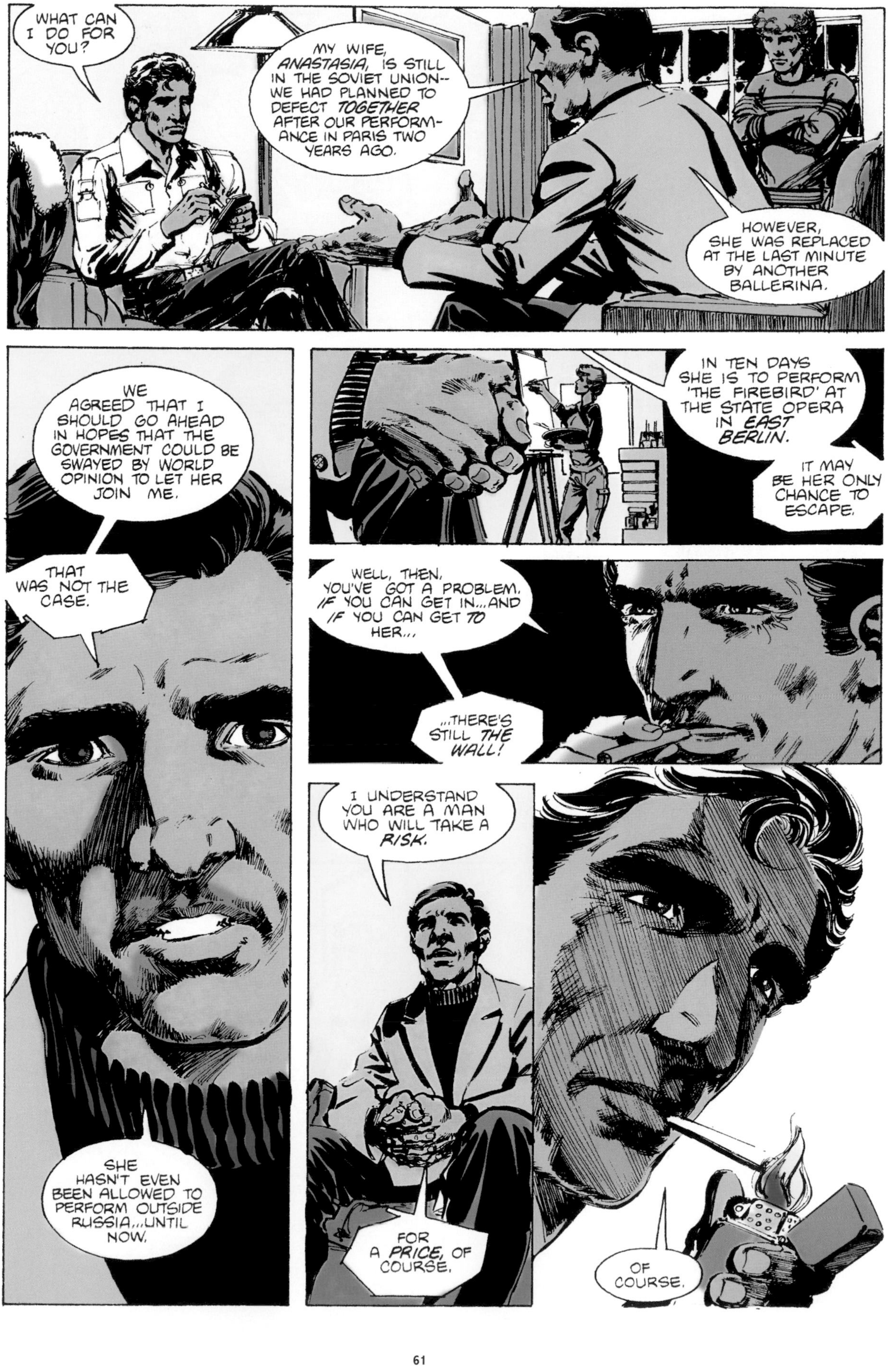
WHAT CAN I DO FOR YOU?
MY WIFE, ANASTASIA, IS STILL IN THE SOVIET UNION-- WE HAD PLANNED TO DEFECT TOGETHER AFTER OUR PERFORMANCE IN PARIS TWO YEARS AGO.
HOWEVER, SHE WAS REPLACED AT THE LAST MINUTE BY ANOTHER BALLERINA.
WE AGREED THAT I SHOULD GO AHEAD IN HOPES THAT THE GOVERNMENT COULD BE SWAYED BY WORLD OPINION TO LET HER JOIN ME.
THAT WAS NOT THE CASE.
SHE HASN'T EVEN BEEN ALLOWED TO PERFORM OUTSIDE RUSSIA...UNTIL NOW.
IN TEN DAYS SHE IS TO PERFORM 'THE FIREBIRD' AT THE STATE OPERA IN EAST BERLIN.
IT MAY BE HER ONLY CHANCE TO ESCAPE.
WELL, THEN, YOU'VE GOT A PROBLEM. IF YOU CAN GET IN...AND IF YOU CAN GET TO HER...
...THERE'S STILL THE WALL!
I UNDERSTAND YOU ARE A MAN WHO WILL TAKE A RISK.
FOR A PRICE, OF COURSE.
OF COURSE.

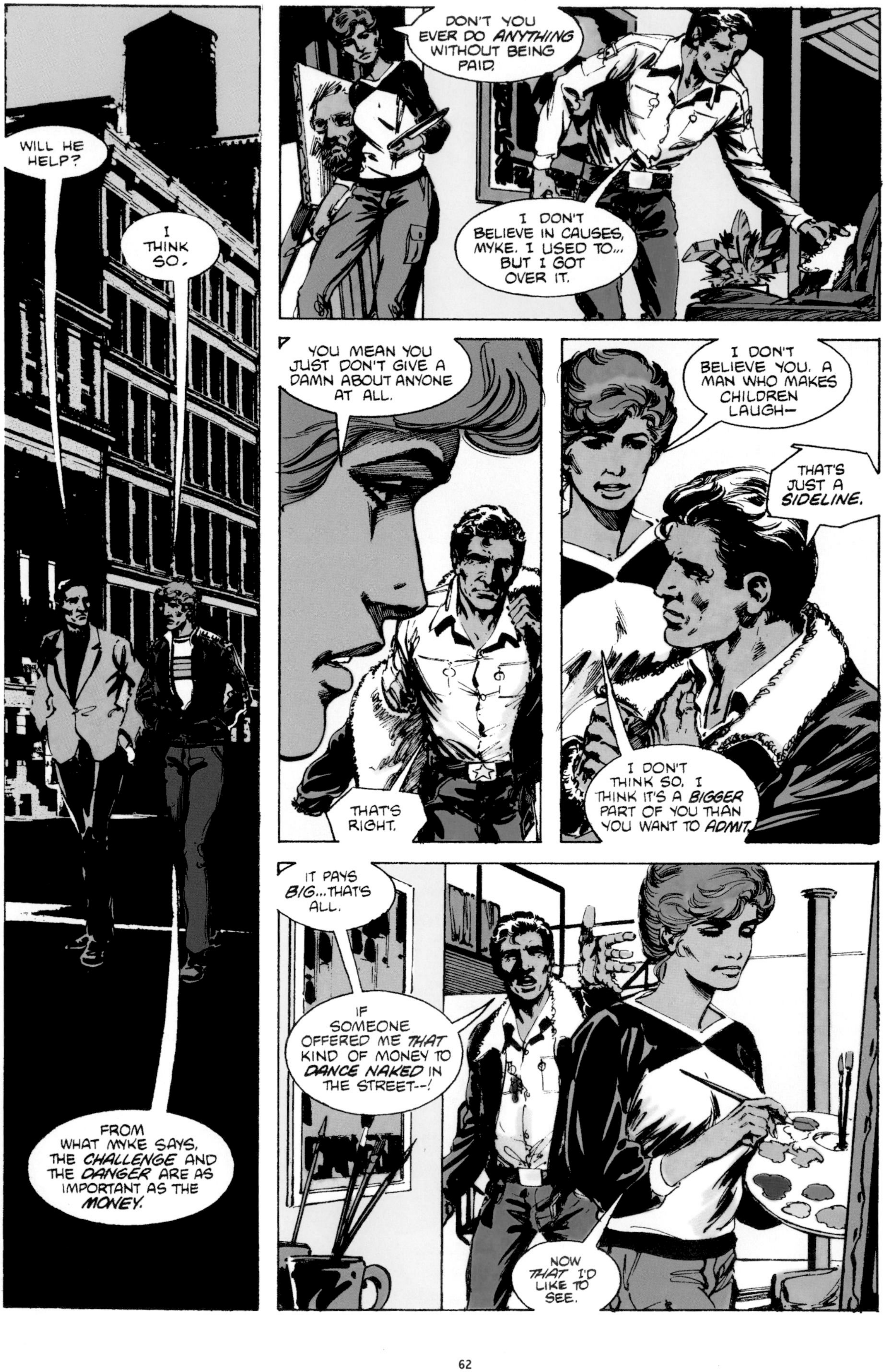
WILL HE HELP?
I THINK SO.
FROM WHAT MYKE SAYS, THE CHALLENGE AND THE DANGER ARE AS IMPORTANT AS THE MONEY.
DON'T YOU EVER DO ANYTHING WITHOUT BEING PAID.
I DON'T BELIEVE IN CAUSES, MYKE. I USED TO... BUT I GOT OVER IT.
YOU MEAN YOU JUST DON'T GIVE A DAMN ABOUT ANYONE AT ALL.
THAT'S RIGHT.
I DON'T BELIEVE YOU. A MAN WHO MAKES CHILDREN LAUGH—
THAT'S JUST A SIDELINE.
I DON'T THINK SO. I THINK IT'S A BIGGER PART OF YOU THAN YOU WANT TO ADMIT.
IT PAYS BIG...THAT'S ALL.
IF SOMEONE OFFERED ME THAT KIND OF MONEY TO DANCE NAKED IN THE STREET--!
NOW THAT I'D LIKE TO SEE.

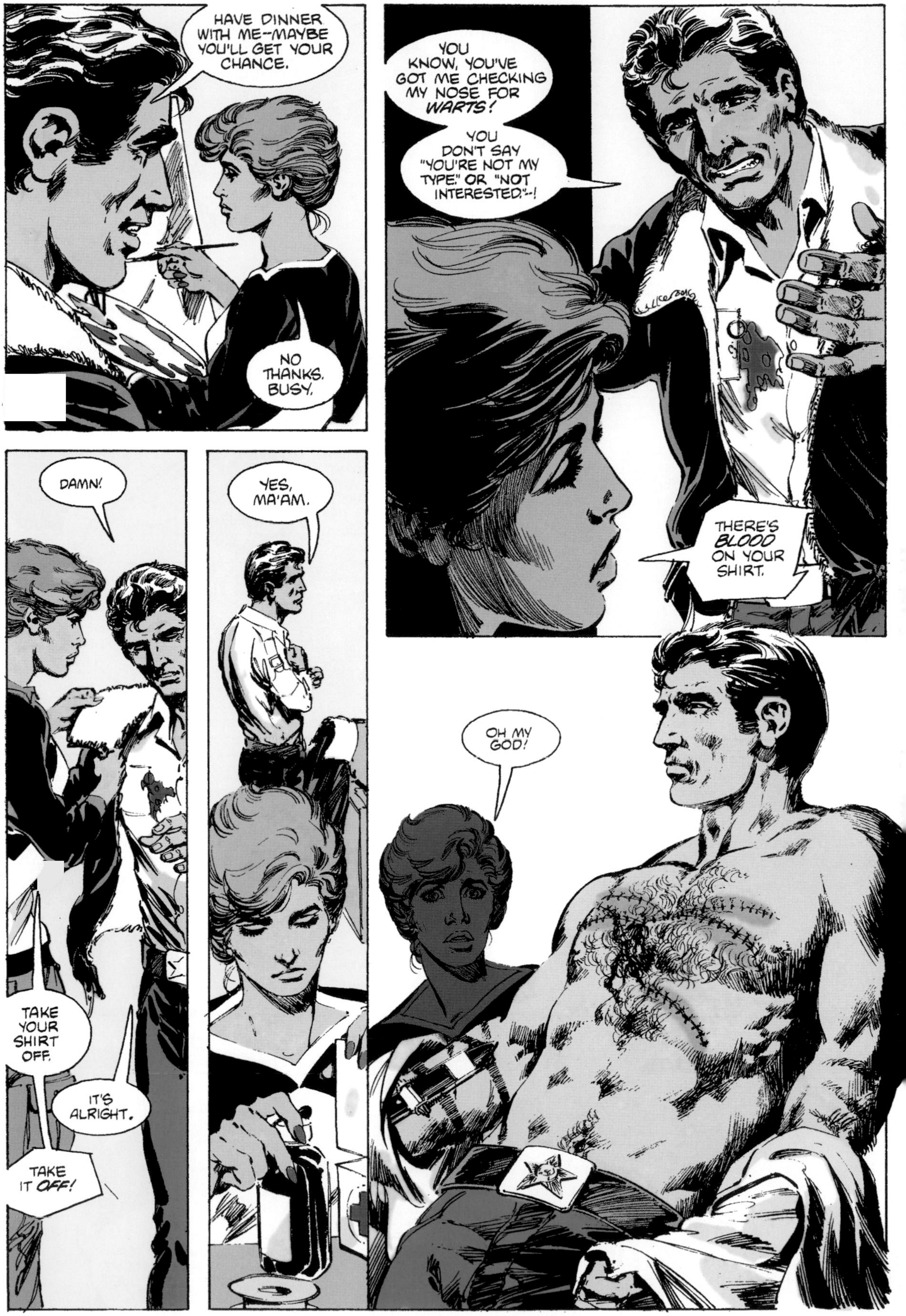
HAVE DINNER WITH ME--MAYBE YOU'LL GET YOUR CHANCE.
NO THANKS. BUSY.
YOU KNOW, YOU'VE GOT ME CHECKING MY NOSE FOR WARTS!
YOU DON'T SAY "YOU'RE NOT MY TYPE." OR "NOT INTERESTED."--!
THERE'S BLOOD ON YOUR SHIRT.
DAMN!
TAKE YOUR SHIRT OFF.
IT'S ALRIGHT.
TAKE IT OFF!
YES, MA'AM.
OH MY GOD!

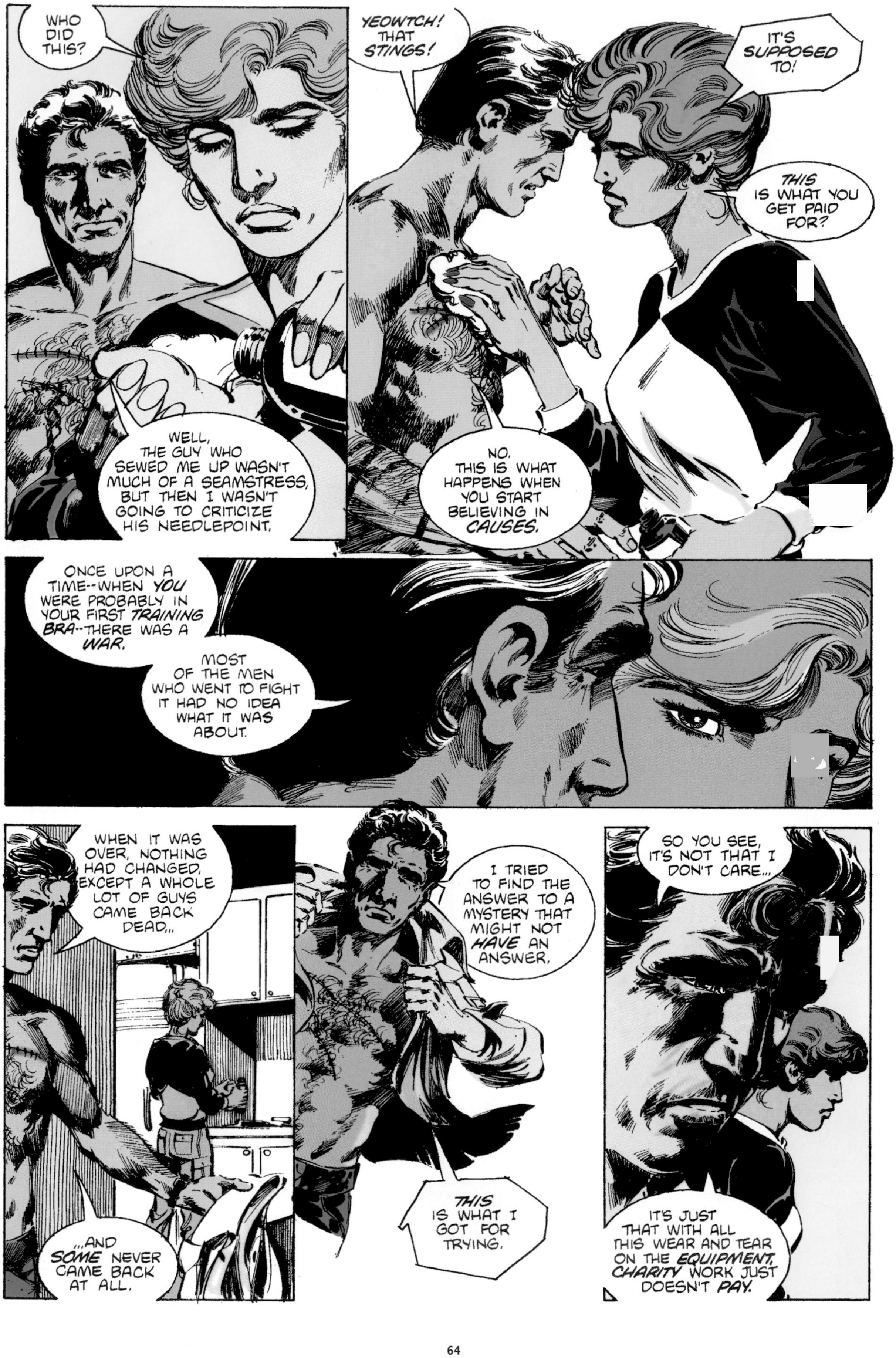
WHO DID THIS?
WELL, THE GUY WHO SEWED ME UP WASN'T MUCH OF A SEAMSTRESS, BUT THEN I WASN'T GOING TO CRITICIZE HIS NEEDLEPOINT.
YEOWTCH! THAT STINGS!
IT'S SUPPOSED TO!
THIS IS WHAT YOU GET PAID FOR?
NO. THIS IS WHAT HAPPENS WHEN YOU START BELIEVING IN CAUSES.
ONCE UPON A TIME--WHEN YOU WERE PROBABLY IN YOUR FIRST TRAINING BRA--THERE WAS A WAR.
MOST OF THE MEN WHO WENT TO FIGHT IT HAD NO IDEA WHAT IT WAS ABOUT.
WHEN IT WAS OVER, NOTHING HAD CHANGED, EXCEPT A WHOLE LOT OF GUYS CAME BACK DEAD...
...AND SOME NEVER CAME BACK AT ALL.
I TRIED TO FIND THE ANSWER TO A MYSTERY THAT MIGHT NOT HAVE AN ANSWER.
THIS IS WHAT I GOT FOR TRYING.
SO YOU SEE, IT'S NOT THAT I DON'T CARE...
IT'S JUST THAT WITH ALL THIS WEAR AND TEAR ON THE EQUIPMENT, CHARITY WORK JUST DOESN'T PAY.

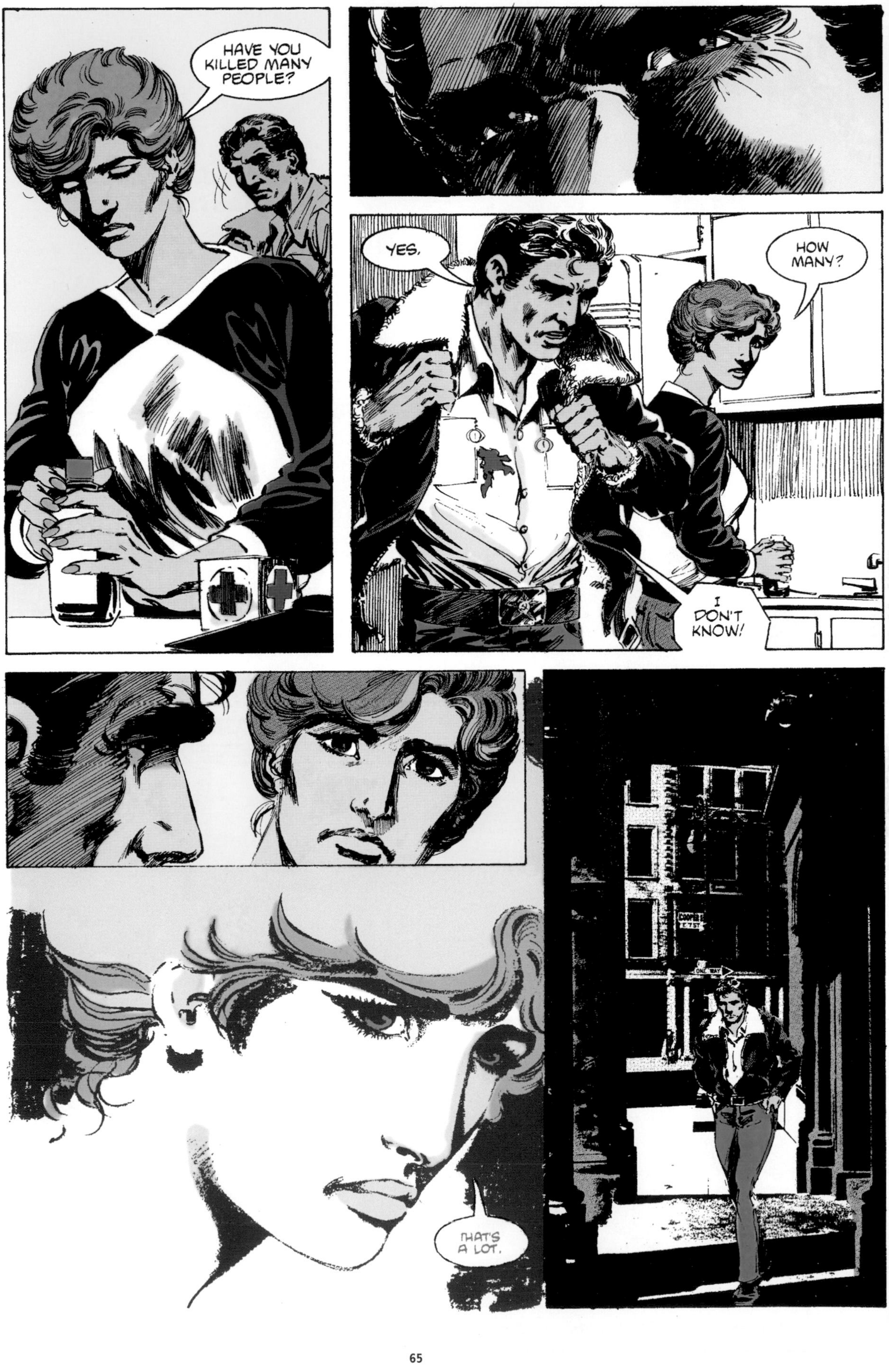
HAVE YOU KILLED MANY PEOPLE?
YES.
HOW MANY?
I DON'T KNOW!
THAT'S A LOT.
ONE WAY

JON **Sable** FREELANCE ™

created, written & illustrated by MIKE GRELL

CHECKPOINT C

YOU ARE LEAVING THE AMERICAN SECTOR

ВЫ ВЫЕЗЖАЕТЕ ИЗ АМЕРИКАНСКОГО СЕКТОРА

VOUS SORTEZ DU SECTEUR AMERICAIN

SIE VERLASSEN DEN AMERIKANISCHEN SEKTO

the WALL

LETTERER: KEN BRUZENAK • COLORIST: JANICE COHEN • EDITOR: MIKE GOLD

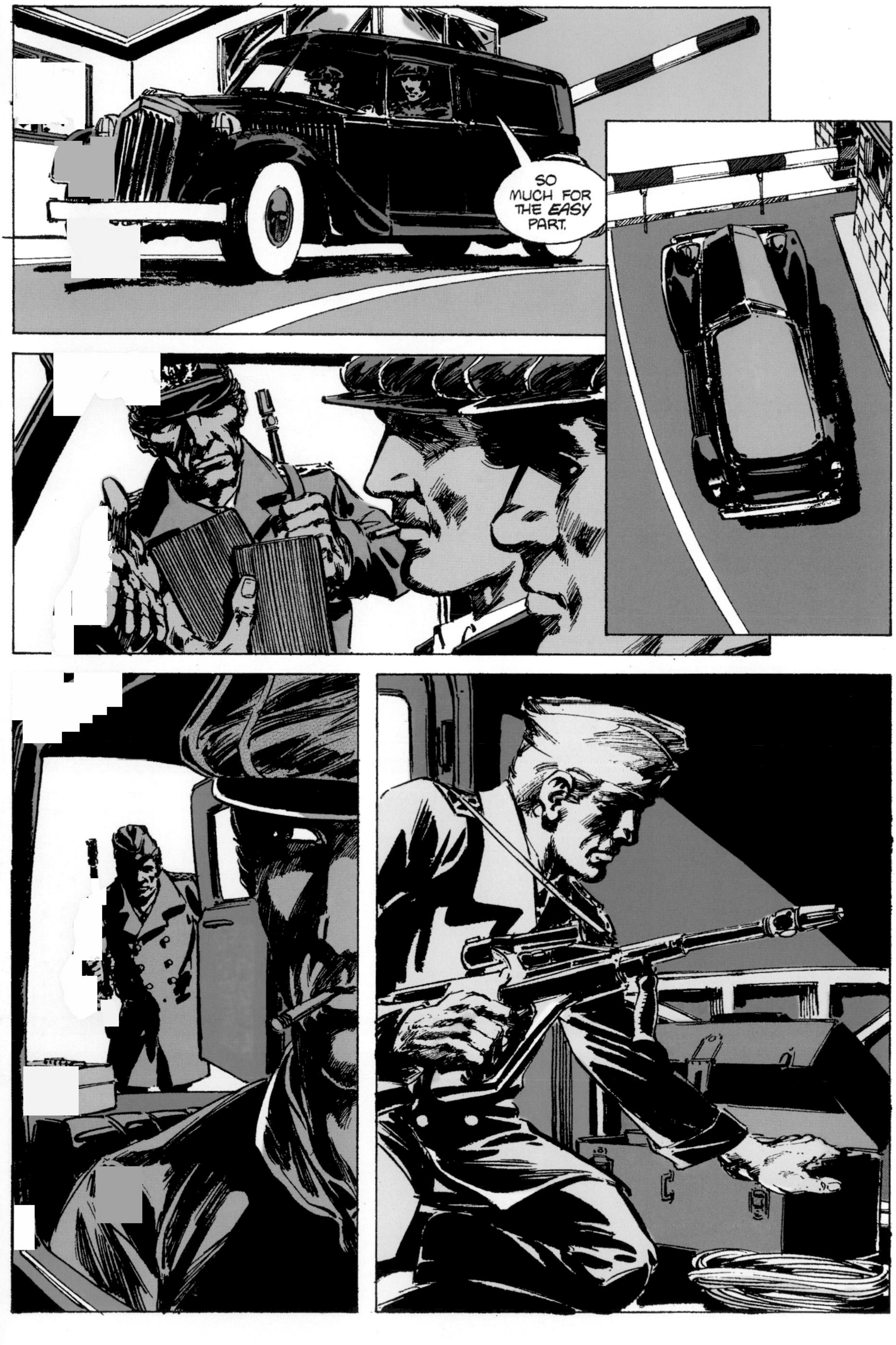
SO MUCH FOR THE EASY PART.

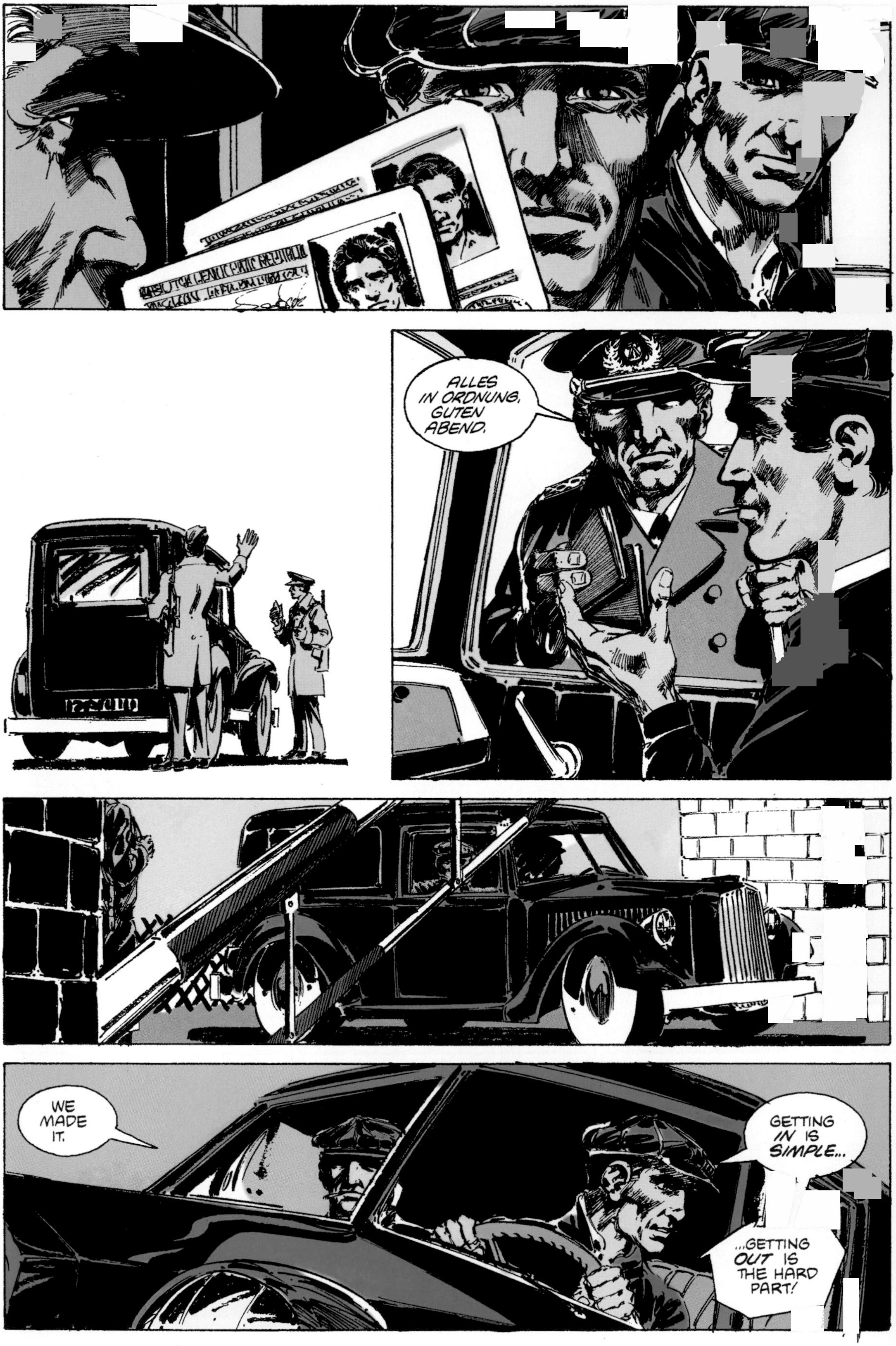
ALLES IN ORDNUNG. GUTEN ABEND.
WE MADE IT.
GETTING IN IS SIMPLE...
...GETTING OUT IS THE HARD PART!

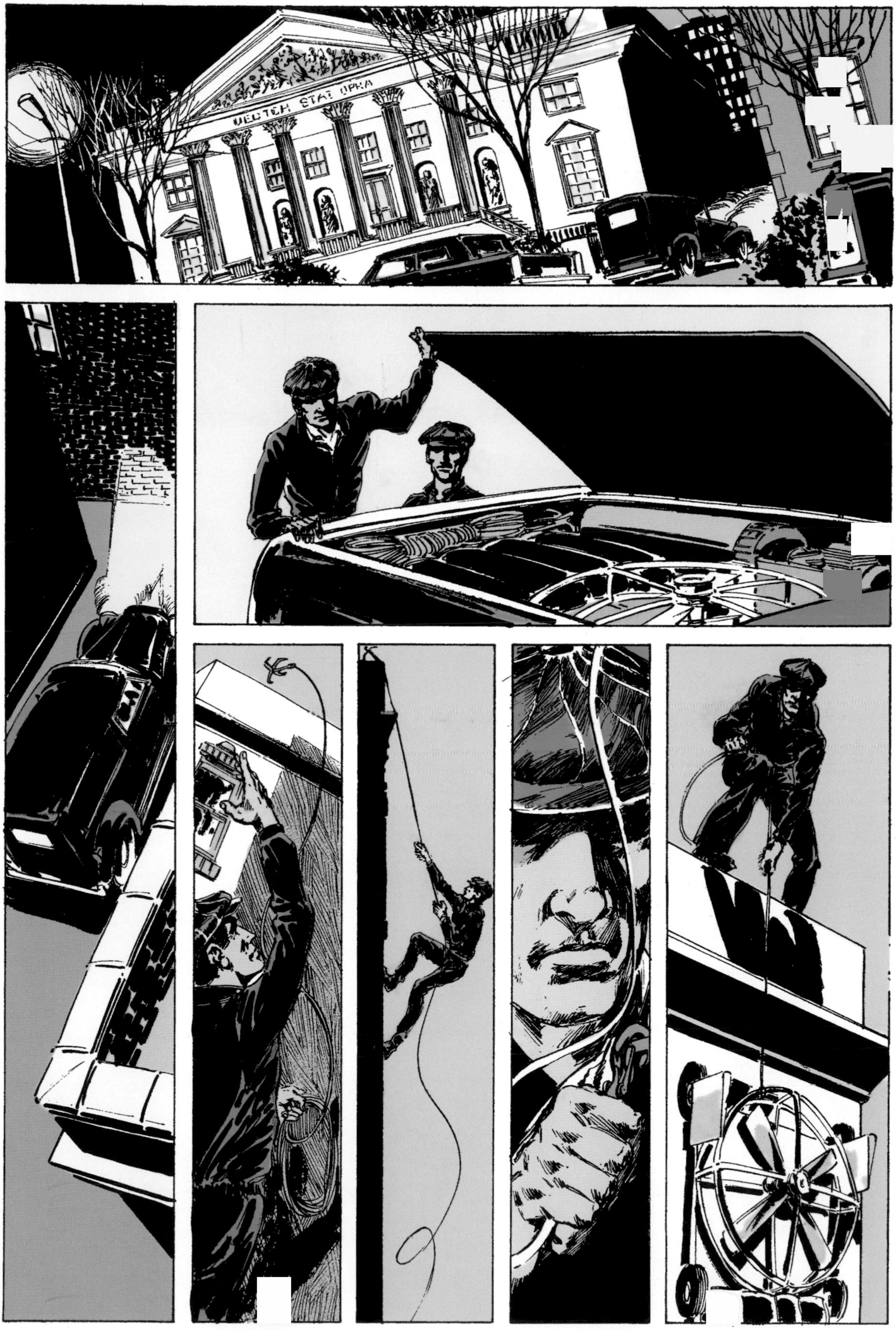

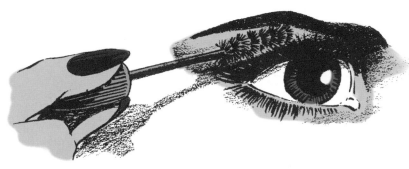

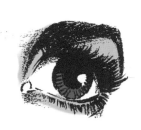

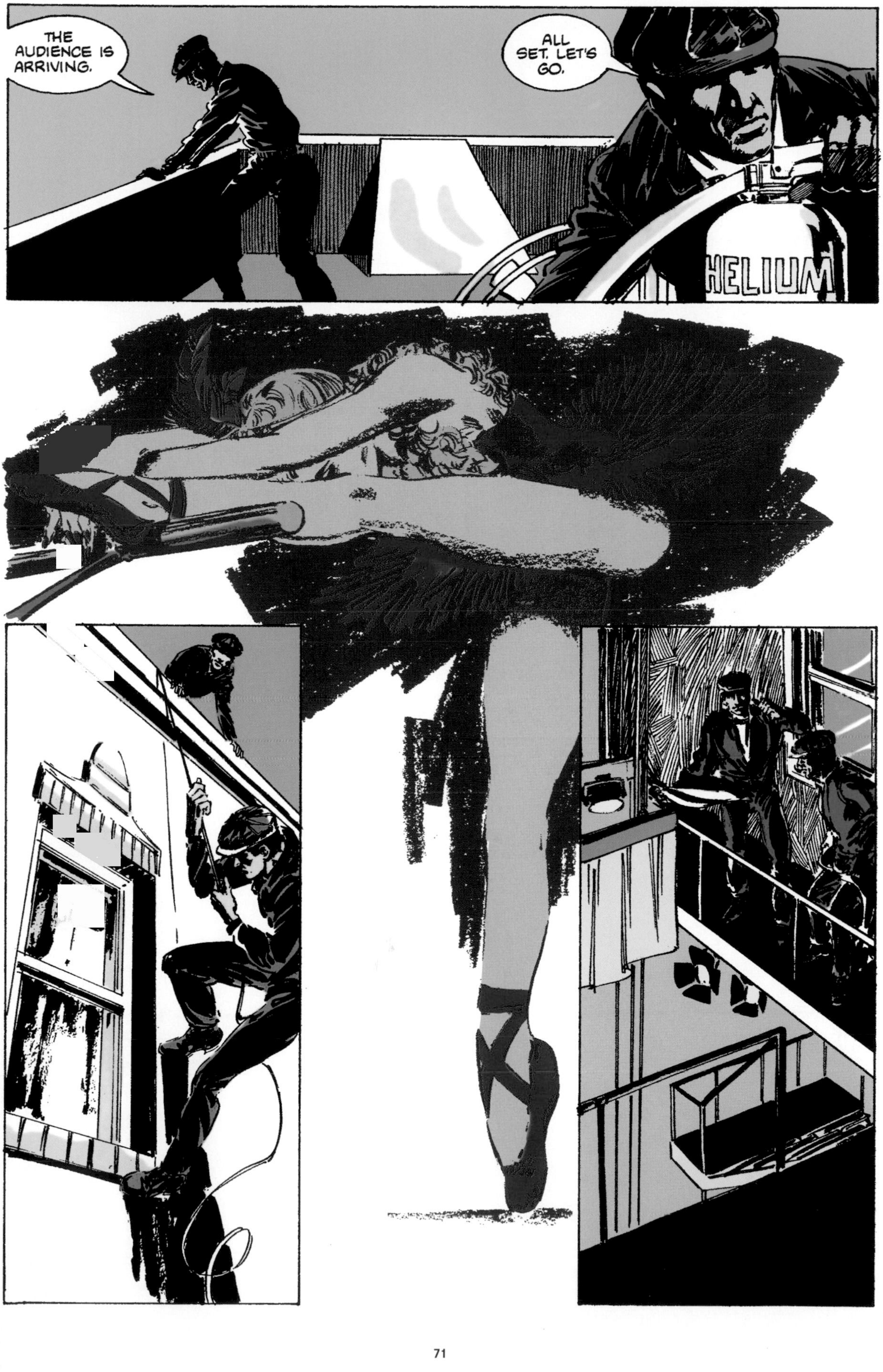
THE AUDIENCE IS ARRIVING.
ALL SET. LET'S GO.
HELIUM

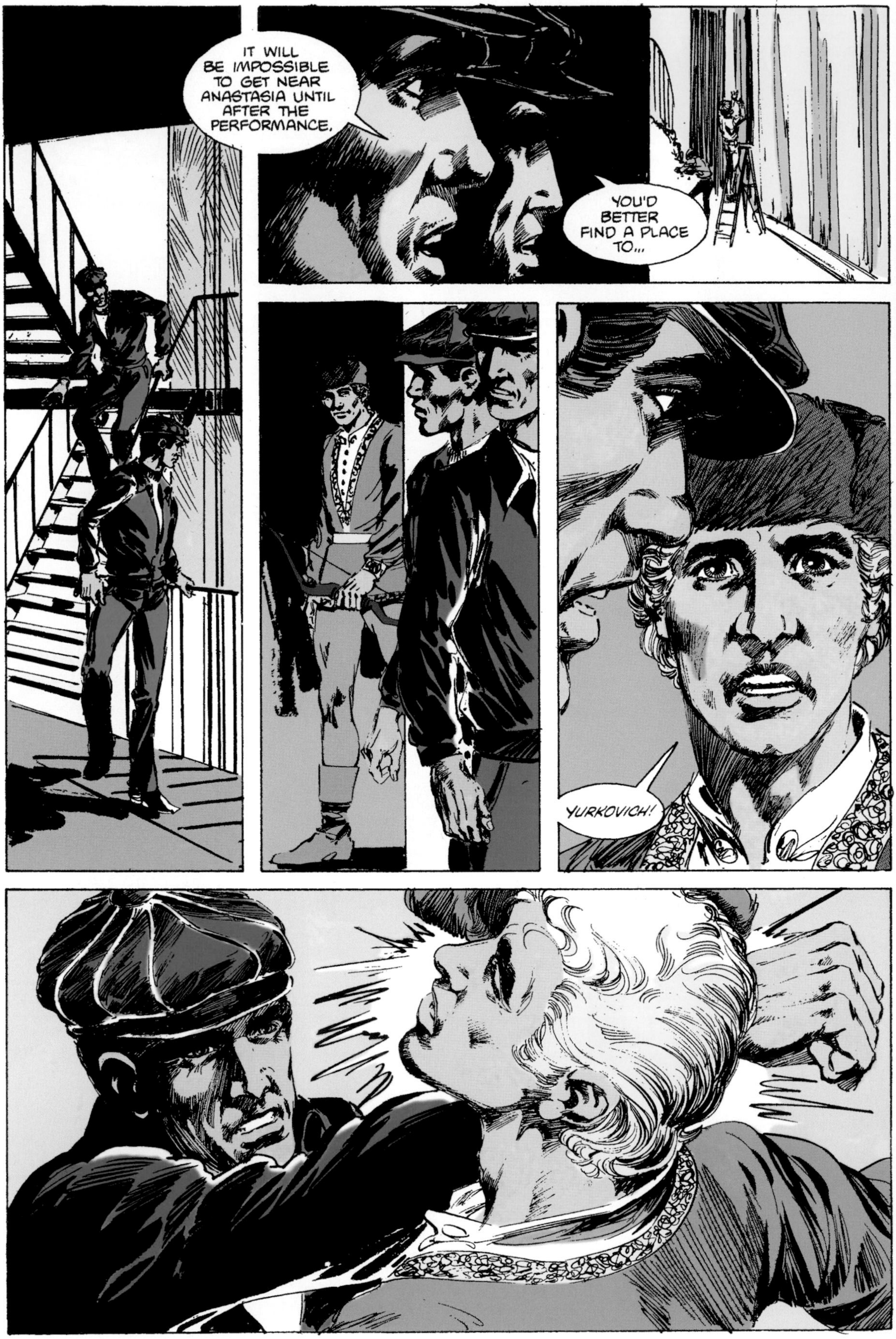
IT WILL BE IMPOSSIBLE TO GET NEAR ANASTASIA UNTIL AFTER THE PERFORMANCE.
YOU'D BETTER FIND A PLACE TO...
YURKOVICH!

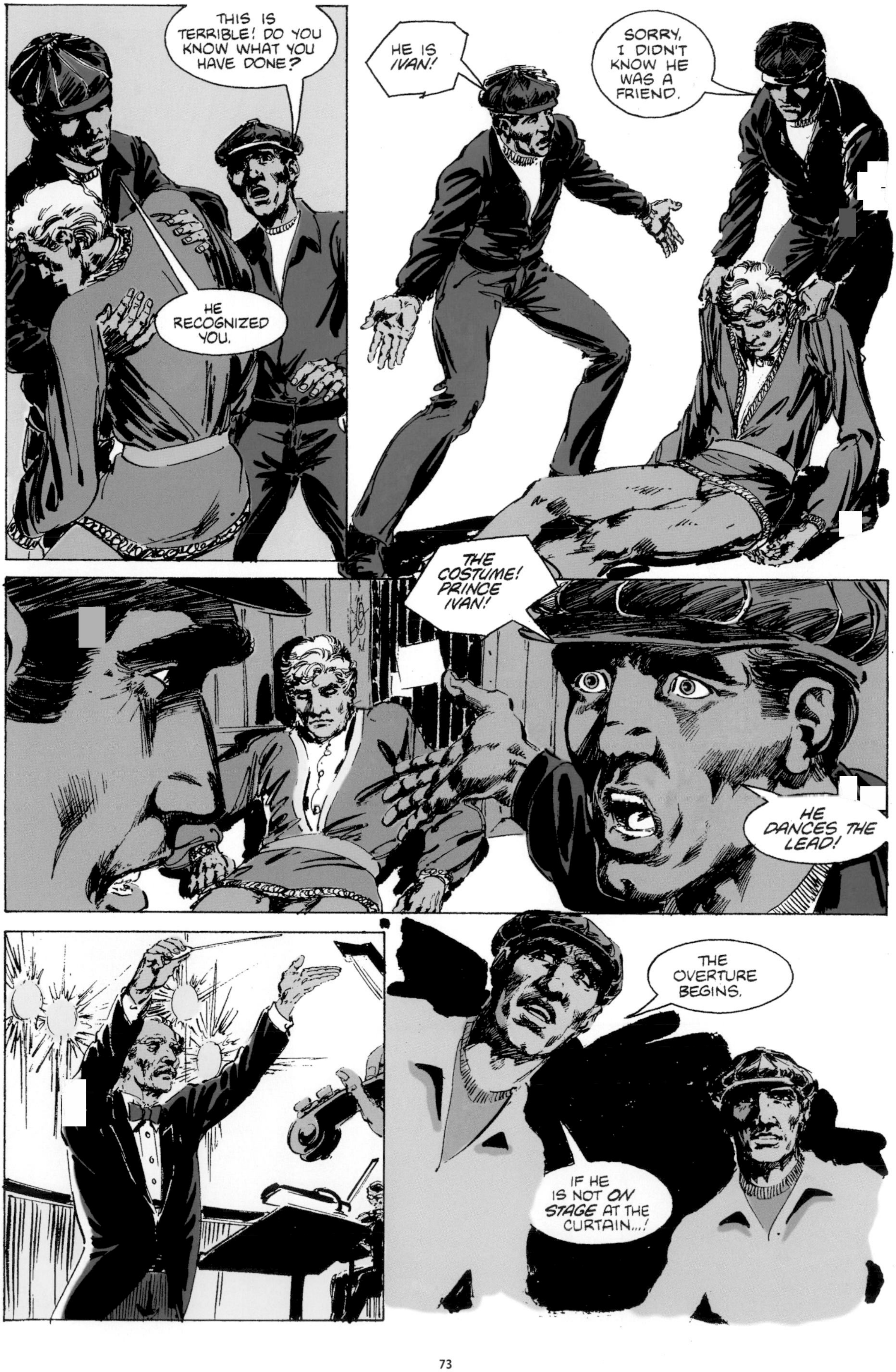
THIS IS TERRIBLE! DO YOU KNOW WHAT YOU HAVE DONE?
HE RECOGNIZED YOU.
HE IS IVAN!
SORRY, I DIDN'T KNOW HE WAS A FRIEND.
THE COSTUME! PRINCE IVAN!
HE DANCES THE LEAD!
THE OVERTURE BEGINS.
IF HE IS NOT ON STAGE AT THE CURTAIN...!

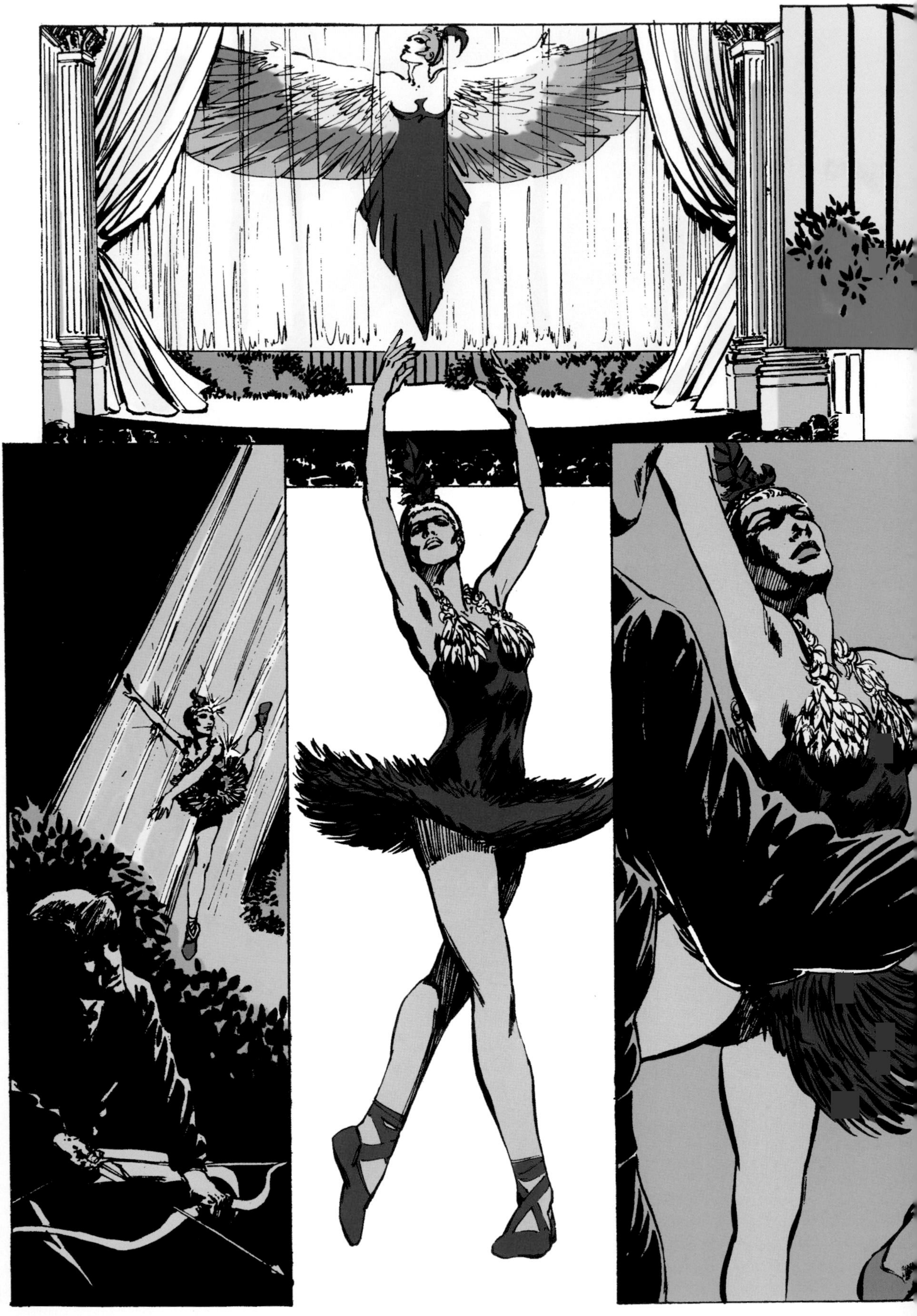

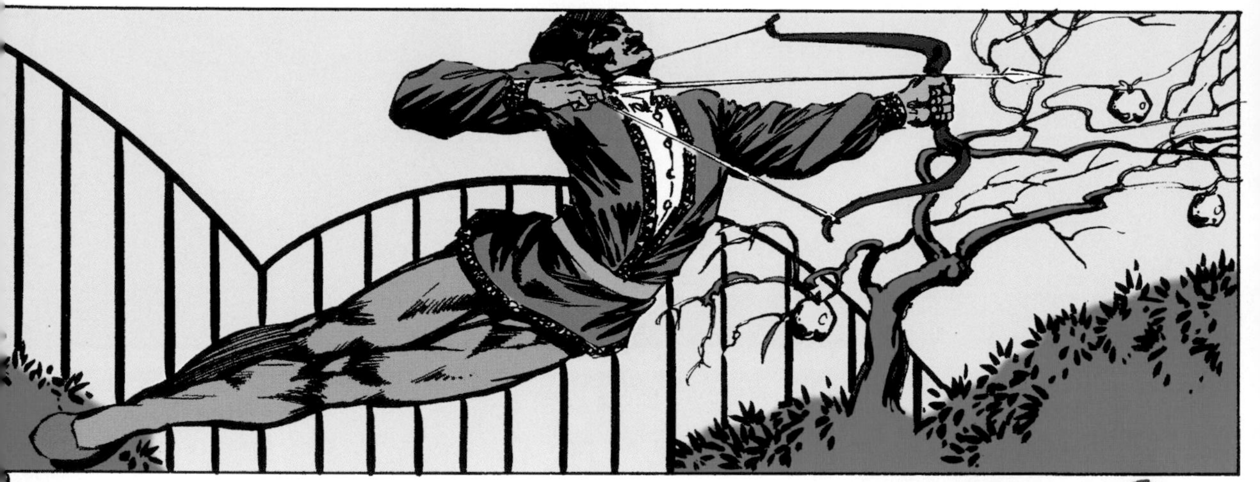

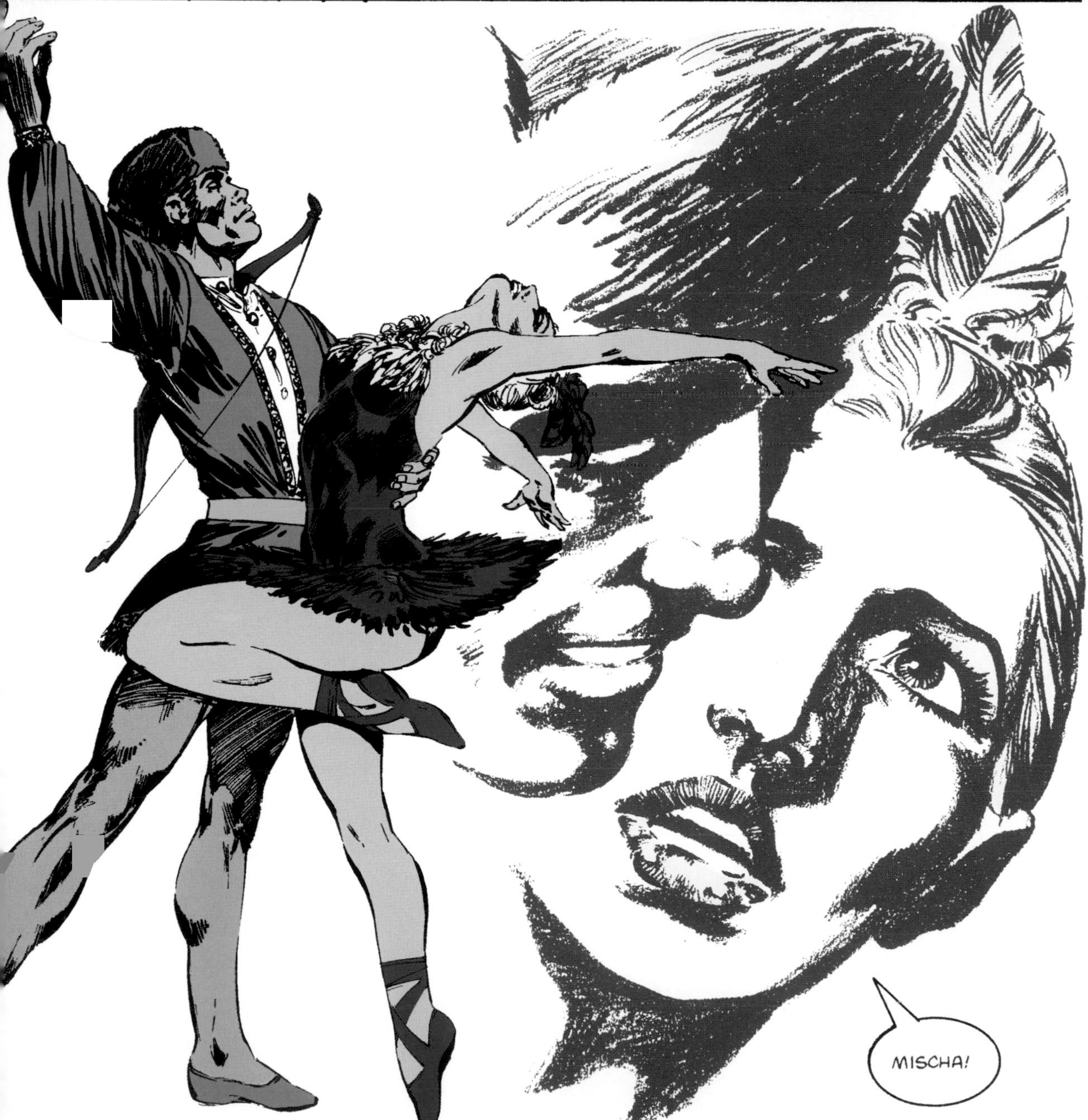
MISCHA!

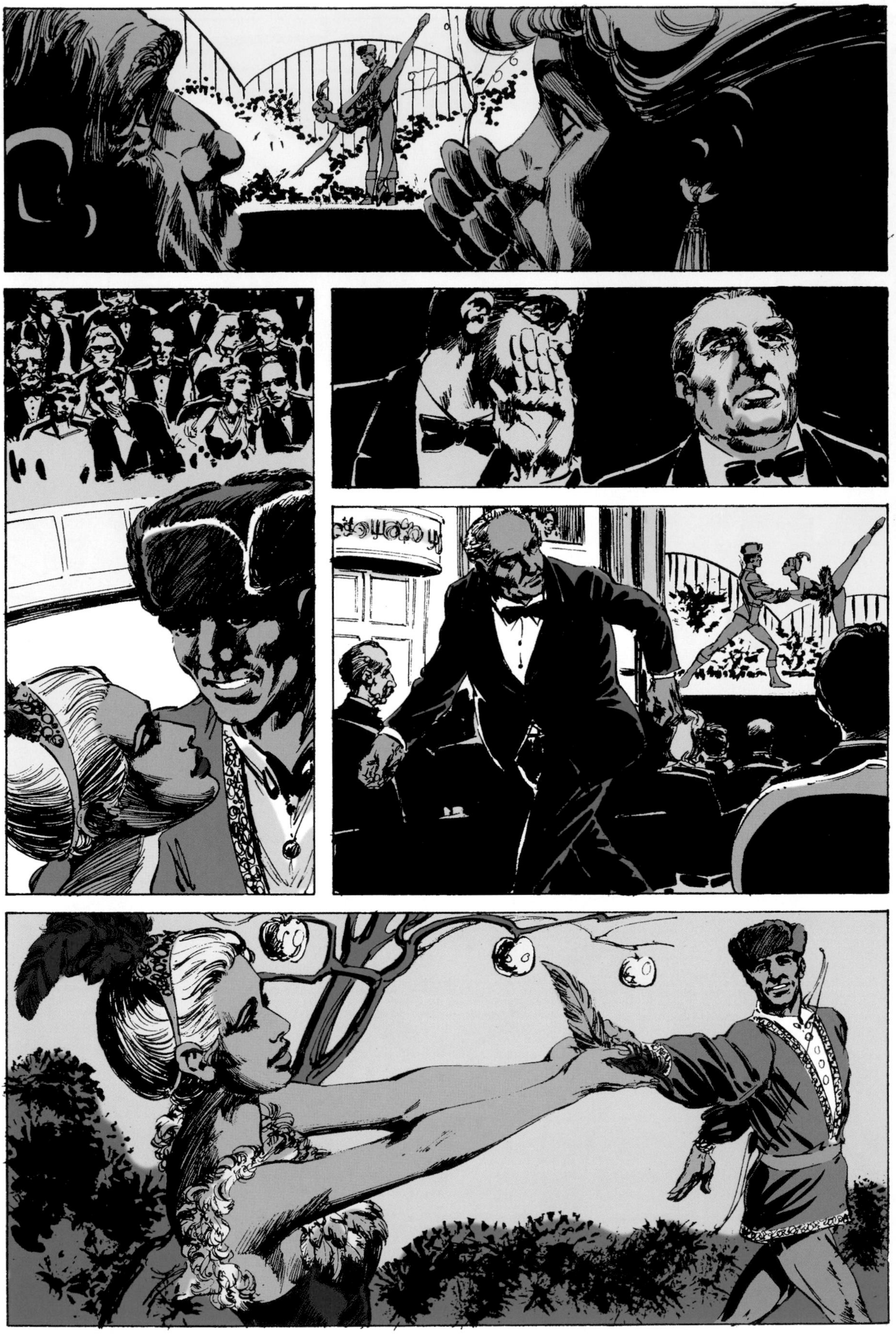

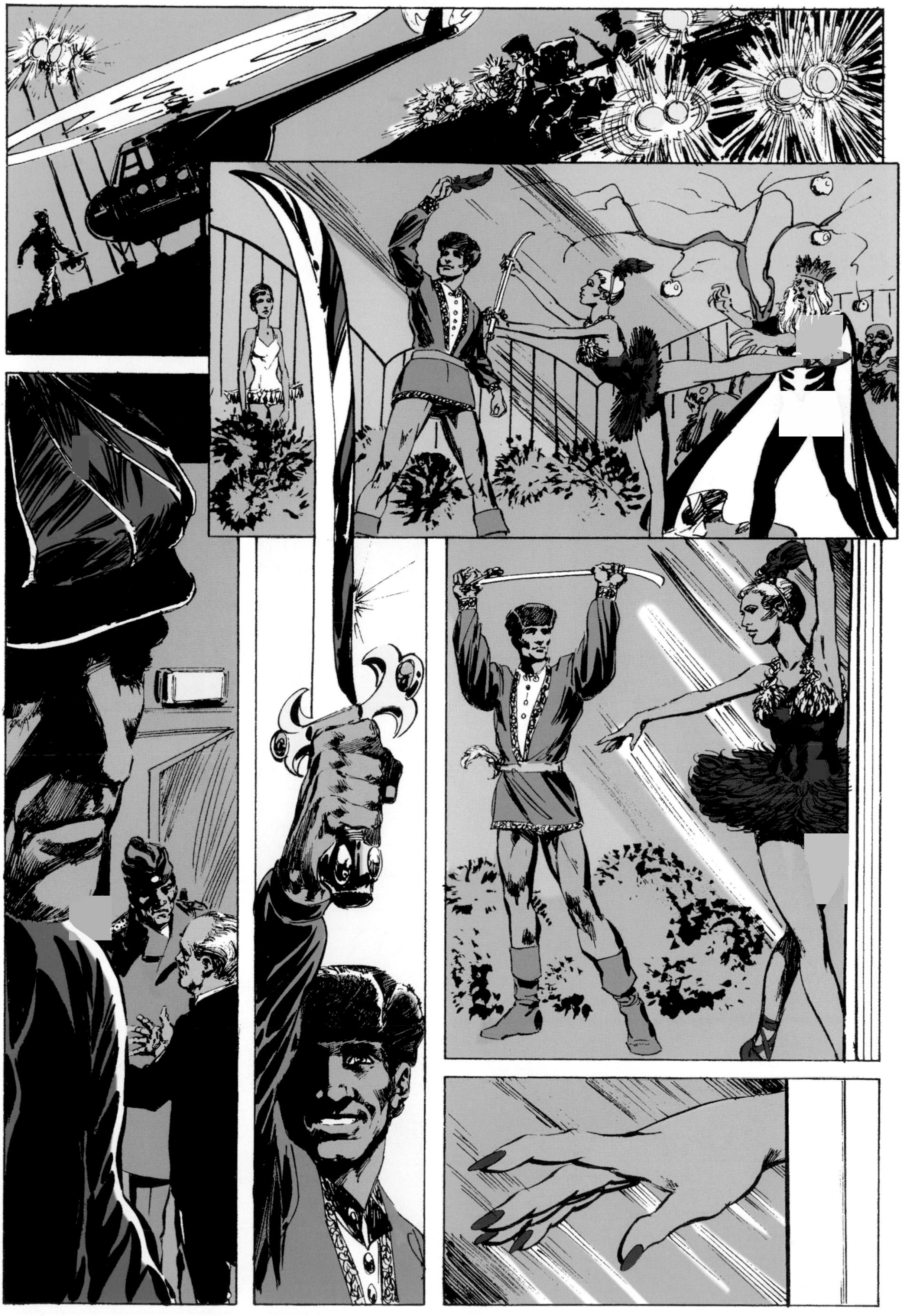

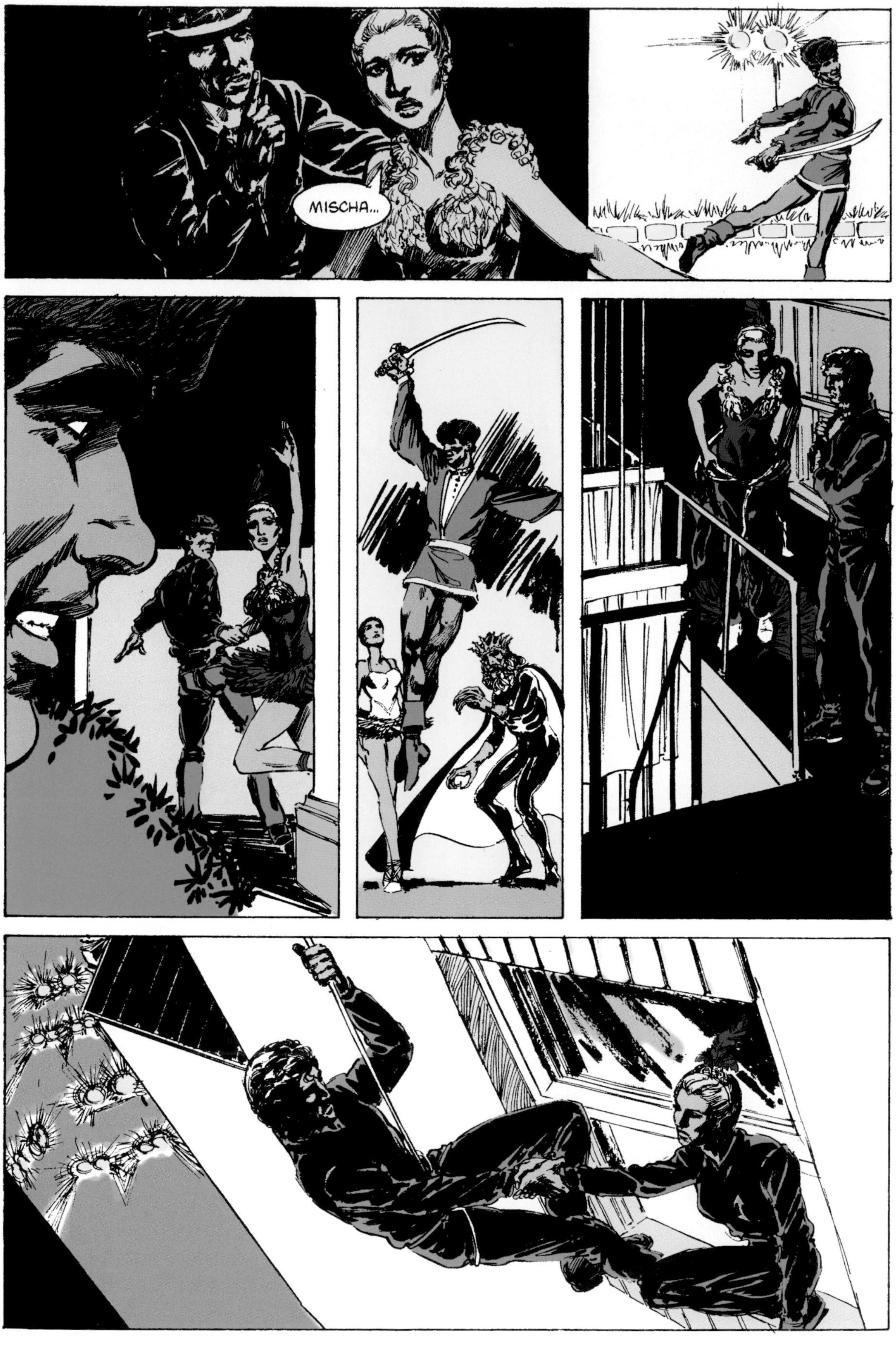
MISCHA...

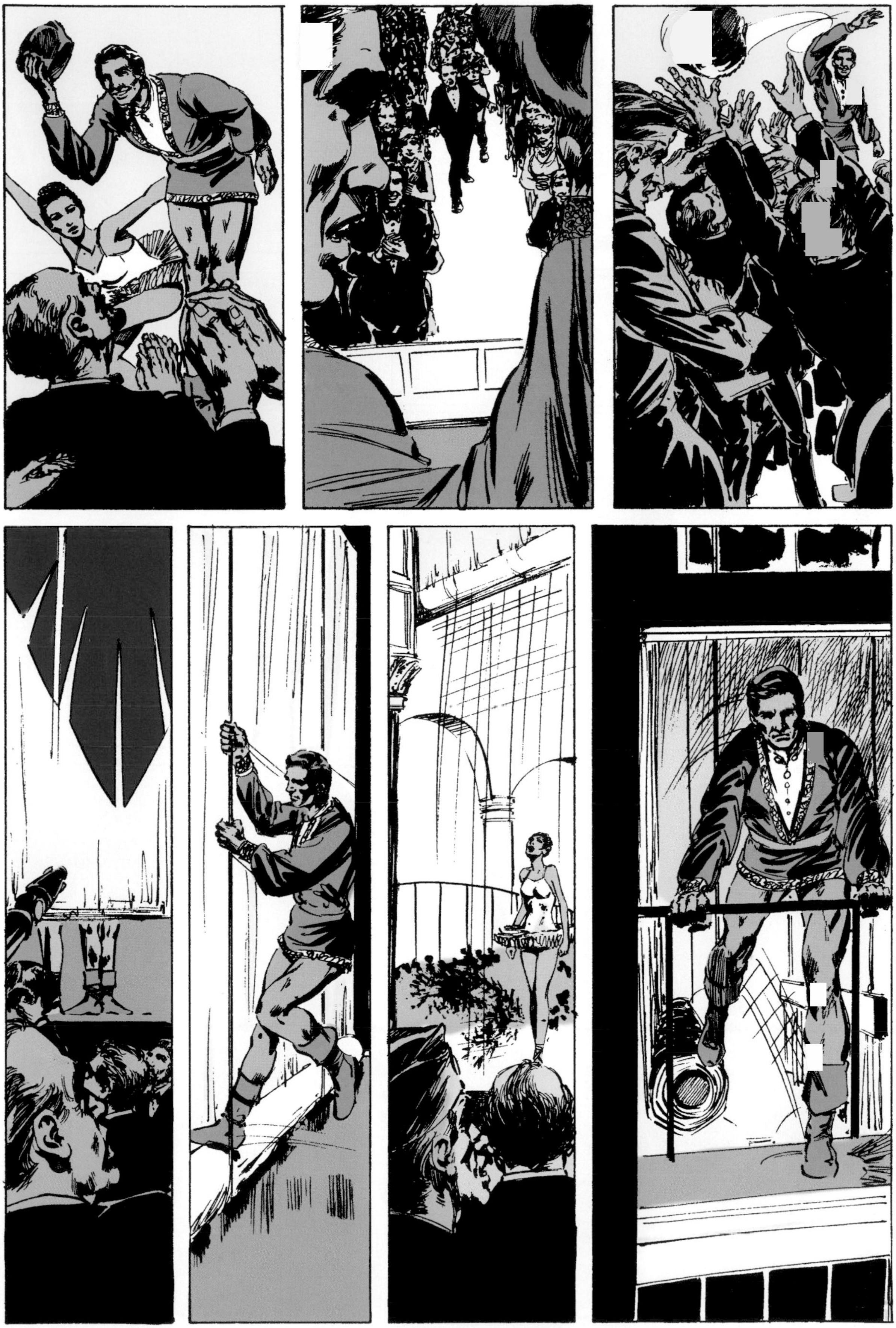

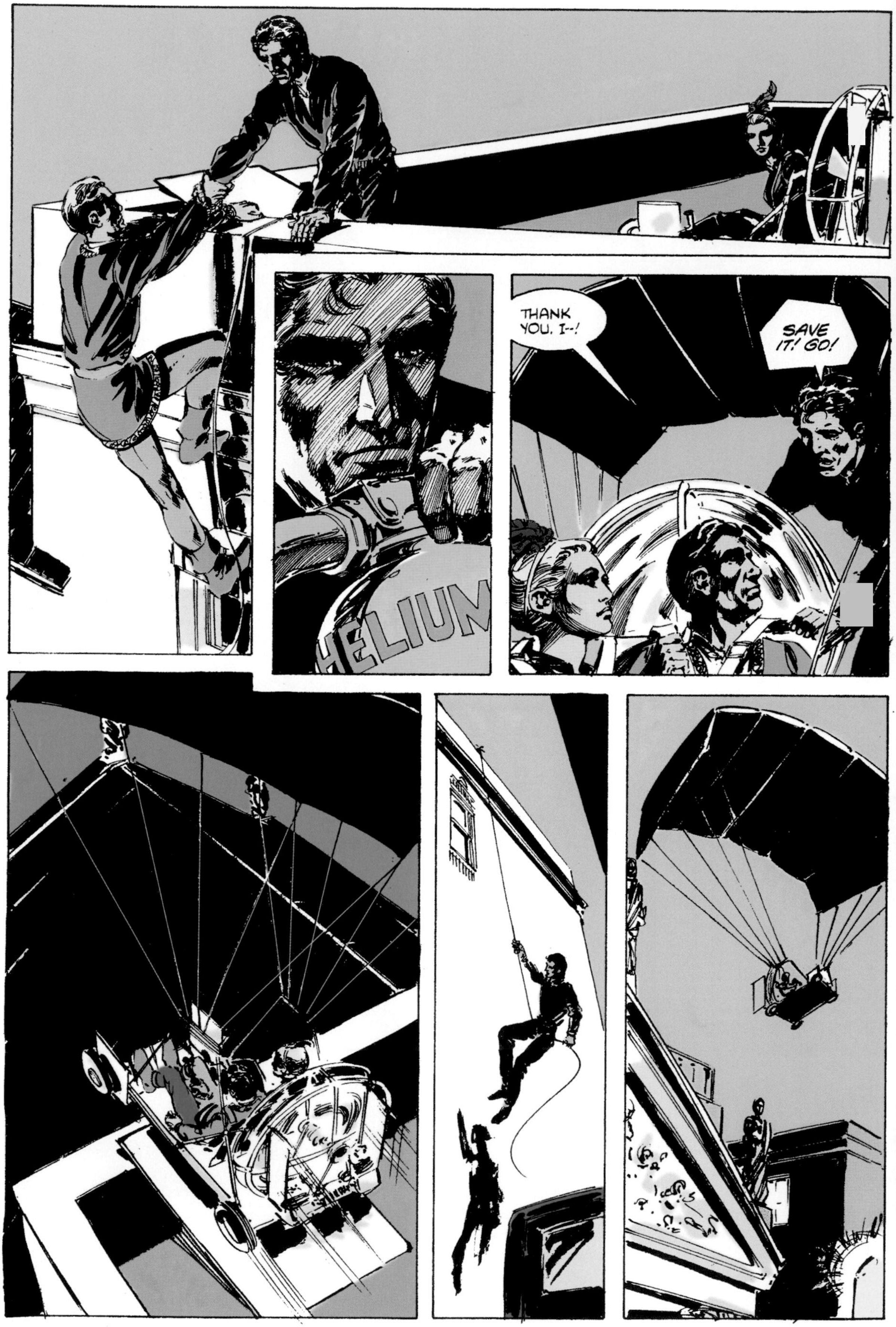
HELIUM
THANK YOU. I--!
SAVE IT! GO!

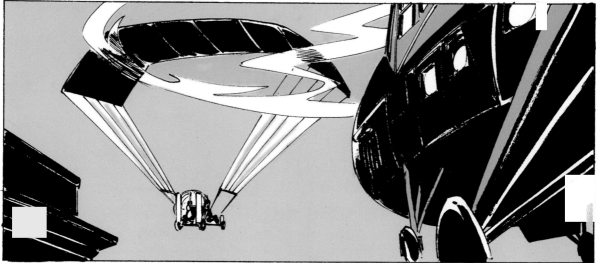

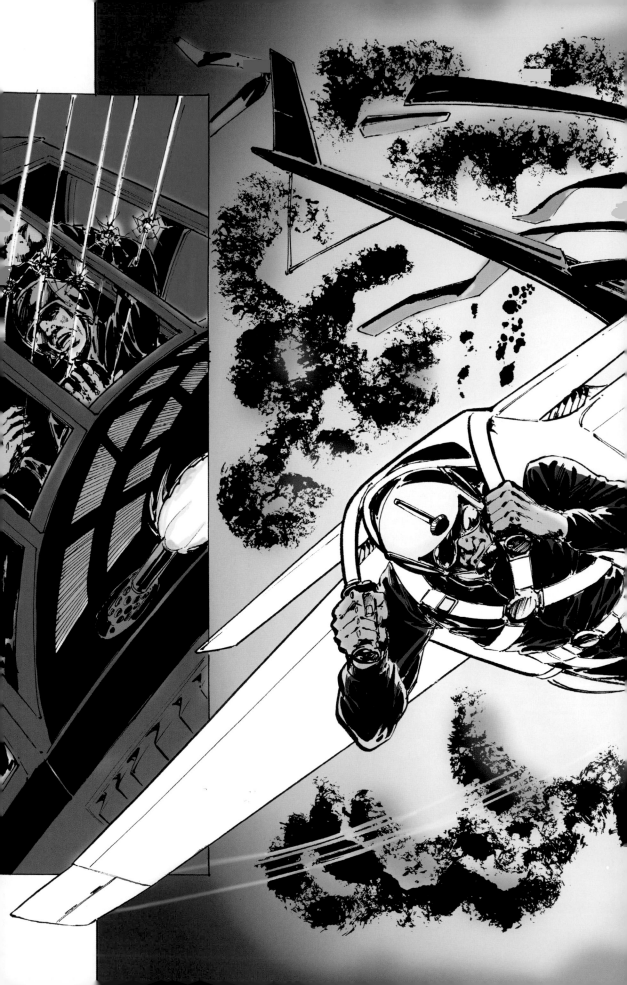

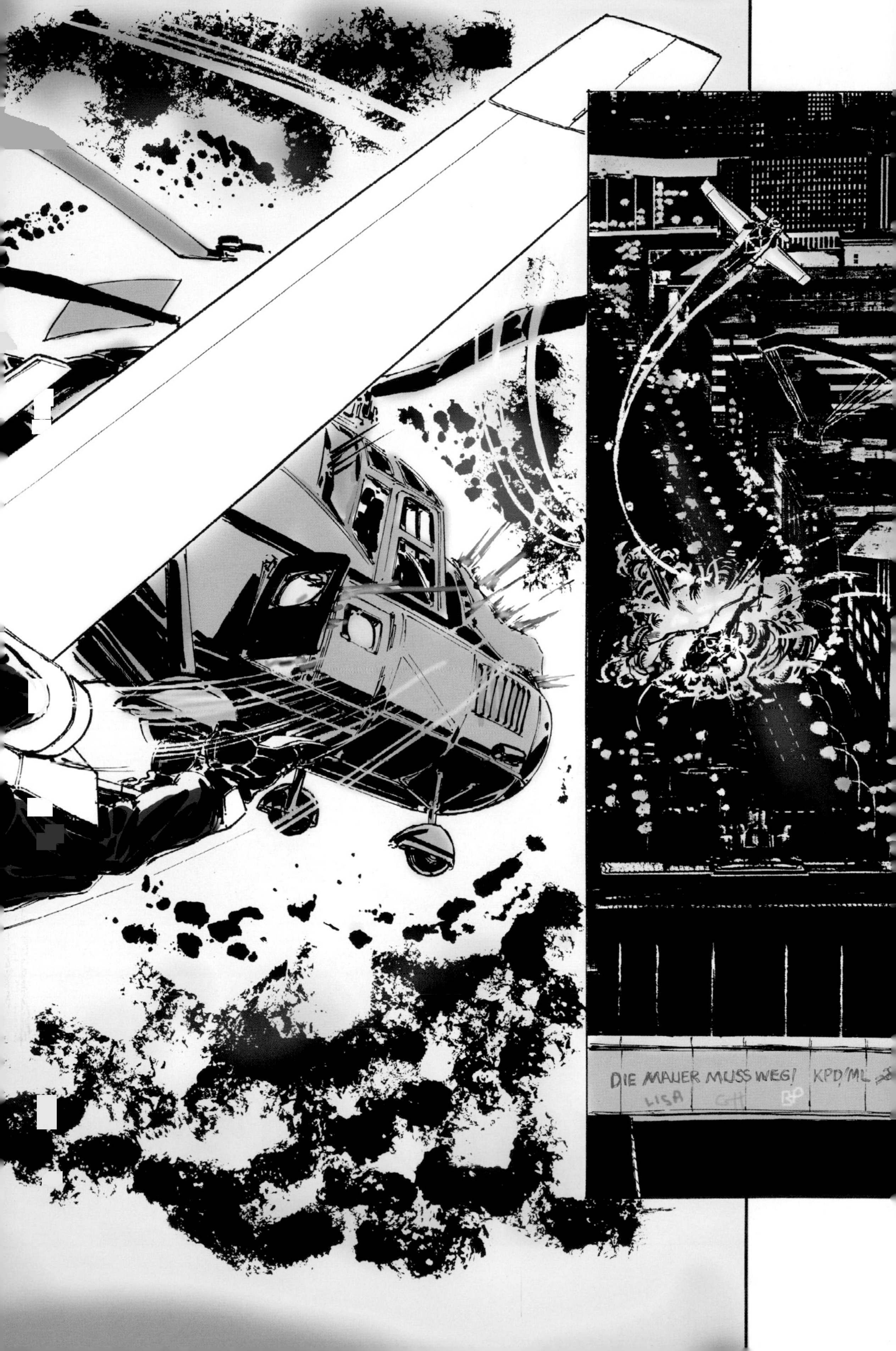
DIE MAUER MUSS WEG! KPD/ML
LISA
GH
BP

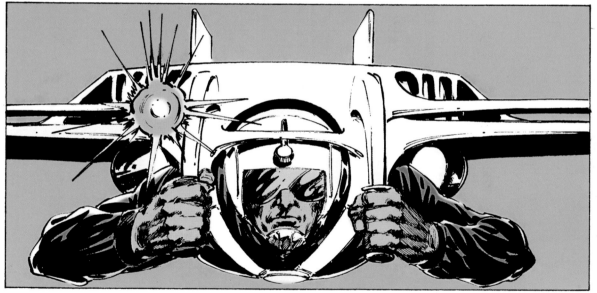

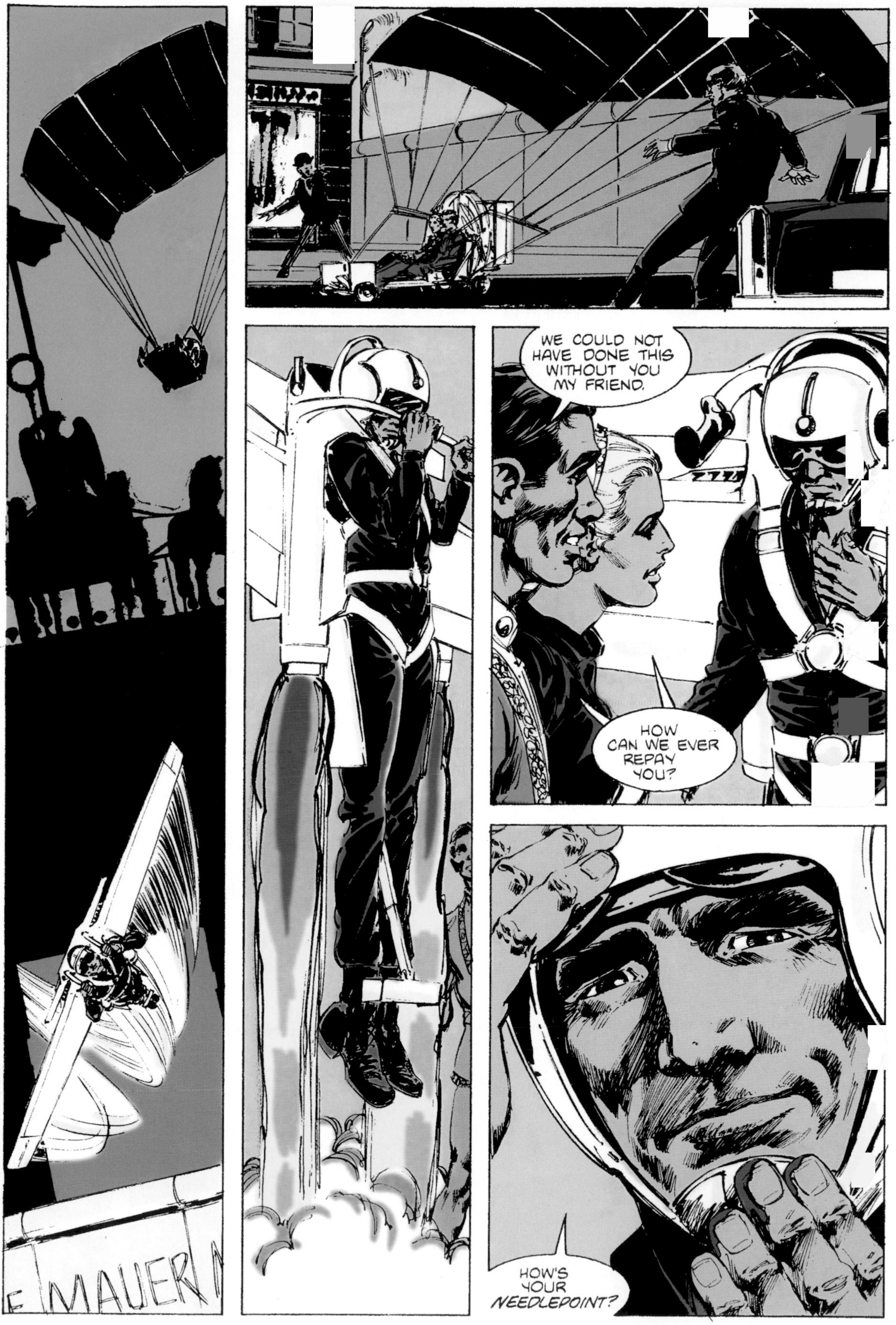
WE COULD NOT HAVE DONE THIS WITHOUT YOU MY FRIEND.
HOW CAN WE EVER REPAY YOU?
HOW'S YOUR NEEDLEPOINT?
MAUER

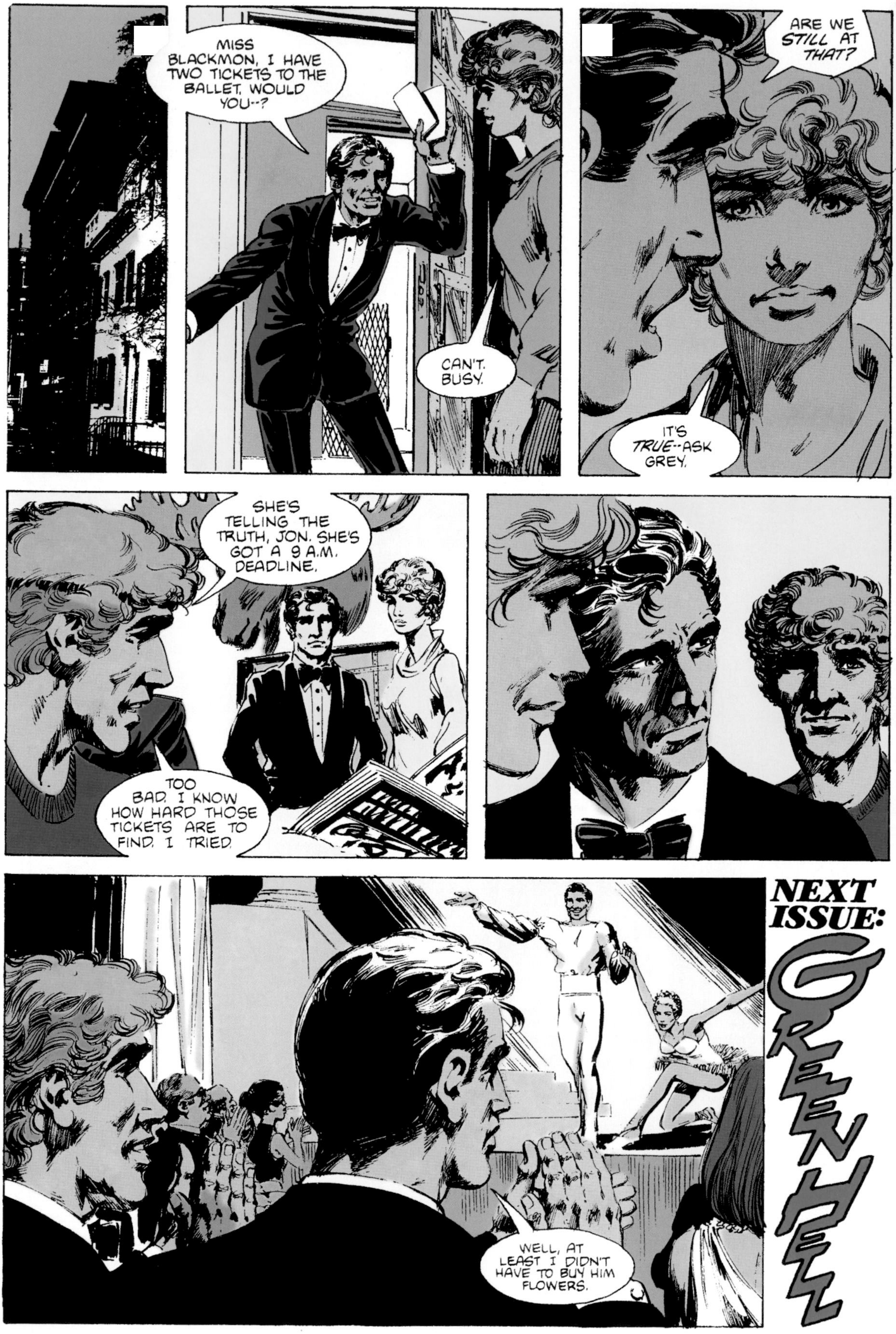

MISS BLACKMON, I HAVE TWO TICKETS TO THE BALLET. WOULD YOU--?
CAN'T. BUSY.
ARE WE STILL AT THAT?
IT'S TRUE--ASK GREY.
SHE'S TELLING THE TRUTH, JON. SHE'S GOT A 9 A.M. DEADLINE.
TOO BAD. I KNOW HOW HARD THOSE TICKETS ARE TO FIND. I TRIED.
WELL, AT LEAST I DIDN'T HAVE TO BUY HIM FLOWERS.
NEXT ISSUE:
GREEN HELL

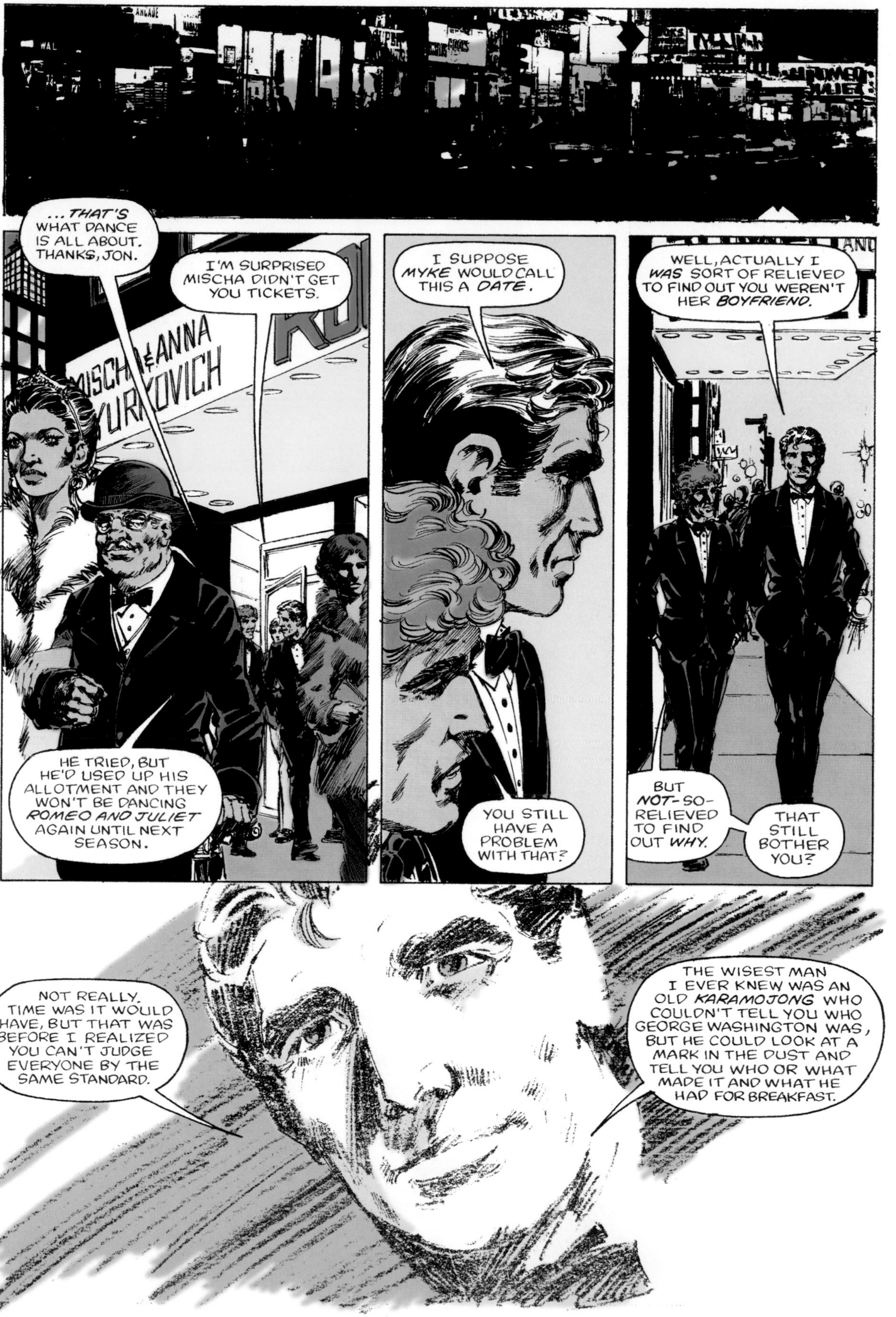
...THAT'S WHAT DANCE IS ALL ABOUT. THANKS, JON.
I'M SURPRISED MISCHA DIDN'T GET YOU TICKETS.
MISCHA & ANNA YURKOVICH
HE TRIED, BUT HE'D USED UP HIS ALLOTMENT AND THEY WON'T BE DANCING ROMEO AND JULIET AGAIN UNTIL NEXT SEASON.
I SUPPOSE MYKE WOULD CALL THIS A DATE.
YOU STILL HAVE A PROBLEM WITH THAT?
WELL, ACTUALLY I WAS SORT OF RELIEVED TO FIND OUT YOU WEREN'T HER BOYFRIEND.
BUT NOT-SO-RELIEVED TO FIND OUT WHY.
THAT STILL BOTHER YOU?
NOT REALLY. TIME WAS IT WOULD HAVE, BUT THAT WAS BEFORE I REALIZED YOU CAN'T JUDGE EVERYONE BY THE SAME STANDARD.
THE WISEST MAN I EVER KNEW WAS AN OLD KARAMOJONG WHO COULDN'T TELL YOU WHO GEORGE WASHINGTON WAS, BUT HE COULD LOOK AT A MARK IN THE DUST AND TELL YOU WHO OR WHAT MADE IT AND WHAT HE HAD FOR BREAKFAST.

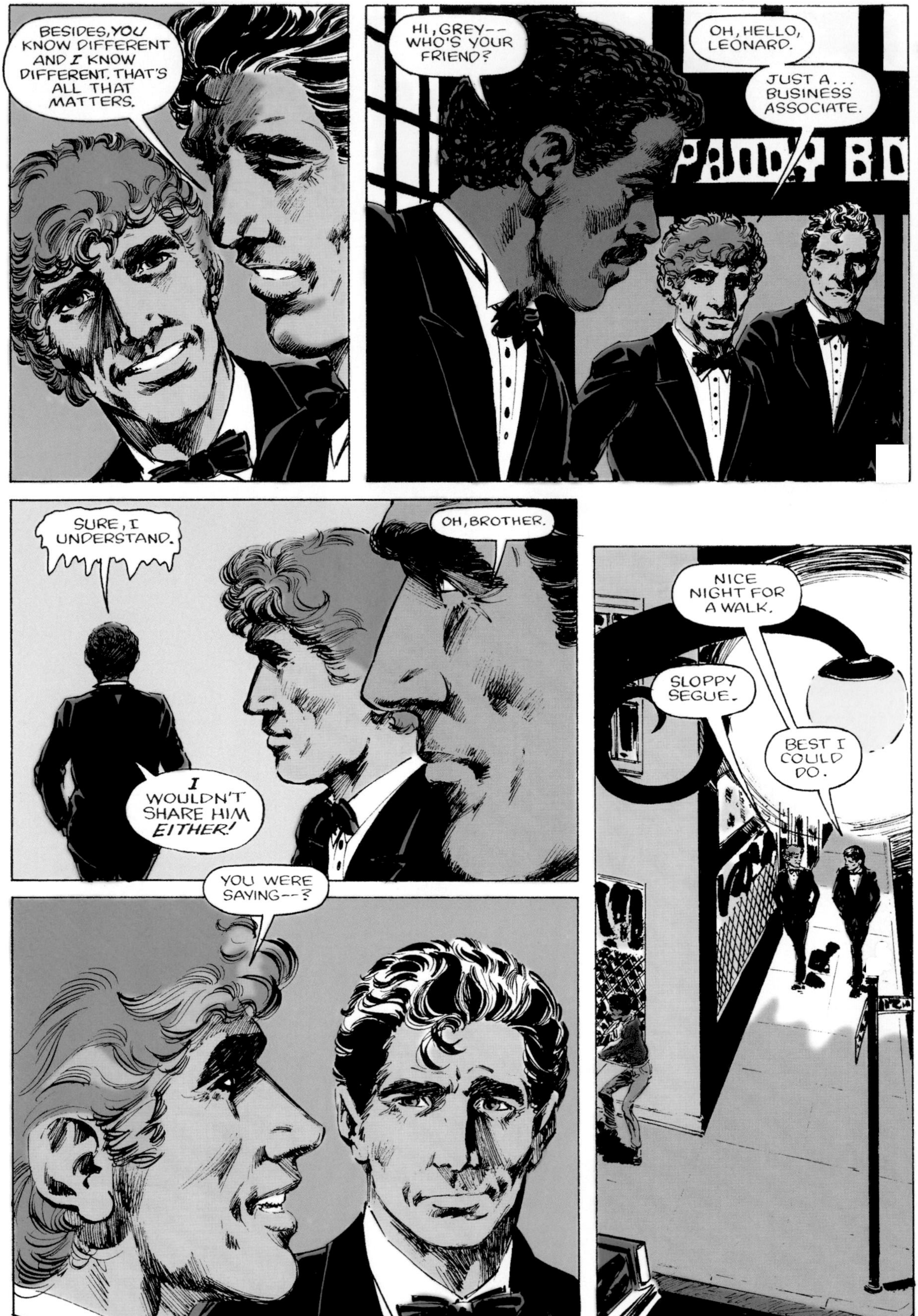
BESIDES, YOU KNOW DIFFERENT AND I KNOW DIFFERENT. THAT'S ALL THAT MATTERS.
HI, GREY-- WHO'S YOUR FRIEND?
OH, HELLO, LEONARD.
JUST A... BUSINESS ASSOCIATE.
SURE, I UNDERSTAND.
OH, BROTHER.
I WOULDN'T SHARE HIM EITHER!
YOU WERE SAYING--?
NICE NIGHT FOR A WALK.
SLOPPY SEGUE.
BEST I COULD DO.

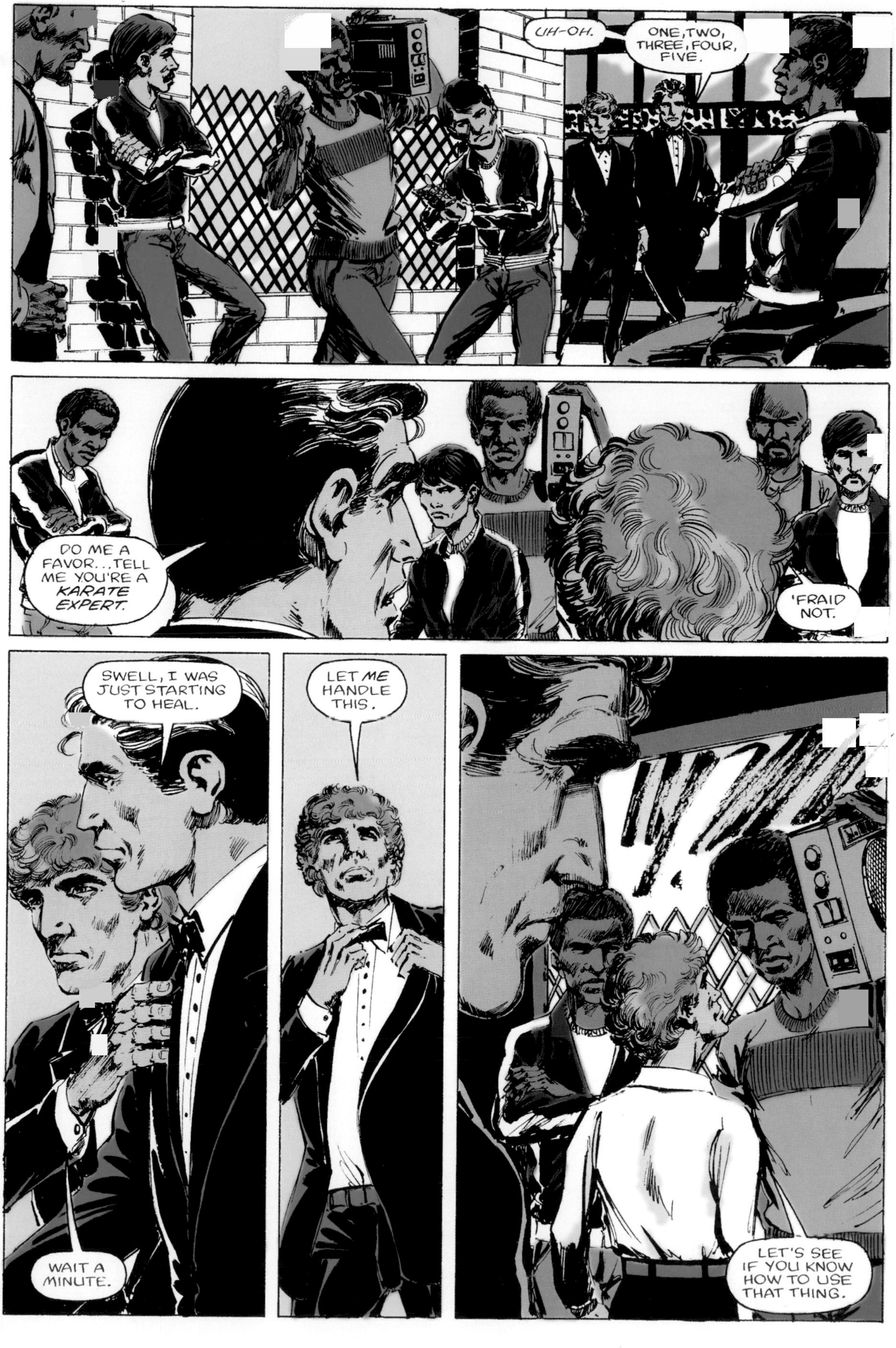
UH-OH.
ONE, TWO, THREE, FOUR, FIVE.
DO ME A FAVOR...TELL ME YOU'RE A *KARATE EXPERT.*
'FRAID NOT.
SWELL, I WAS JUST STARTING TO HEAL.
WAIT A MINUTE.
LET *ME* HANDLE THIS.
LET'S SEE IF YOU KNOW HOW TO USE THAT THING.

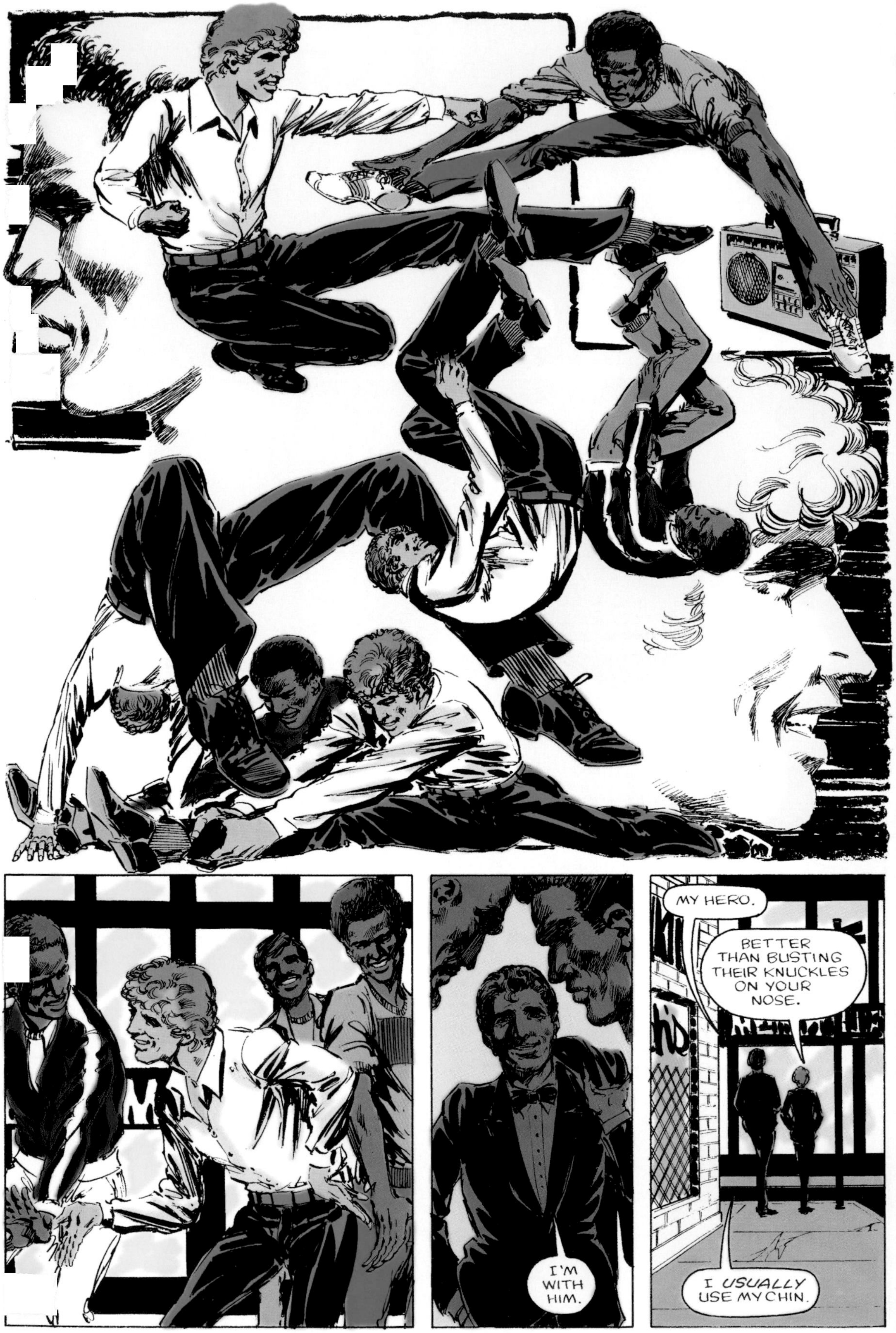
I'M WITH HIM.
MY HERO.
BETTER THAN BUSTING THEIR KNUCKLES ON YOUR NOSE.
I USUALLY USE MY CHIN.

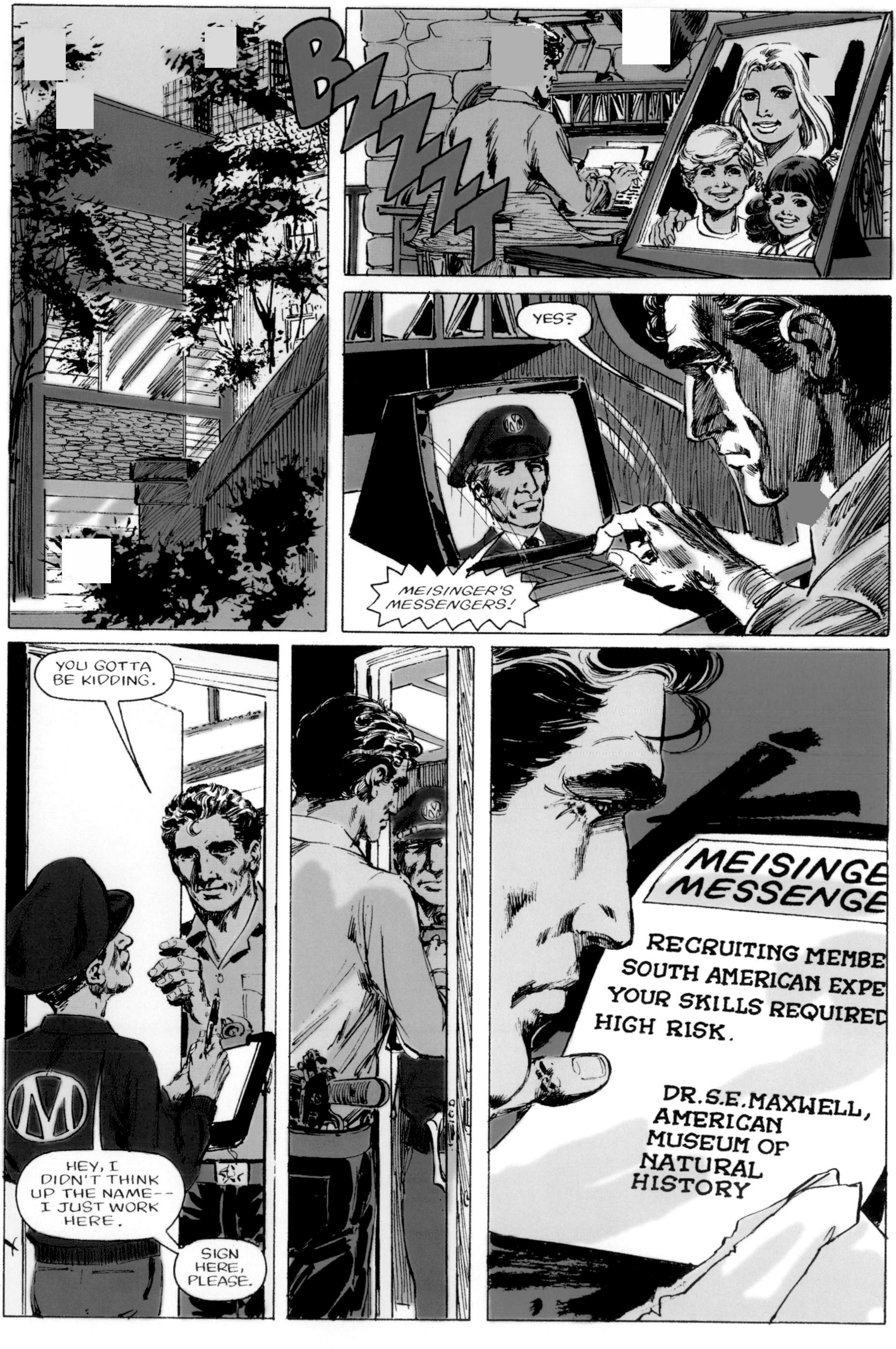
BZZZZZ
YES?
MEISINGER'S MESSENGERS!
YOU GOTTA BE KIDDING.
HEY, I DIDN'T THINK UP THE NAME-- I JUST WORK HERE.
SIGN HERE, PLEASE.
MEISINGE
MESSENGE
RECRUITING MEMBE
SOUTH AMERICAN EXPE
YOUR SKILLS REQUIRED
HIGH RISK.
DR. S.E. MAXWELL,
AMERICAN
MUSEUM OF
NATURAL
HISTORY

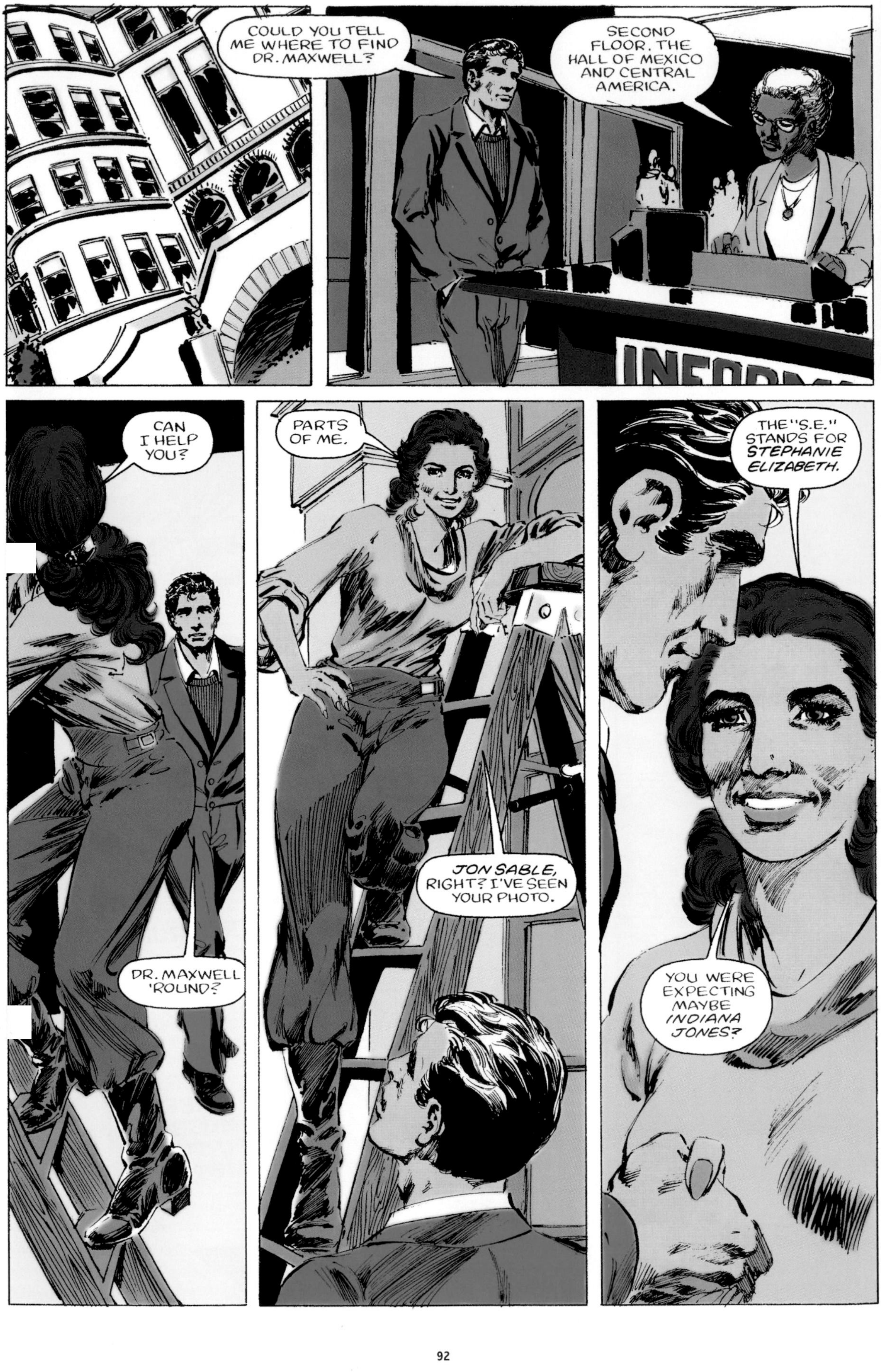
COULD YOU TELL ME WHERE TO FIND DR. MAXWELL?
SECOND FLOOR. THE HALL OF MEXICO AND CENTRAL AMERICA.
INFORM
CAN I HELP YOU?
DR. MAXWELL 'ROUND?
PARTS OF ME.
JON SABLE, RIGHT? I'VE SEEN YOUR PHOTO.
THE "S.E." STANDS FOR STEPHANIE ELIZABETH.
YOU WERE EXPECTING MAYBE INDIANA JONES?

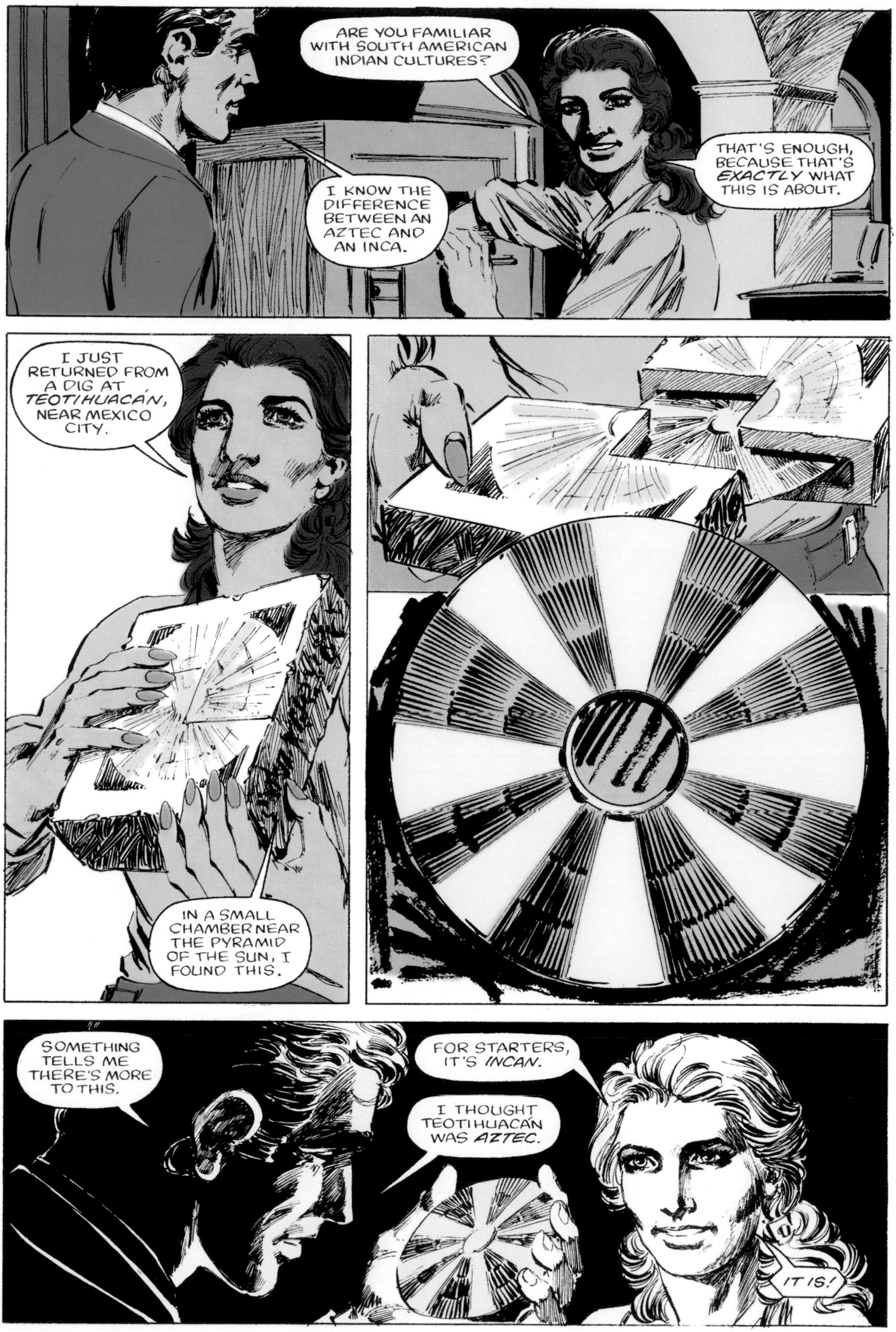
ARE YOU FAMILIAR WITH SOUTH AMERICAN INDIAN CULTURES?
I KNOW THE DIFFERENCE BETWEEN AN AZTEC AND AN INCA.
THAT'S ENOUGH, BECAUSE THAT'S *EXACTLY* WHAT THIS IS ABOUT.
I JUST RETURNED FROM A DIG AT *TEOTIHUACÁN*, NEAR MEXICO CITY.
IN A SMALL CHAMBER NEAR THE PYRAMID OF THE SUN, I FOUND THIS.
SOMETHING TELLS ME THERE'S MORE TO THIS.
FOR STARTERS, IT'S *INCAN*.
I THOUGHT TEOTIHUACÁN WAS *AZTEC*.
IT IS!

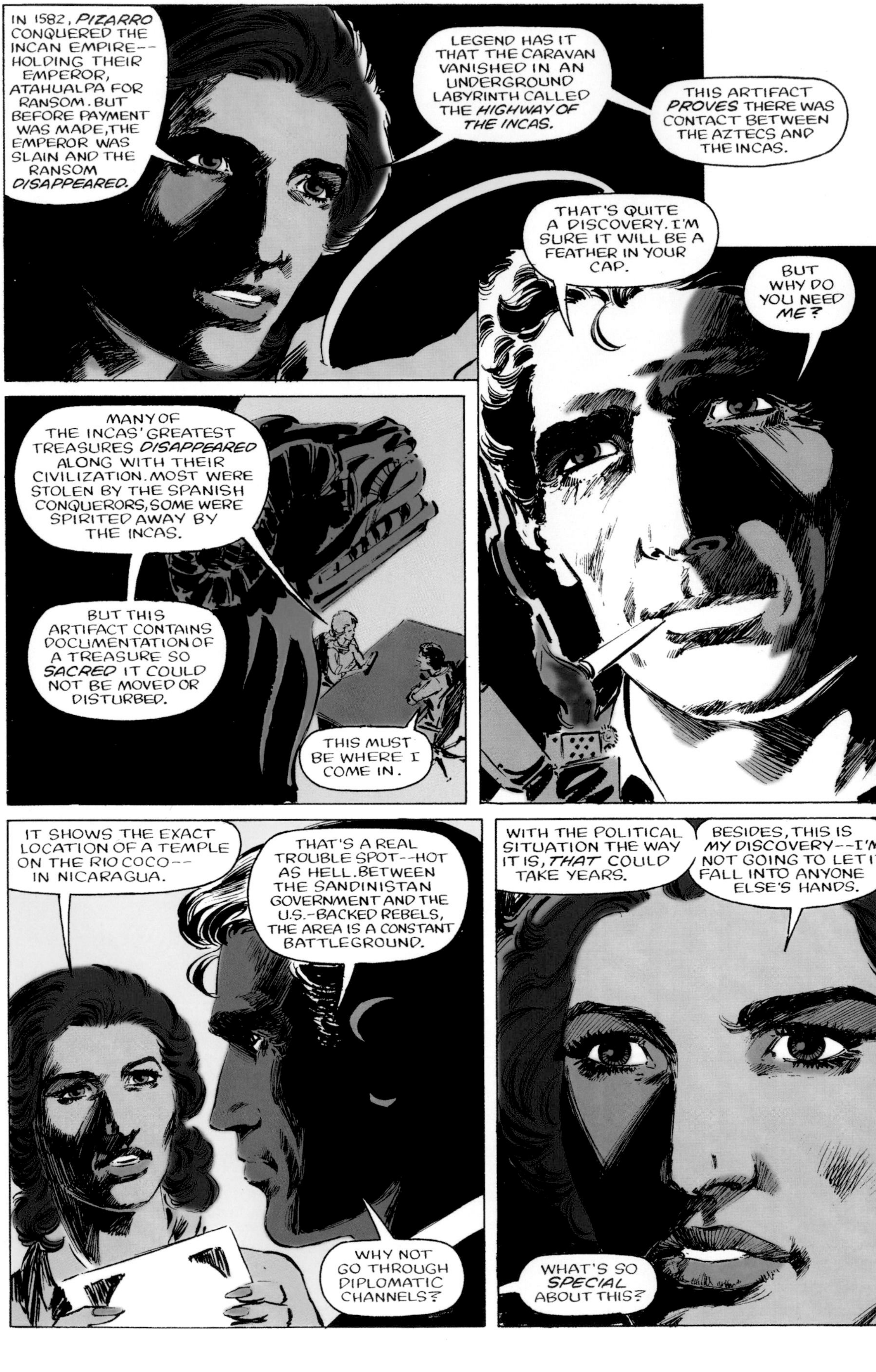
IN 1582, PIZARRO CONQUERED THE INCAN EMPIRE--HOLDING THEIR EMPEROR, ATAHUALPA FOR RANSOM. BUT BEFORE PAYMENT WAS MADE, THE EMPEROR WAS SLAIN AND THE RANSOM DISAPPEARED.
LEGEND HAS IT THAT THE CARAVAN VANISHED IN AN UNDERGROUND LABYRINTH CALLED THE HIGHWAY OF THE INCAS.
THIS ARTIFACT PROVES THERE WAS CONTACT BETWEEN THE AZTECS AND THE INCAS.
THAT'S QUITE A DISCOVERY. I'M SURE IT WILL BE A FEATHER IN YOUR CAP.
BUT WHY DO YOU NEED ME?
MANY OF THE INCAS' GREATEST TREASURES DISAPPEARED ALONG WITH THEIR CIVILIZATION. MOST WERE STOLEN BY THE SPANISH CONQUERORS, SOME WERE SPIRITED AWAY BY THE INCAS.
BUT THIS ARTIFACT CONTAINS DOCUMENTATION OF A TREASURE SO SACRED IT COULD NOT BE MOVED OR DISTURBED.
THIS MUST BE WHERE I COME IN.
IT SHOWS THE EXACT LOCATION OF A TEMPLE ON THE RIO COCO--IN NICARAGUA.
THAT'S A REAL TROUBLE SPOT--HOT AS HELL. BETWEEN THE SANDINISTAN GOVERNMENT AND THE U.S.-BACKED REBELS, THE AREA IS A CONSTANT BATTLEGROUND.
WHY NOT GO THROUGH DIPLOMATIC CHANNELS?
WITH THE POLITICAL SITUATION THE WAY IT IS, THAT COULD TAKE YEARS.
BESIDES, THIS IS MY DISCOVERY--I'M NOT GOING TO LET IT FALL INTO ANYONE ELSE'S HANDS.
WHAT'S SO SPECIAL ABOUT THIS?

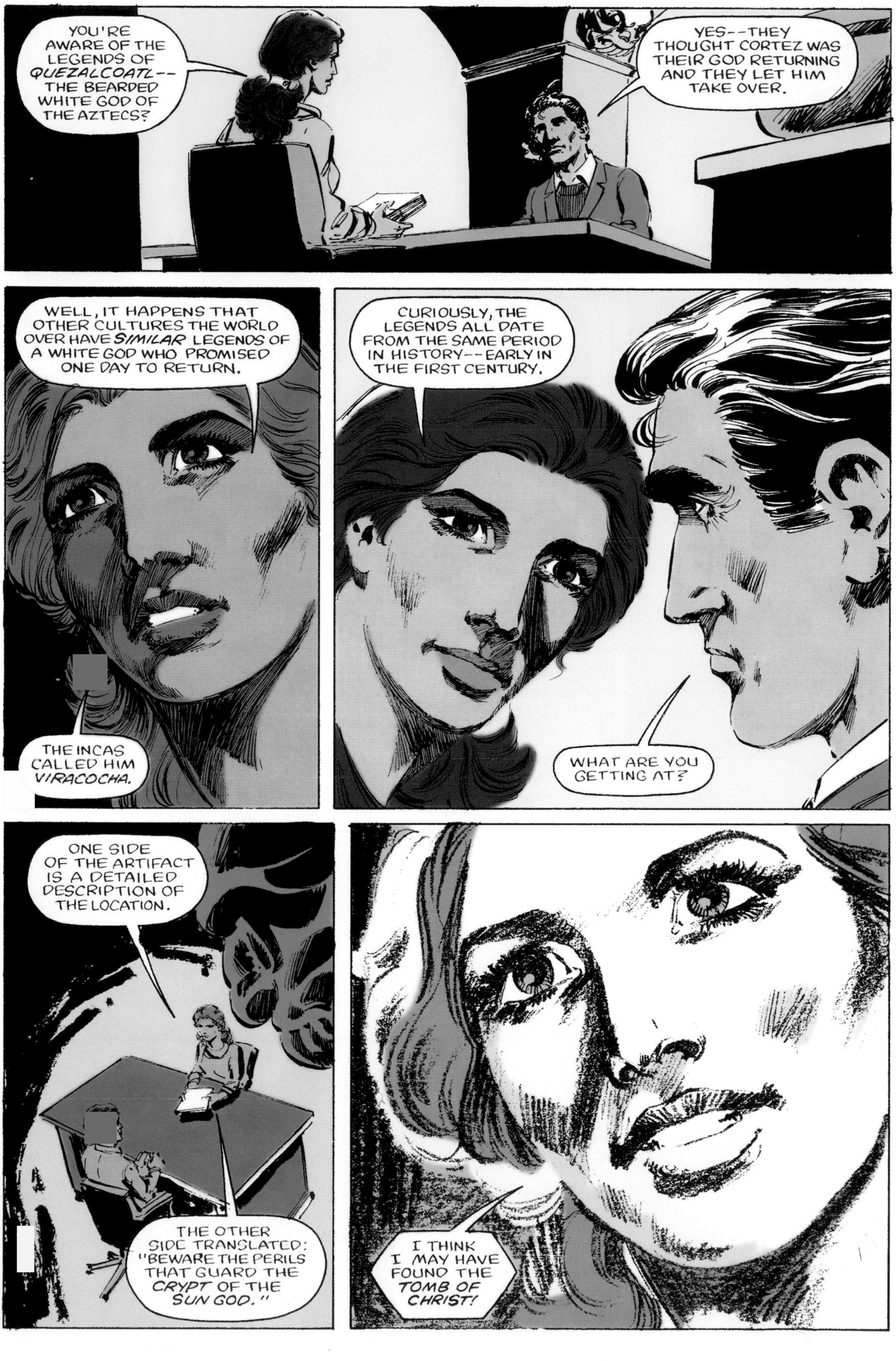
YOU'RE AWARE OF THE LEGENDS OF QUEZALCOATL-- THE BEARDED WHITE GOD OF THE AZTECS?
YES--THEY THOUGHT CORTEZ WAS THEIR GOD RETURNING AND THEY LET HIM TAKE OVER.
WELL, IT HAPPENS THAT OTHER CULTURES THE WORLD OVER HAVE SIMILAR LEGENDS OF A WHITE GOD WHO PROMISED ONE DAY TO RETURN.
THE INCAS CALLED HIM VIRACOCHA.
CURIOUSLY, THE LEGENDS ALL DATE FROM THE SAME PERIOD IN HISTORY--EARLY IN THE FIRST CENTURY.
WHAT ARE YOU GETTING AT?
ONE SIDE OF THE ARTIFACT IS A DETAILED DESCRIPTION OF THE LOCATION.
THE OTHER SIDE TRANSLATED: "BEWARE THE PERILS THAT GUARD THE CRYPT OF THE SUN GOD."
I THINK I MAY HAVE FOUND THE TOMB OF CHRIST!

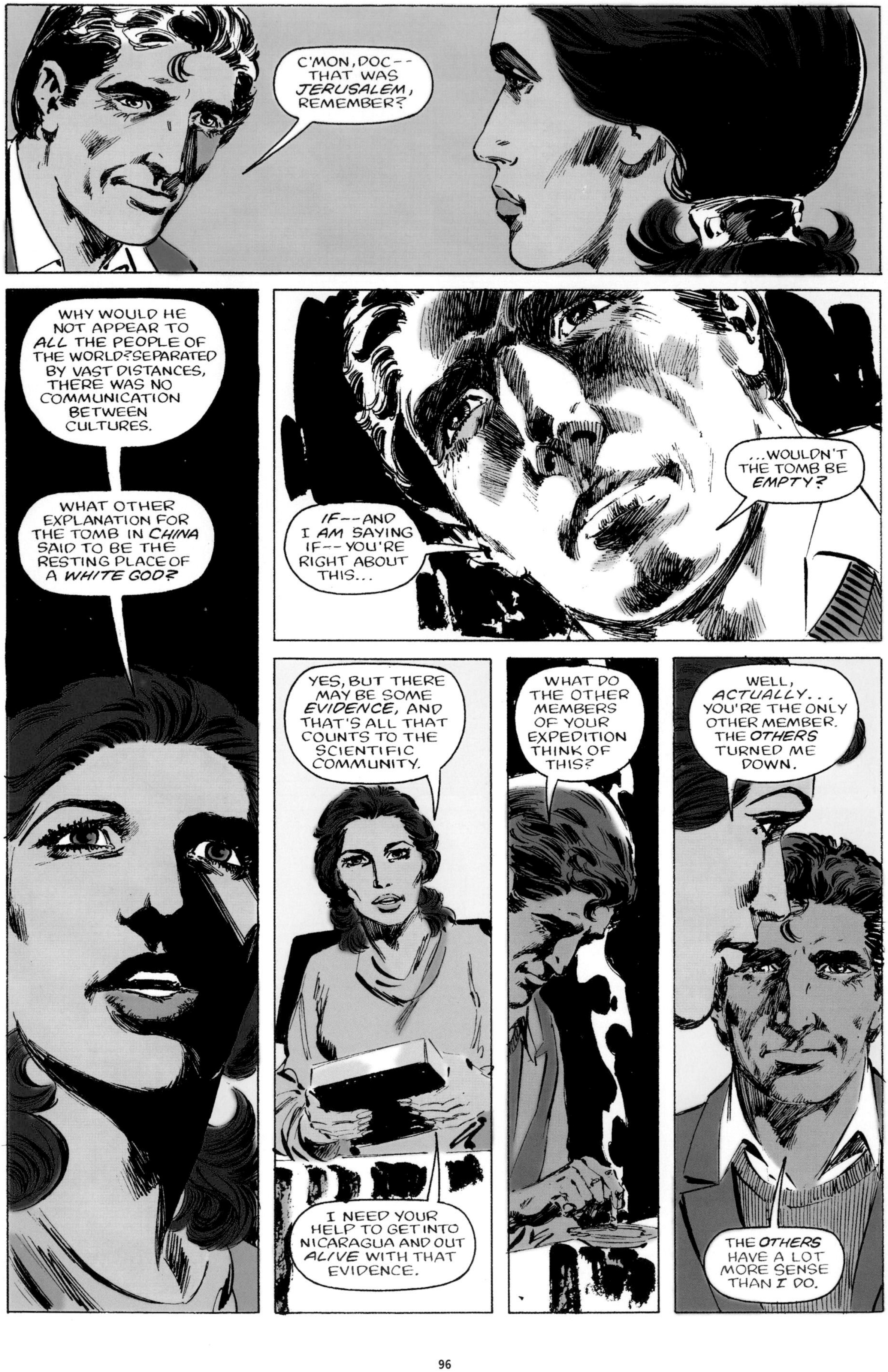

C'MON, DOC-- THAT WAS *JERUSALEM*, REMEMBER?
WHY WOULD HE NOT APPEAR TO *ALL* THE PEOPLE OF THE WORLD? SEPARATED BY VAST DISTANCES, THERE WAS NO COMMUNICATION BETWEEN CULTURES.
WHAT OTHER EXPLANATION FOR THE TOMB IN *CHINA* SAID TO BE THE RESTING PLACE OF A *WHITE GOD?*
IF--AND I *AM* SAYING IF-- YOU'RE RIGHT ABOUT THIS...
...WOULDN'T THE TOMB BE *EMPTY?*
YES, BUT THERE MAY BE SOME *EVIDENCE*, AND THAT'S ALL THAT COUNTS TO THE SCIENTIFIC COMMUNITY.
I NEED YOUR HELP TO GET INTO NICARAGUA AND OUT *ALIVE* WITH THAT EVIDENCE.
WHAT DO THE OTHER MEMBERS OF YOUR EXPEDITION THINK OF THIS?
WELL, *ACTUALLY*... YOU'RE THE ONLY OTHER MEMBER. THE *OTHERS* TURNED ME DOWN.
THE *OTHERS* HAVE A LOT MORE SENSE THAN *I* DO.

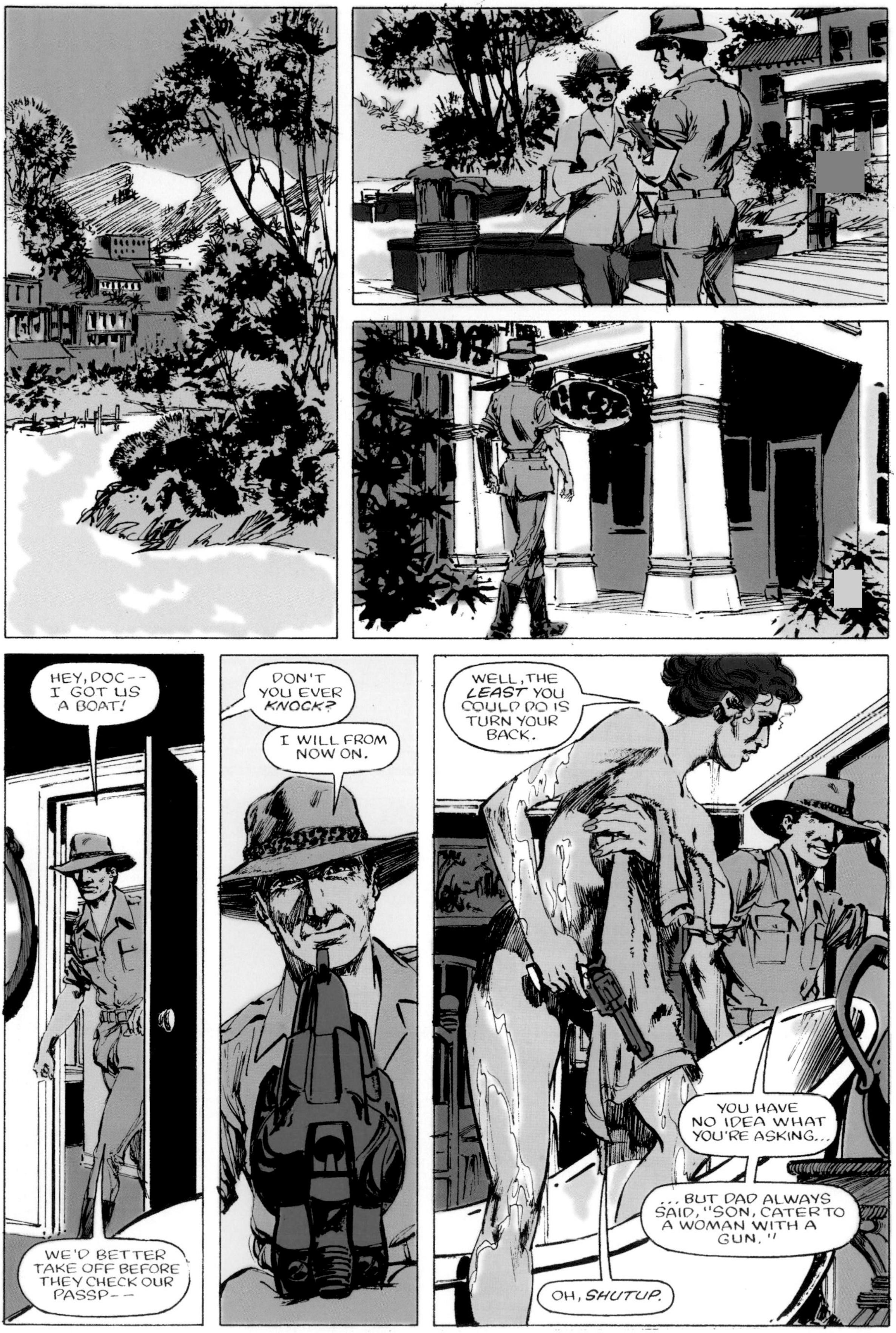
HEY, DOC-- I GOT US A BOAT!
WE'D BETTER TAKE OFF BEFORE THEY CHECK OUR PASSP--
DON'T YOU EVER KNOCK?
I WILL FROM NOW ON.
WELL, THE LEAST YOU COULD DO IS TURN YOUR BACK.
YOU HAVE NO IDEA WHAT YOU'RE ASKING...
...BUT DAD ALWAYS SAID, "SON, CATER TO A WOMAN WITH A GUN."
OH, SHUTUP.

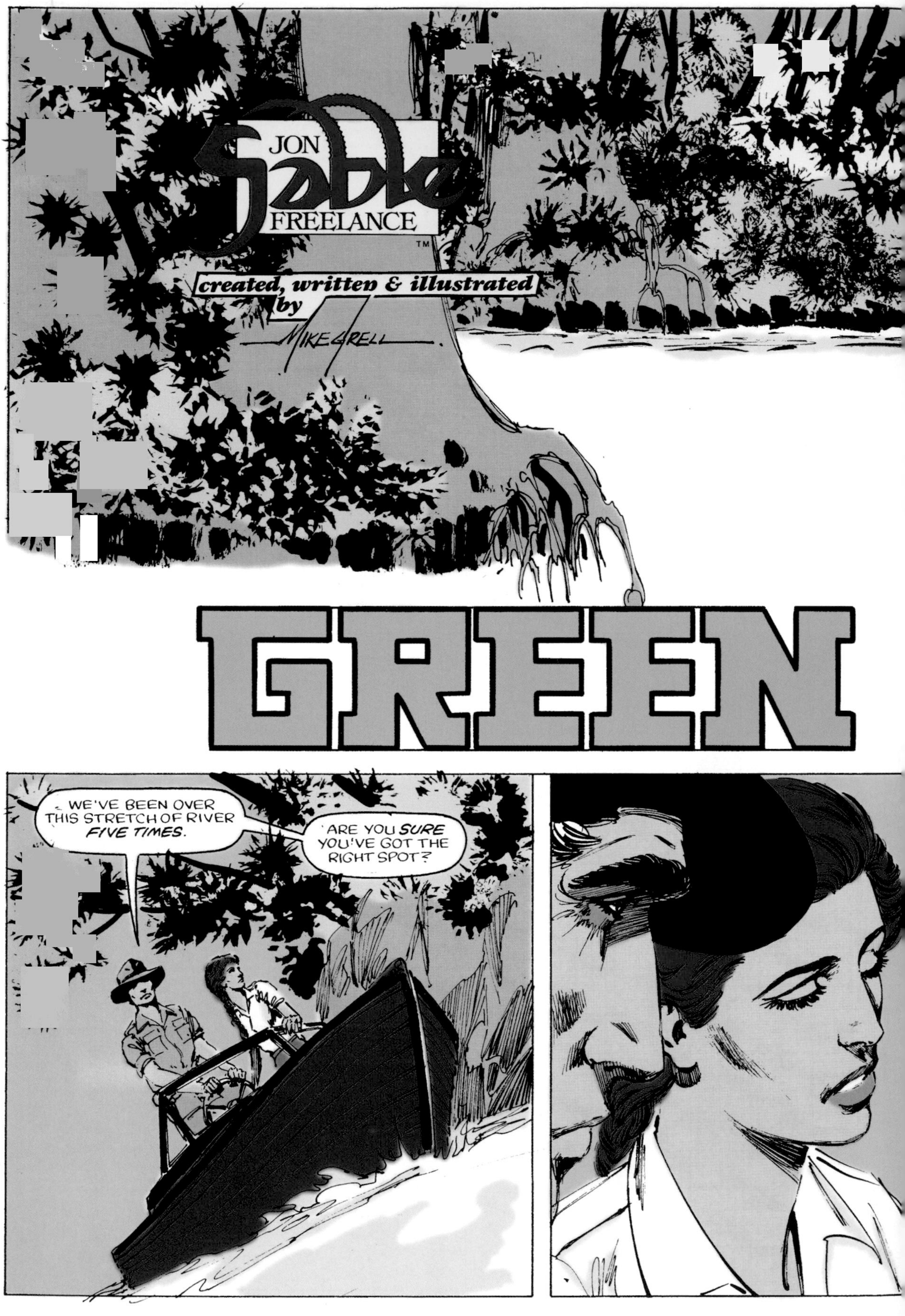
JON Sable FREELANCE ™
created, written & illustrated by
MIKE GRELL
GREEN
WE'VE BEEN OVER THIS STRETCH OF RIVER FIVE TIMES.
ARE YOU SURE YOU'VE GOT THE RIGHT SPOT?

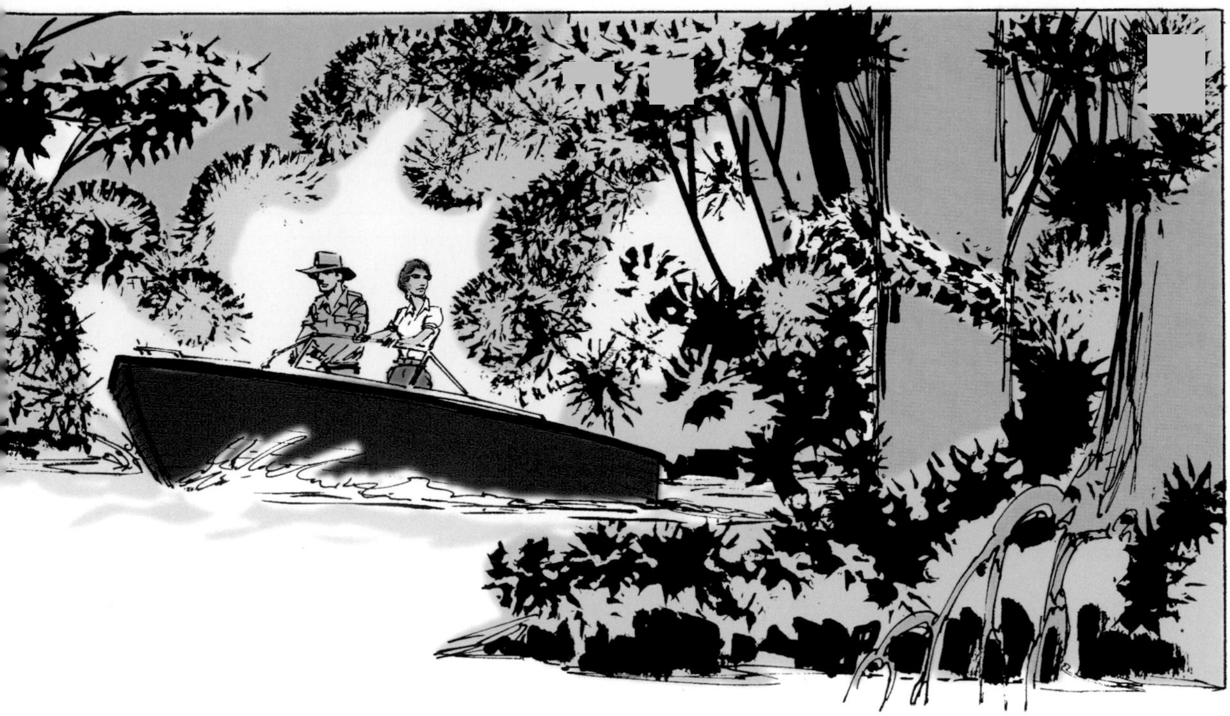

HELL

JANICE CHIANG
LETTERER
JANICE COHEN
COLORIST
MIKE GOLD
EDITOR

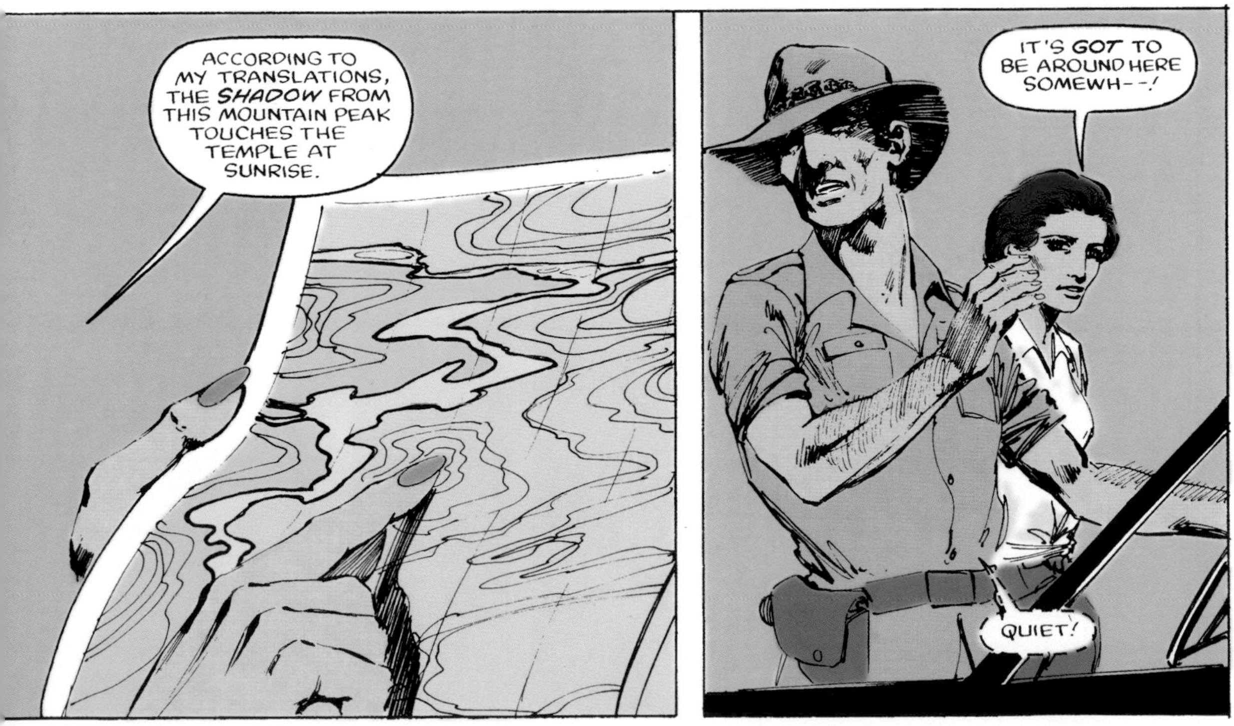
ACCORDING TO MY TRANSLATIONS, THE SHADOW FROM THIS MOUNTAIN PEAK TOUCHES THE TEMPLE AT SUNRISE.
IT'S GOT TO BE AROUND HERE SOMEWH--!
QUIET!

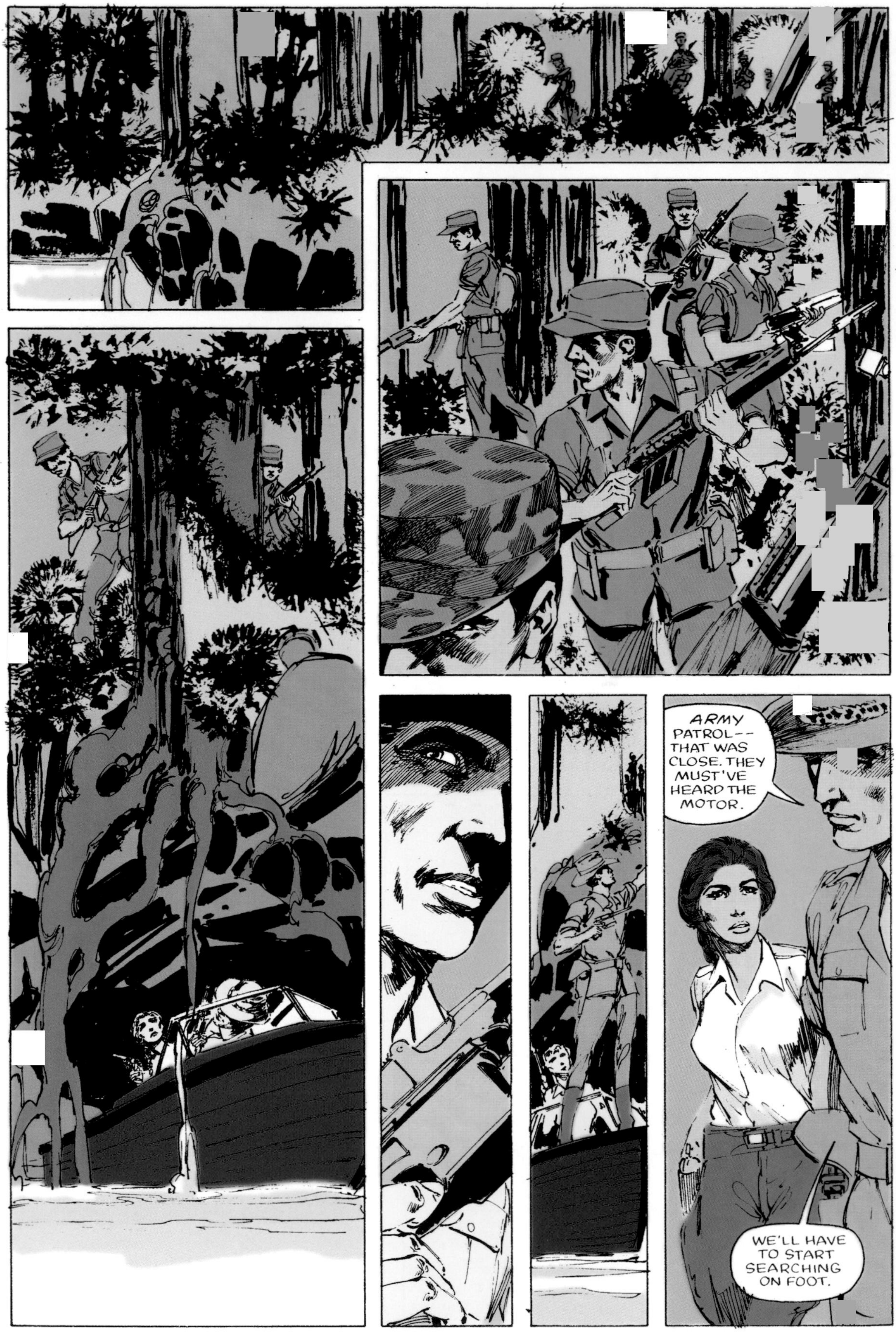
ARMY PATROL-- THAT WAS CLOSE. THEY MUST'VE HEARD THE MOTOR.
WE'LL HAVE TO START SEARCHING ON FOOT.

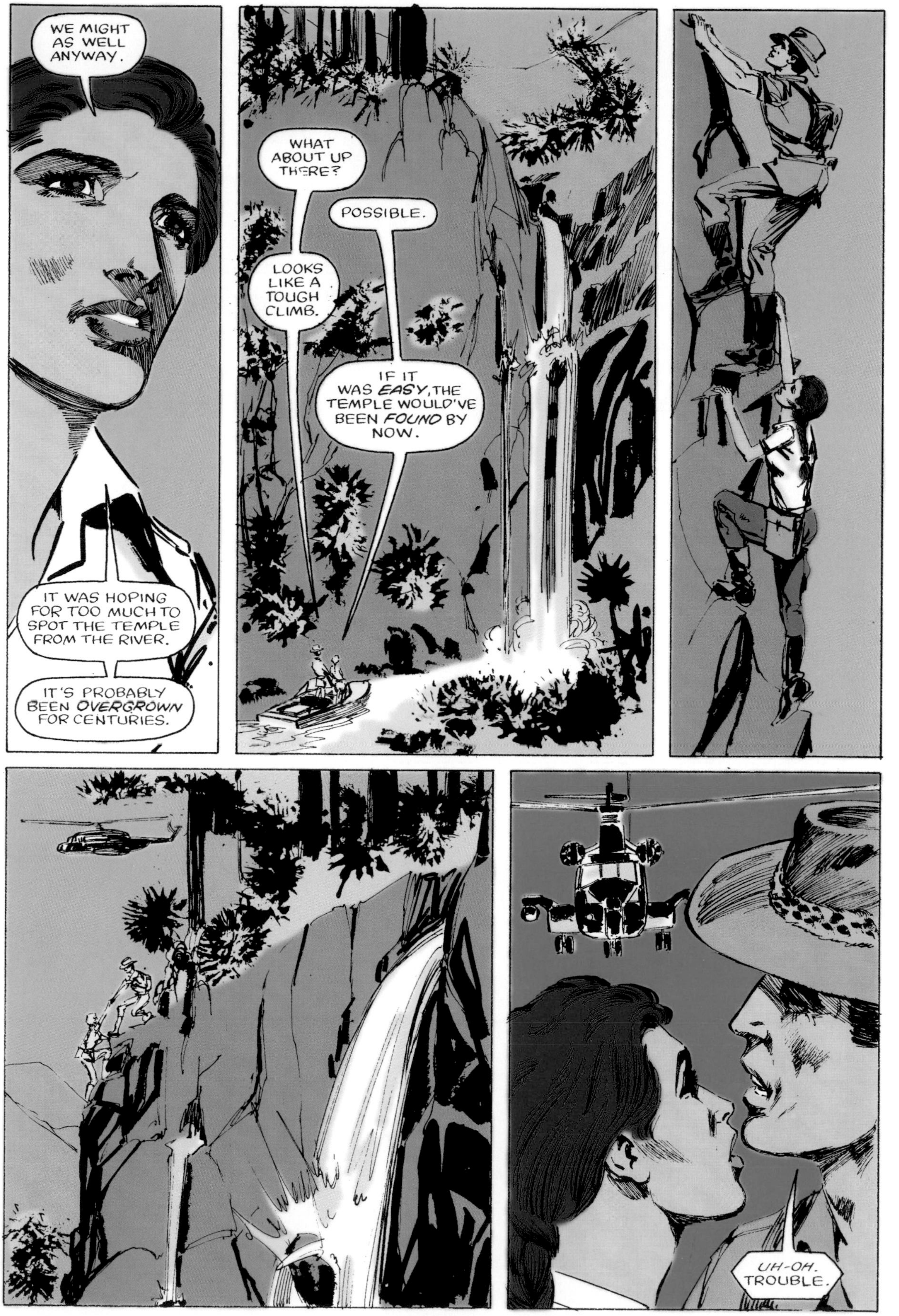
WE MIGHT AS WELL ANYWAY.
IT WAS HOPING FOR TOO MUCH TO SPOT THE TEMPLE FROM THE RIVER.
IT'S PROBABLY BEEN OVERGROWN FOR CENTURIES.
WHAT ABOUT UP THERE?
POSSIBLE.
LOOKS LIKE A TOUGH CLIMB.
IF IT WAS EASY, THE TEMPLE WOULD'VE BEEN FOUND BY NOW.
UH-OH. TROUBLE.

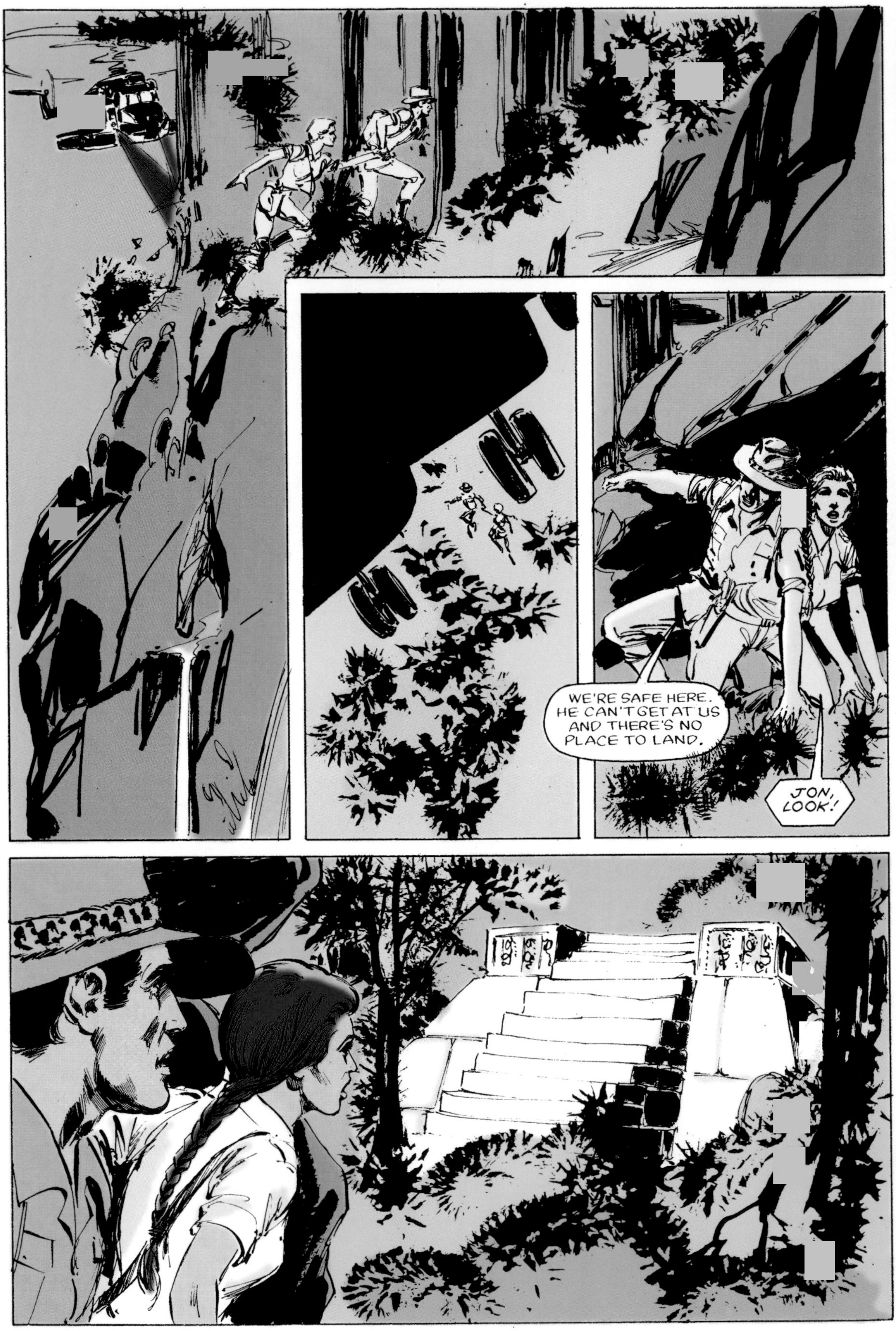
WE'RE SAFE HERE. HE CAN'T GET AT US AND THERE'S NO PLACE TO LAND.
JON, LOOK!

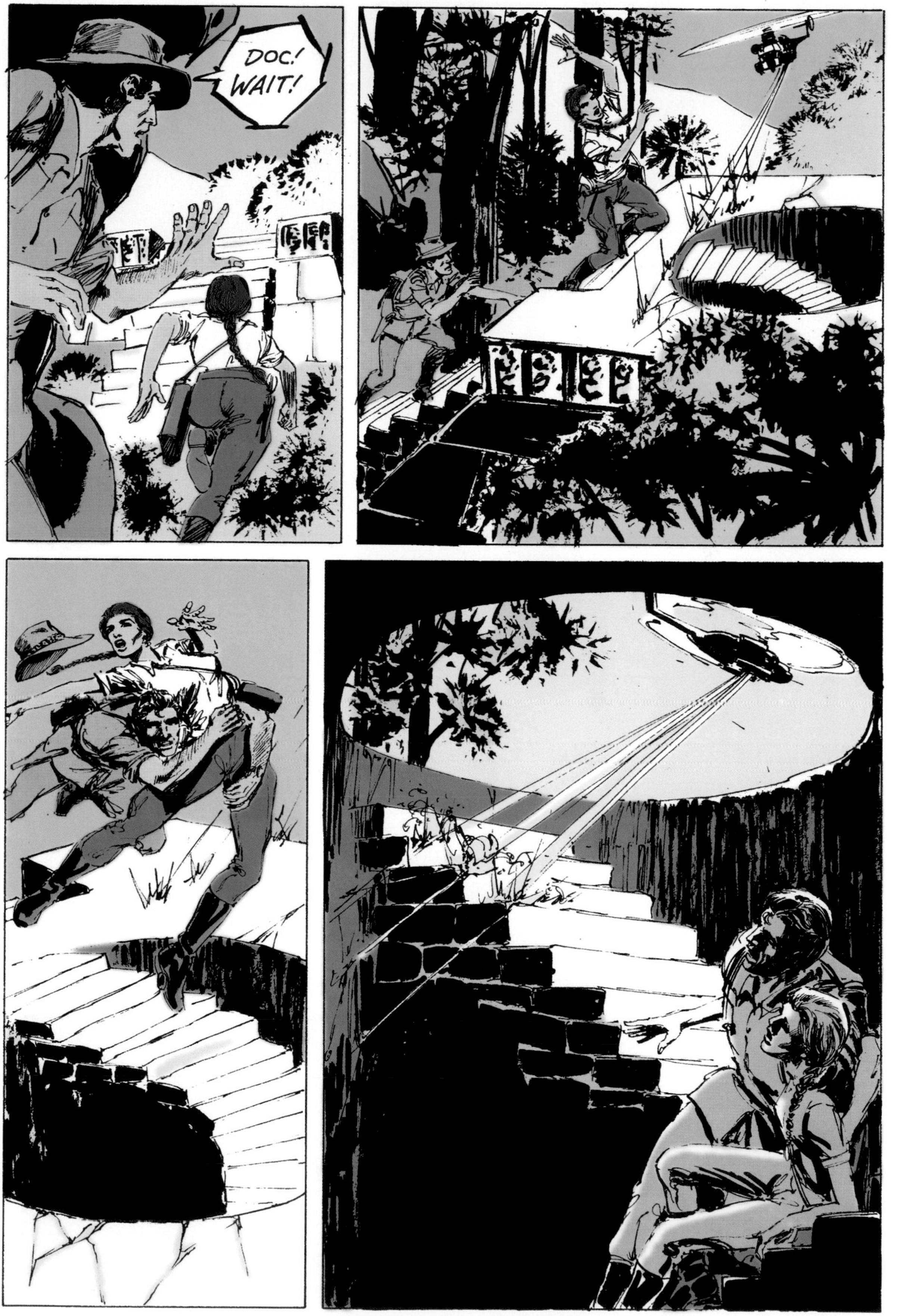
DOC! WAIT!

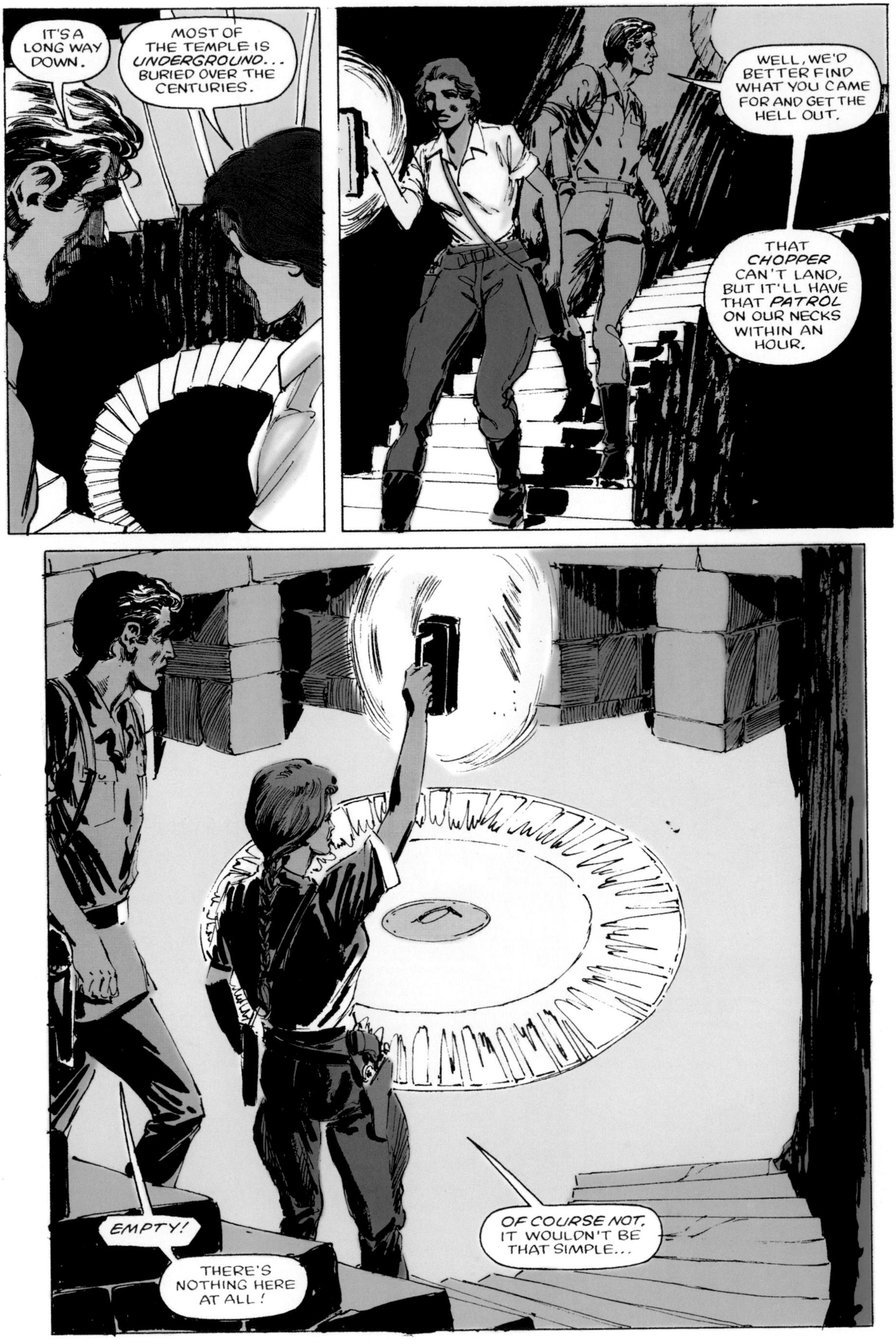
IT'S A LONG WAY DOWN.
MOST OF THE TEMPLE IS UNDERGROUND... BURIED OVER THE CENTURIES.
WELL, WE'D BETTER FIND WHAT YOU CAME FOR AND GET THE HELL OUT.
THAT CHOPPER CAN'T LAND, BUT IT'LL HAVE THAT PATROL ON OUR NECKS WITHIN AN HOUR.
EMPTY!
THERE'S NOTHING HERE AT ALL!
OF COURSE NOT, IT WOULDN'T BE THAT SIMPLE...

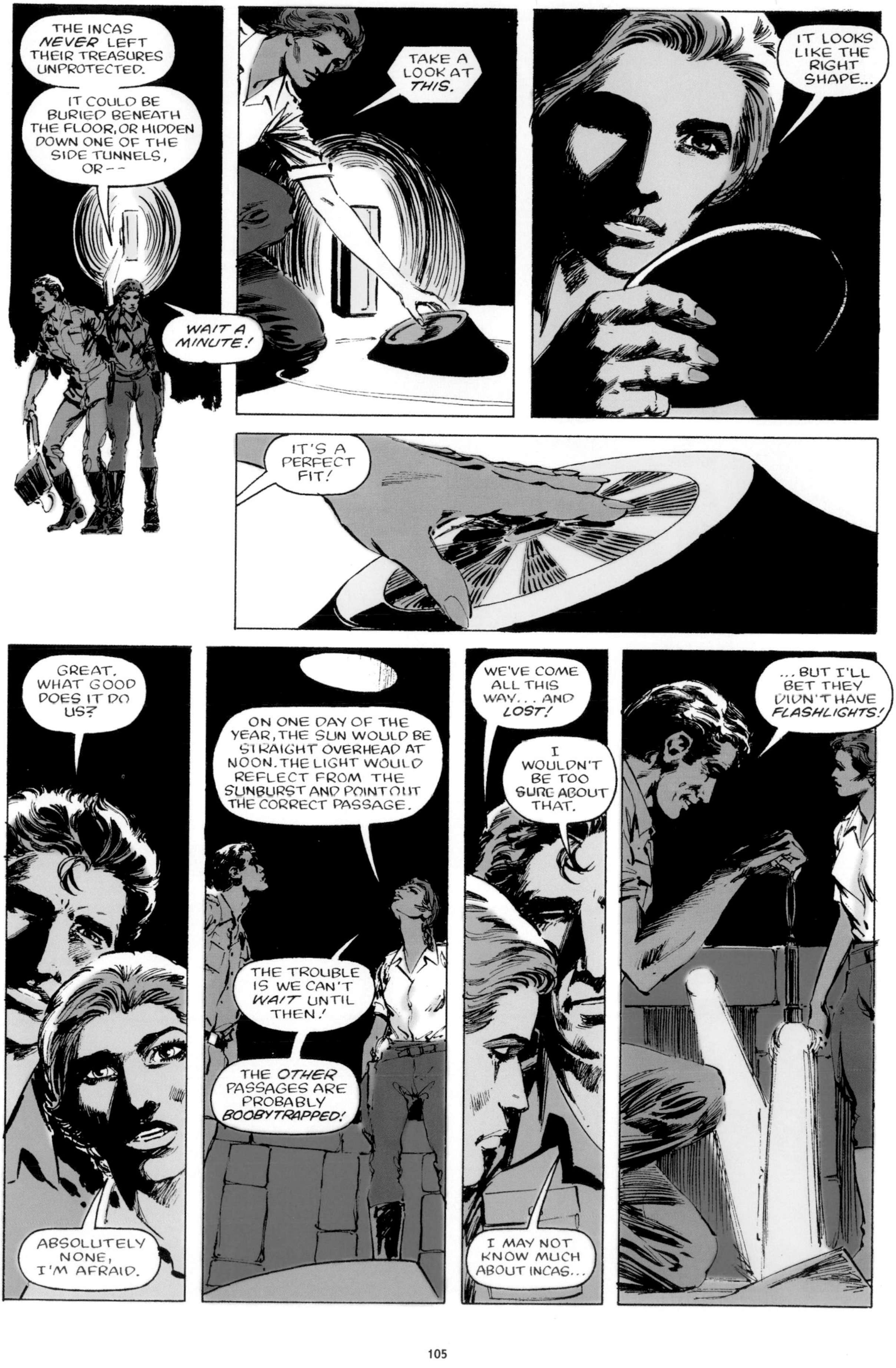
THE INCAS NEVER LEFT THEIR TREASURES UNPROTECTED.
IT COULD BE BURIED BENEATH THE FLOOR, OR HIDDEN DOWN ONE OF THE SIDE TUNNELS, OR--
WAIT A MINUTE!
TAKE A LOOK AT THIS.
IT LOOKS LIKE THE RIGHT SHAPE...
IT'S A PERFECT FIT!
GREAT. WHAT GOOD DOES IT DO US?
ABSOLUTELY NONE, I'M AFRAID.
ON ONE DAY OF THE YEAR, THE SUN WOULD BE STRAIGHT OVERHEAD AT NOON. THE LIGHT WOULD REFLECT FROM THE SUNBURST AND POINT OUT THE CORRECT PASSAGE.
THE TROUBLE IS WE CAN'T WAIT UNTIL THEN!
THE OTHER PASSAGES ARE PROBABLY BOOBYTRAPPED!
WE'VE COME ALL THIS WAY... AND LOST!
I WOULDN'T BE TOO SURE ABOUT THAT.
I MAY NOT KNOW MUCH ABOUT INCAS...
...BUT I'LL BET THEY DIDN'T HAVE FLASHLIGHTS!

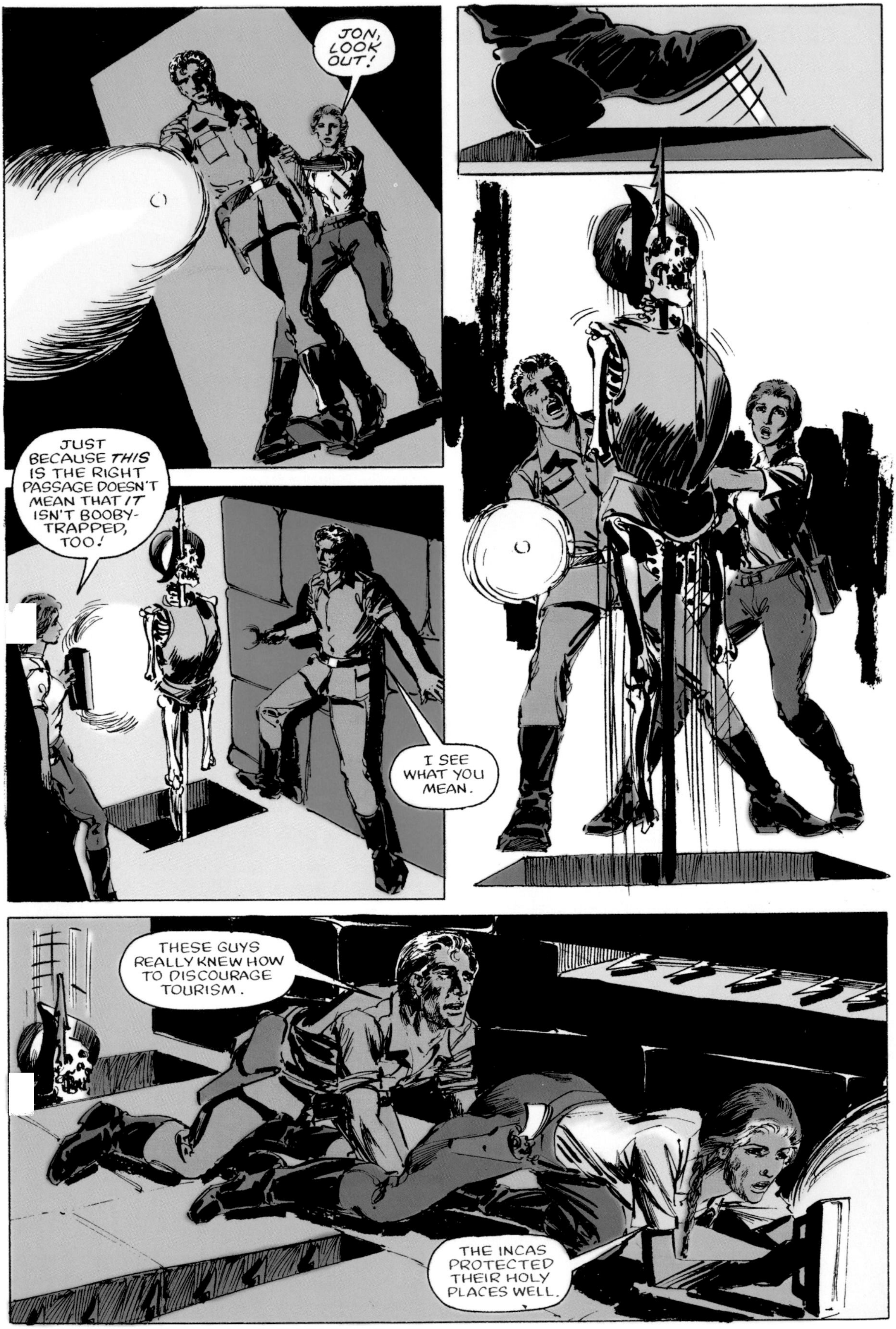
JON, LOOK OUT!
JUST BECAUSE THIS IS THE RIGHT PASSAGE DOESN'T MEAN THAT IT ISN'T BOOBY-TRAPPED, TOO!
I SEE WHAT YOU MEAN.
THESE GUYS REALLY KNEW HOW TO DISCOURAGE TOURISM.
THE INCAS PROTECTED THEIR HOLY PLACES WELL.

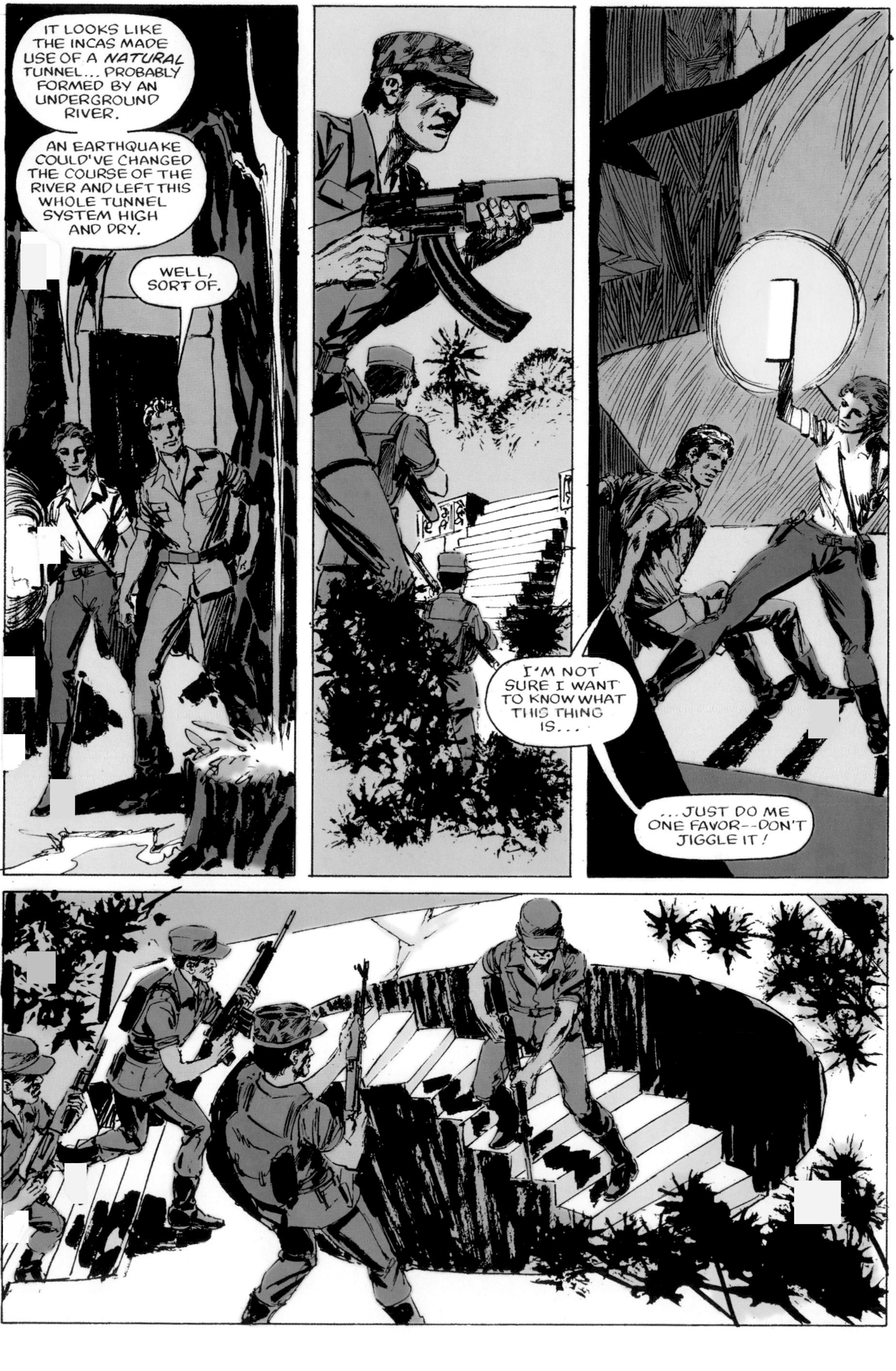
IT LOOKS LIKE THE INCAS MADE USE OF A *NATURAL* TUNNEL... PROBABLY FORMED BY AN UNDERGROUND RIVER.
AN EARTHQUAKE COULD'VE CHANGED THE COURSE OF THE RIVER AND LEFT THIS WHOLE TUNNEL SYSTEM HIGH AND DRY.
WELL, SORT OF.
I'M NOT SURE I WANT TO KNOW WHAT THIS THING IS...
...JUST DO ME ONE FAVOR--DON'T JIGGLE IT!

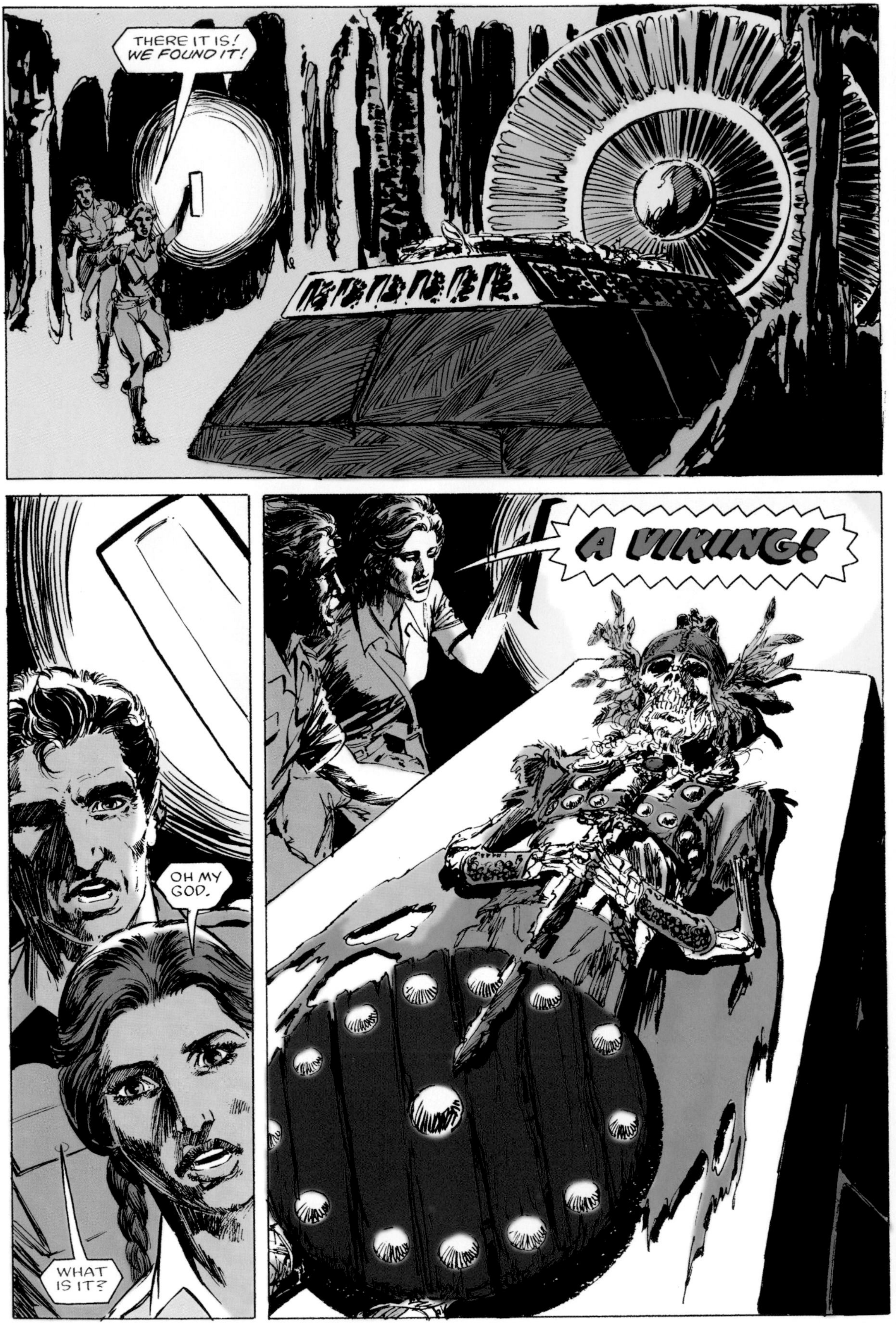
THERE IT IS! WE FOUND IT!
OH MY GOD.
WHAT IS IT?
A VIKING!

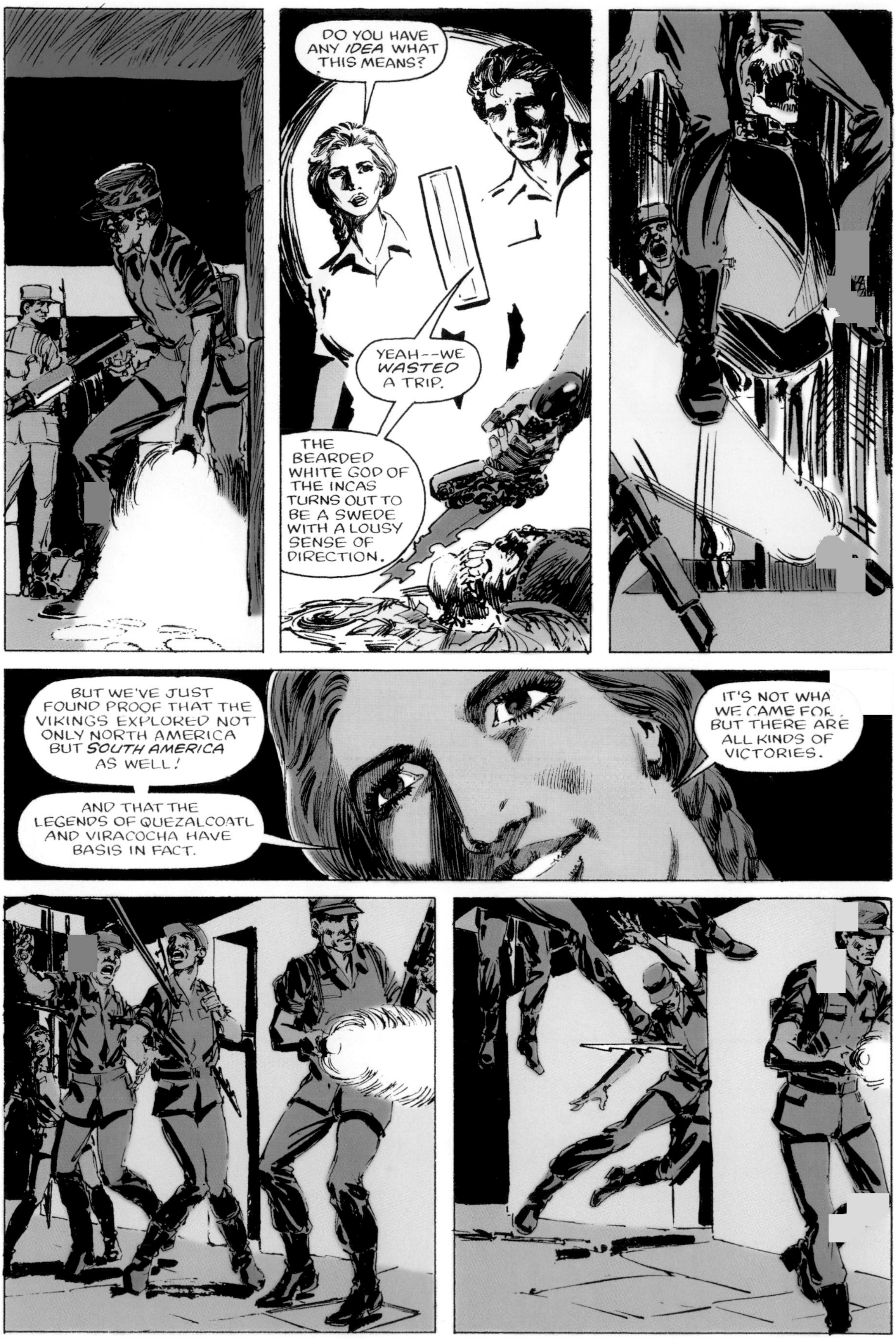
DO YOU HAVE ANY *IDEA* WHAT THIS MEANS?
YEAH--WE *WASTED* A TRIP.
THE BEARDED WHITE GOD OF THE INCAS TURNS OUT TO BE A SWEDE WITH A LOUSY SENSE OF DIRECTION.
BUT WE'VE JUST FOUND PROOF THAT THE VIKINGS EXPLORED NOT ONLY NORTH AMERICA BUT *SOUTH AMERICA* AS WELL!
AND THAT THE LEGENDS OF QUEZALCOATL AND VIRACOCHA HAVE BASIS IN FACT.
IT'S NOT WHA WE CAME FOR, BUT THERE ARE ALL KINDS OF VICTORIES.

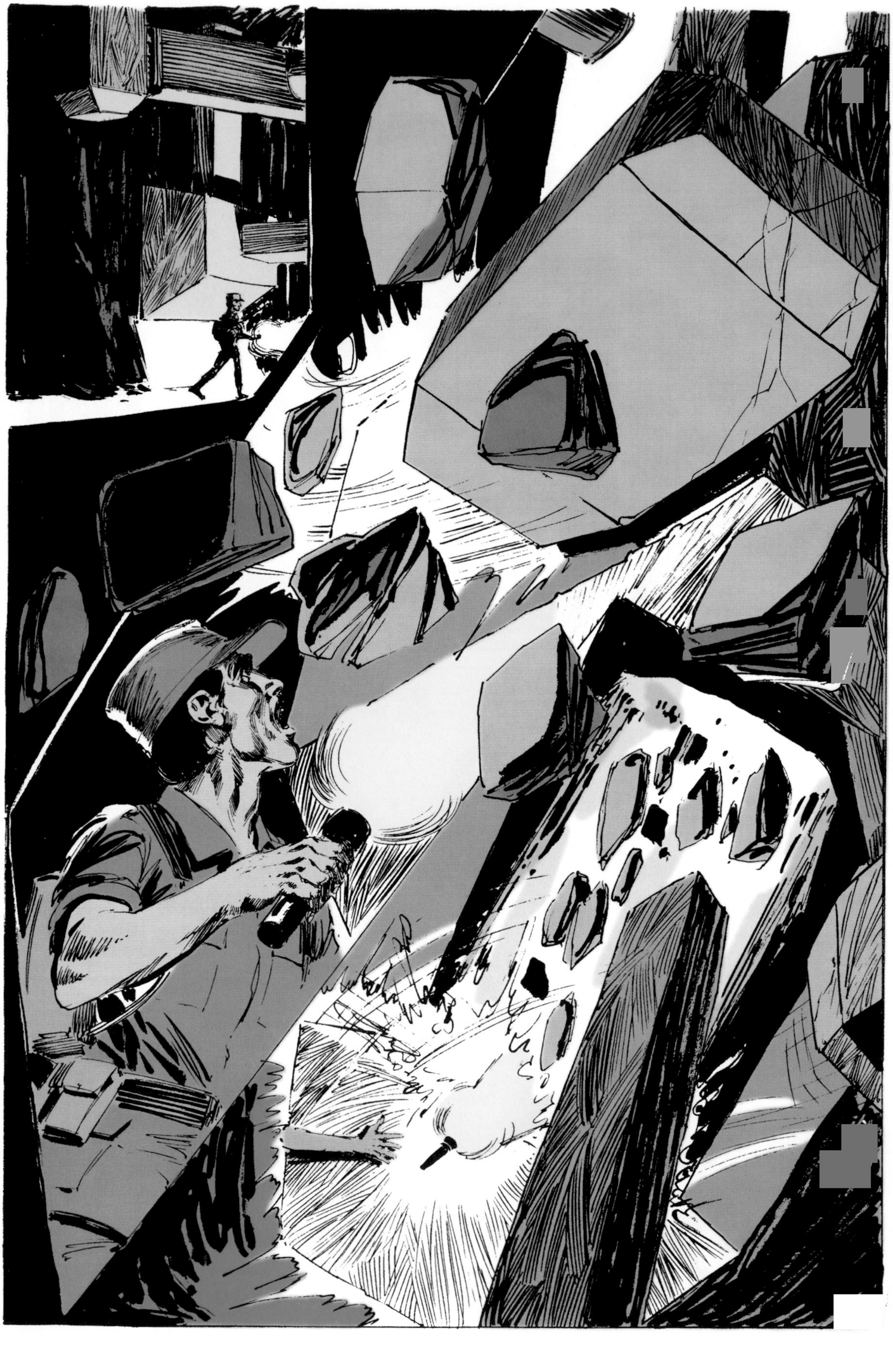

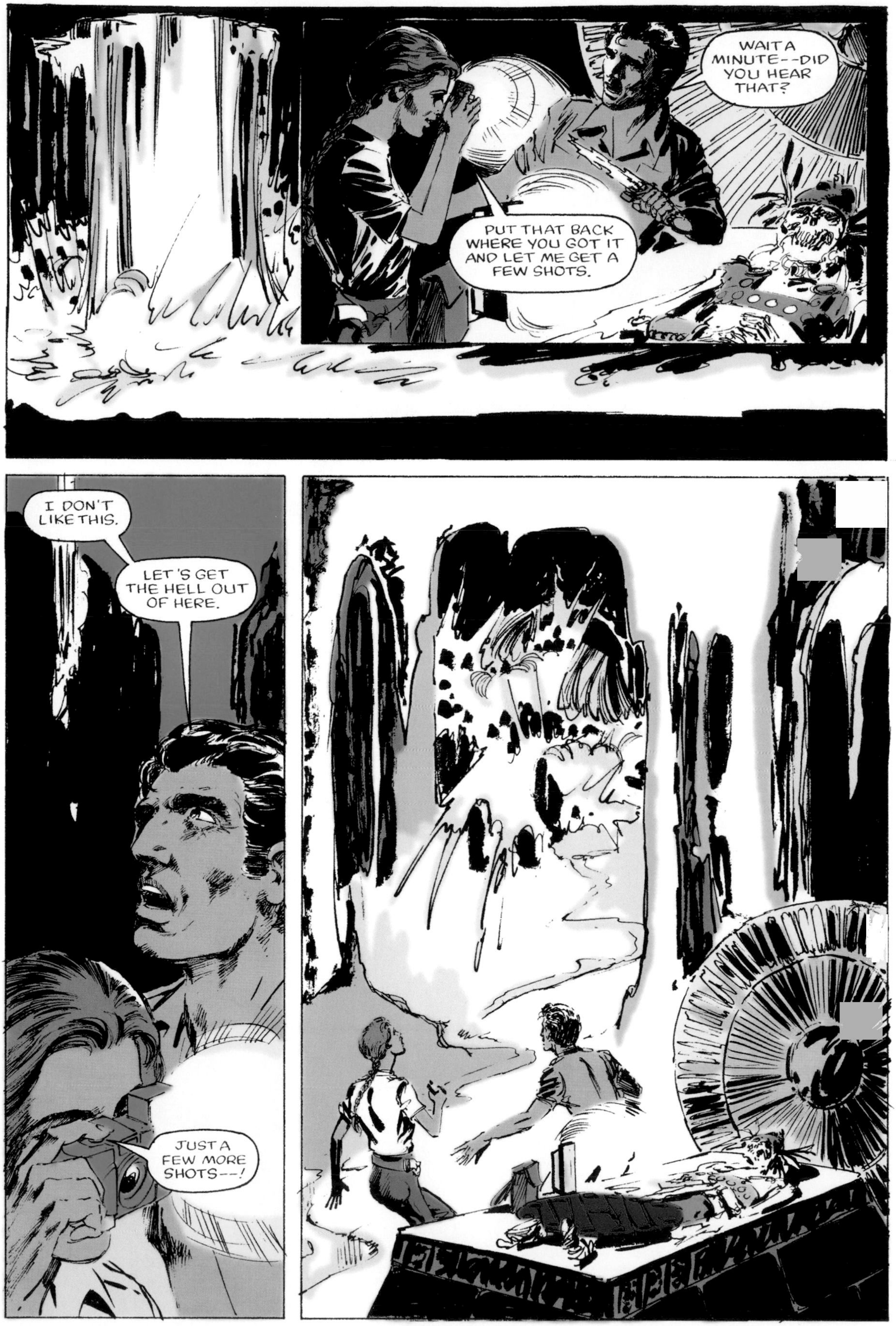
WAIT A MINUTE--DID YOU HEAR THAT?
PUT THAT BACK WHERE YOU GOT IT AND LET ME GET A FEW SHOTS.
I DON'T LIKE THIS.
LET'S GET THE HELL OUT OF HERE.
JUST A FEW MORE SHOTS--!

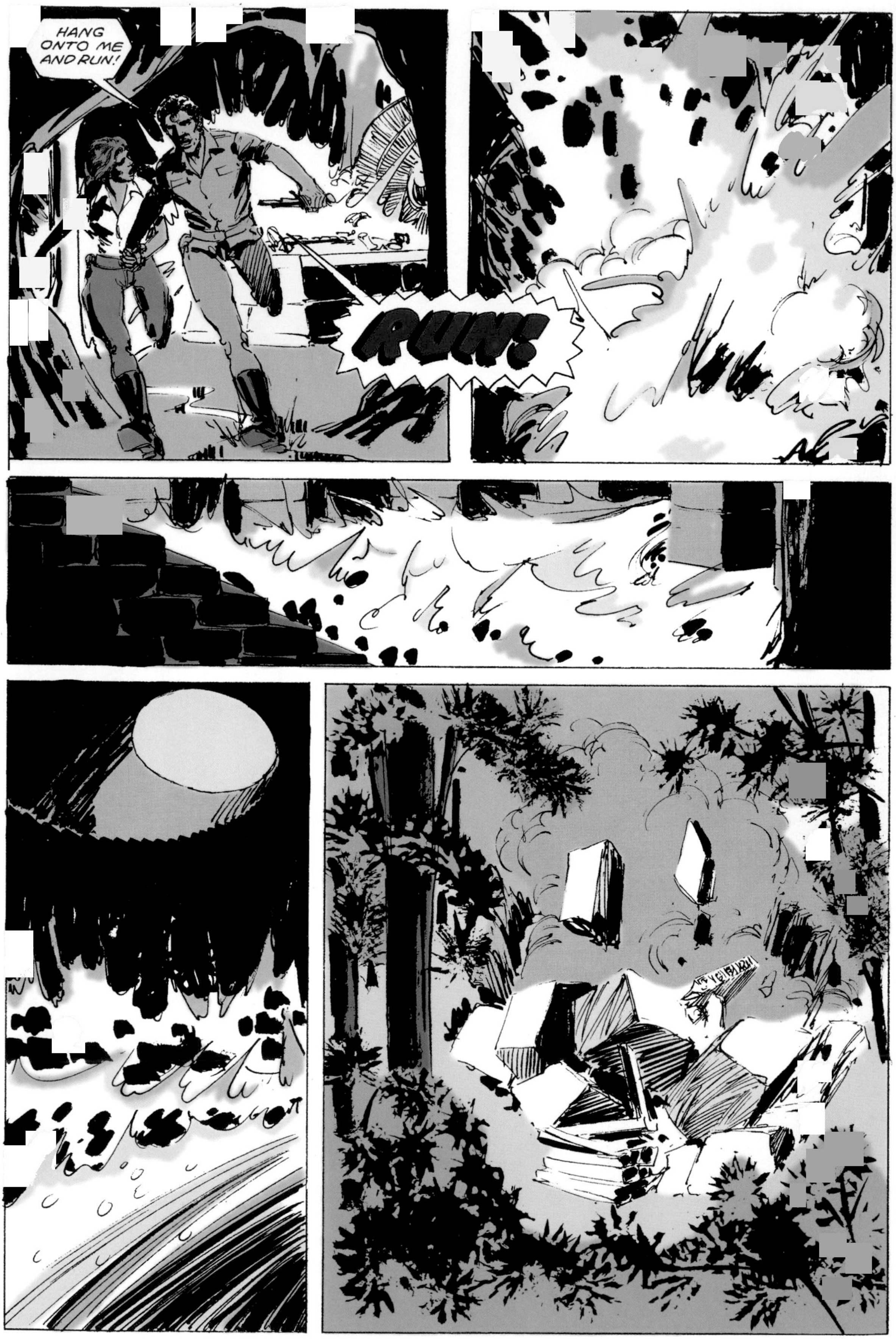
HANG ONTO ME AND RUN!
RUN!

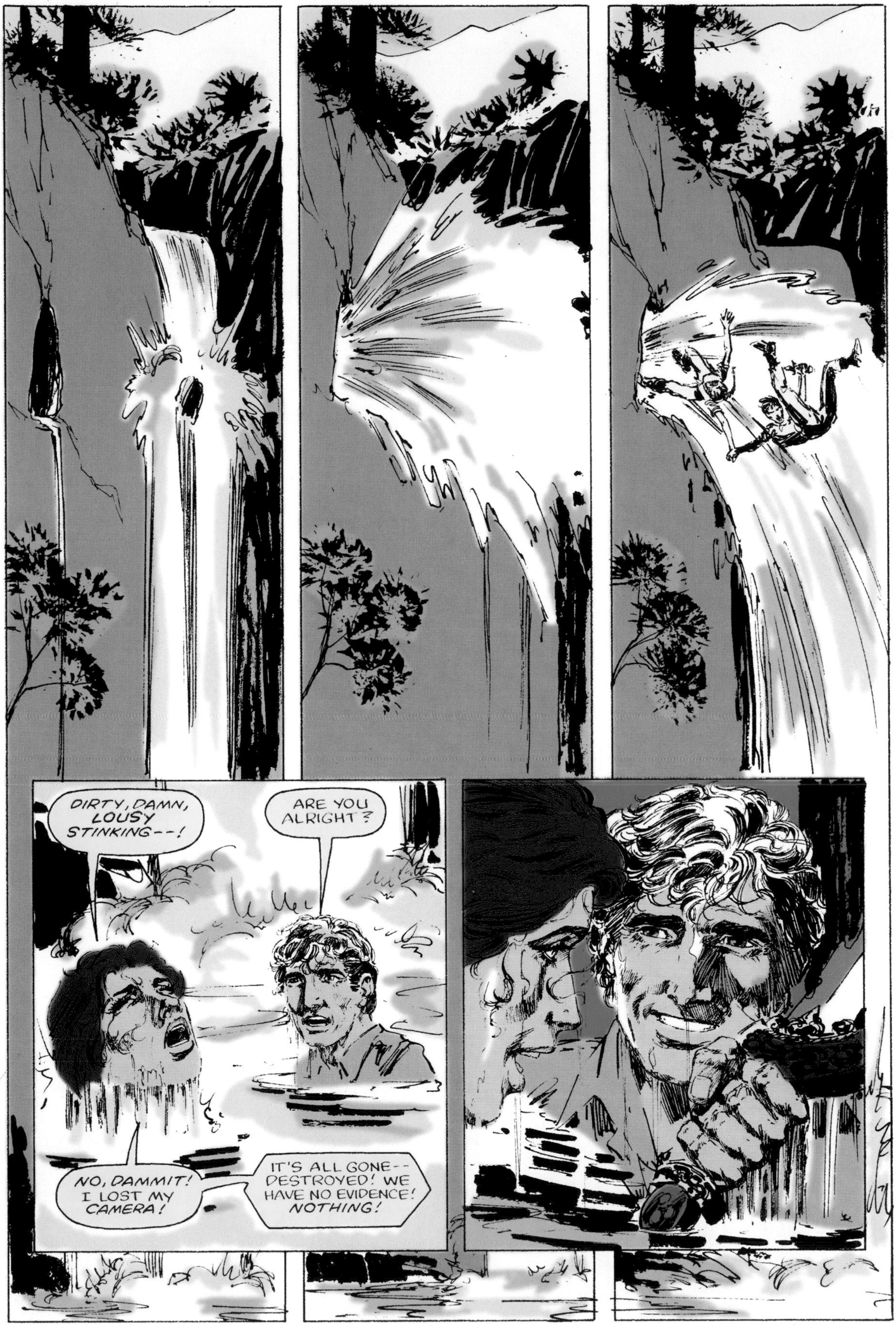
DIRTY, DAMN, LOUSY STINKING--!
ARE YOU ALRIGHT?
NO, DAMMIT! I LOST MY CAMERA!
IT'S ALL GONE-- DESTROYED! WE HAVE NO EVIDENCE! NOTHING!

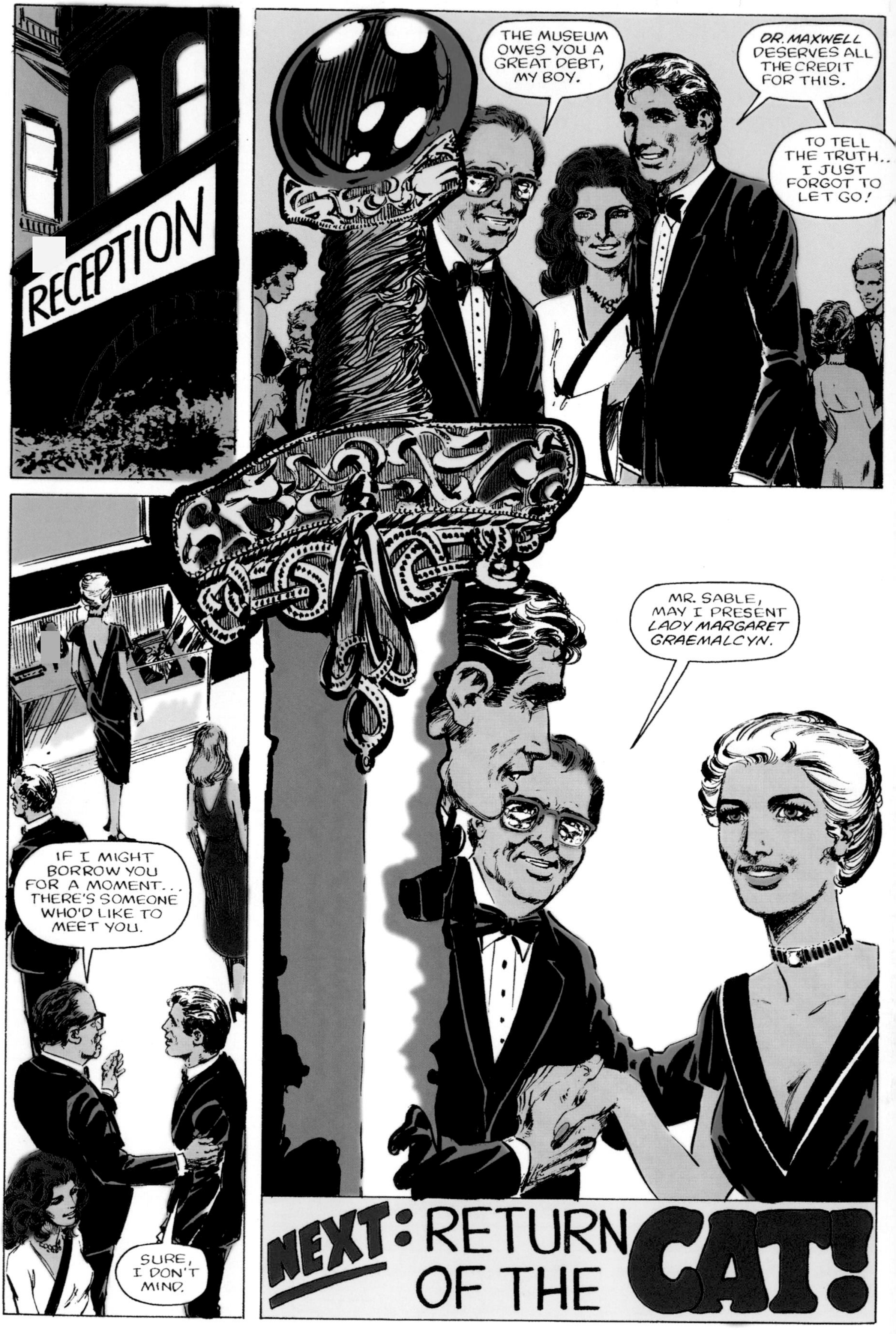
RECEPTION
THE MUSEUM OWES YOU A GREAT DEBT, MY BOY.
DR. MAXWELL DESERVES ALL THE CREDIT FOR THIS.
TO TELL THE TRUTH.. I JUST FORGOT TO LET GO!
IF I MIGHT BORROW YOU FOR A MOMENT... THERE'S SOMEONE WHO'D LIKE TO MEET YOU.
SURE, I DON'T MIND.
MR. SABLE, MAY I PRESENT LADY MARGARET GRAEMALCYN.
NEXT: RETURN OF THE CAT!

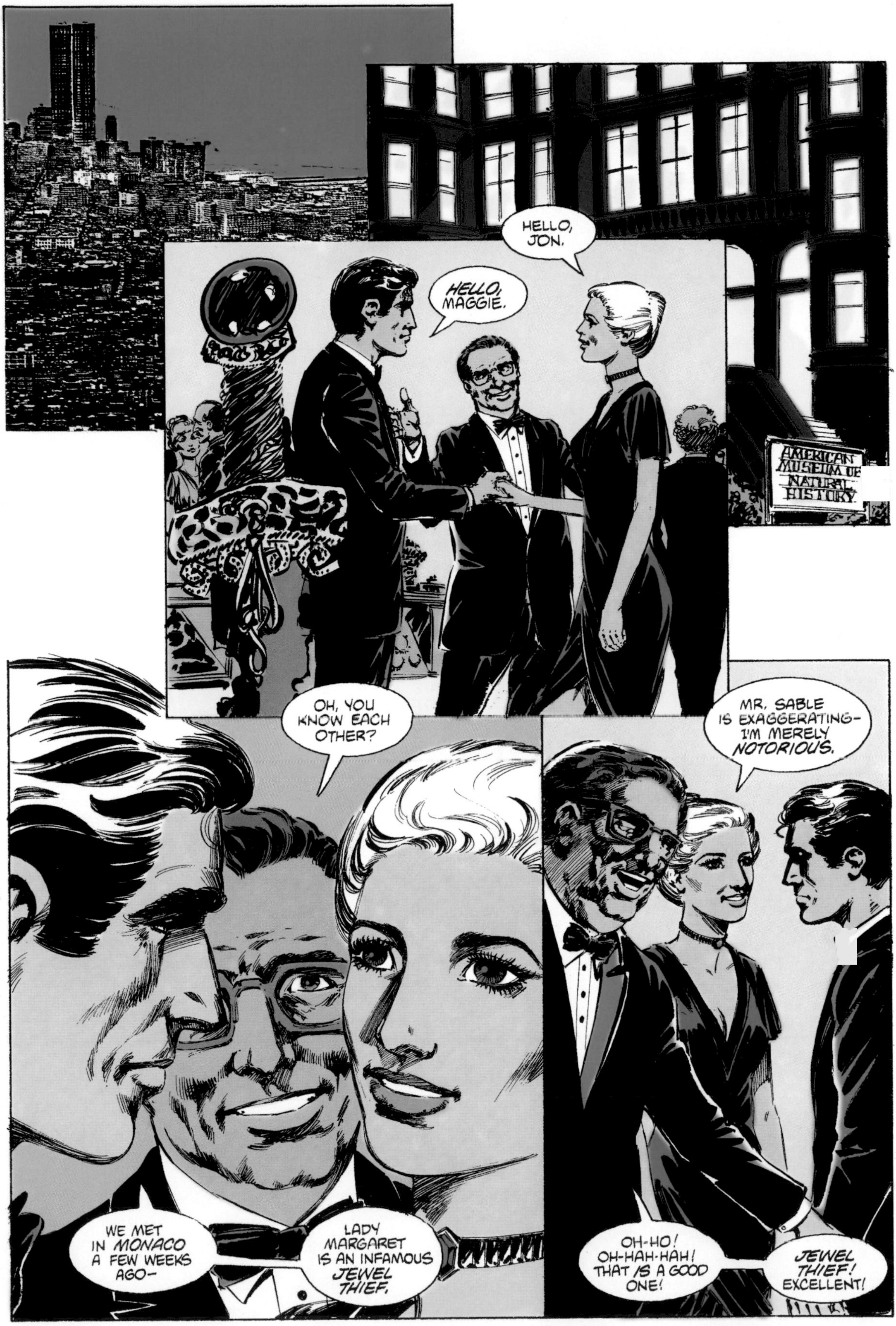
AMERICAN MUSEUM OF NATURAL HISTORY
HELLO, JON.
HELLO, MAGGIE.
OH, YOU KNOW EACH OTHER?
WE MET IN MONACO A FEW WEEKS AGO-
LADY MARGARET IS AN INFAMOUS JEWEL THIEF.
MR. SABLE IS EXAGGERATING- I'M MERELY NOTORIOUS.
OH-HO! OH-HAH-HAH! THAT IS A GOOD ONE!
JEWEL THIEF! EXCELLENT!

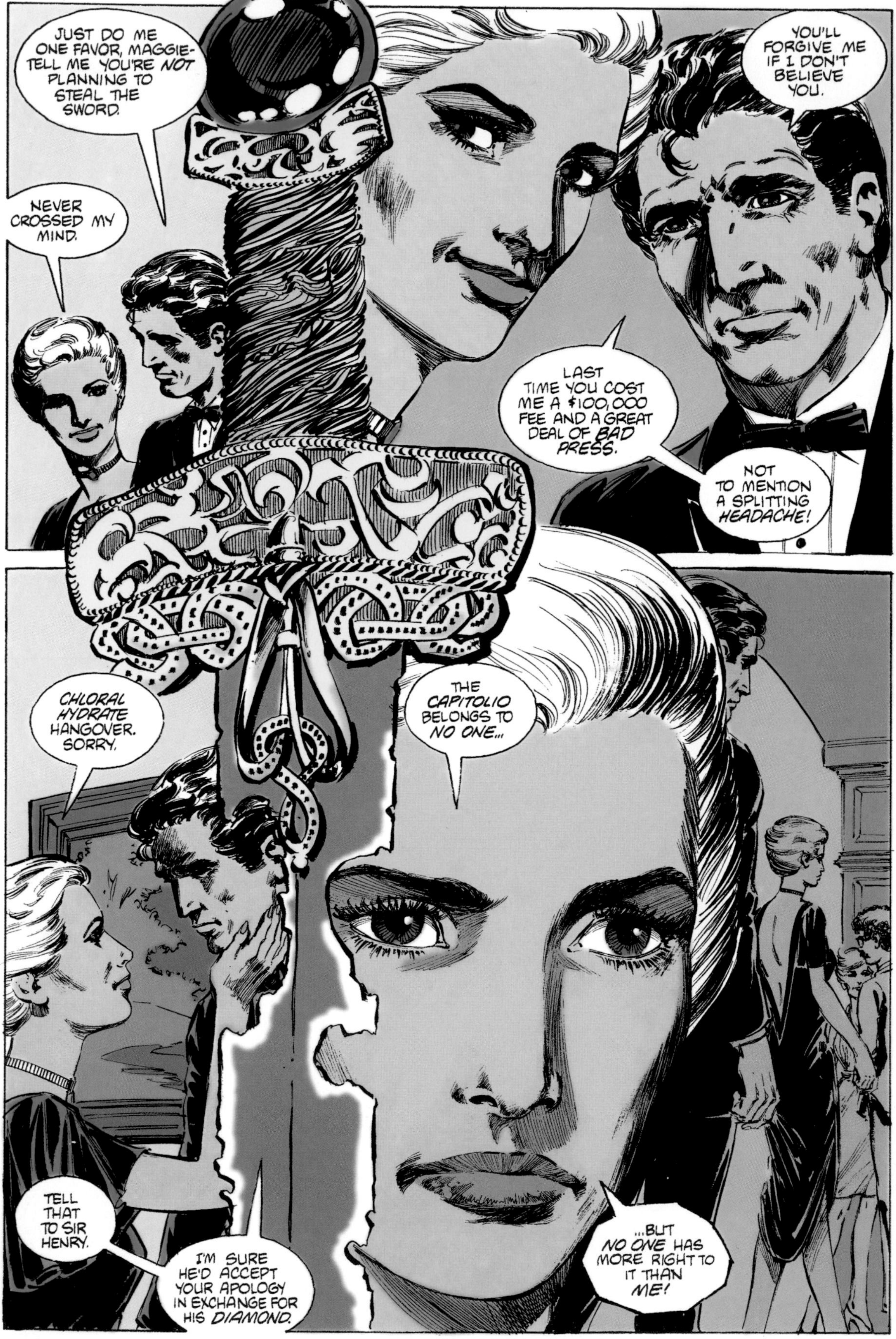
JUST DO ME ONE FAVOR, MAGGIE- TELL ME YOU'RE NOT PLANNING TO STEAL THE SWORD.
NEVER CROSSED MY MIND.
YOU'LL FORGIVE ME IF I DON'T BELIEVE YOU.
LAST TIME YOU COST ME A $100,000 FEE AND A GREAT DEAL OF BAD PRESS.
NOT TO MENTION A SPLITTING HEADACHE!
CHLORAL HYDRATE HANGOVER. SORRY.
THE CAPITOLIO BELONGS TO NO ONE...
TELL THAT TO SIR HENRY.
I'M SURE HE'D ACCEPT YOUR APOLOGY IN EXCHANGE FOR HIS DIAMOND.
...BUT NO ONE HAS MORE RIGHT TO IT THAN ME!

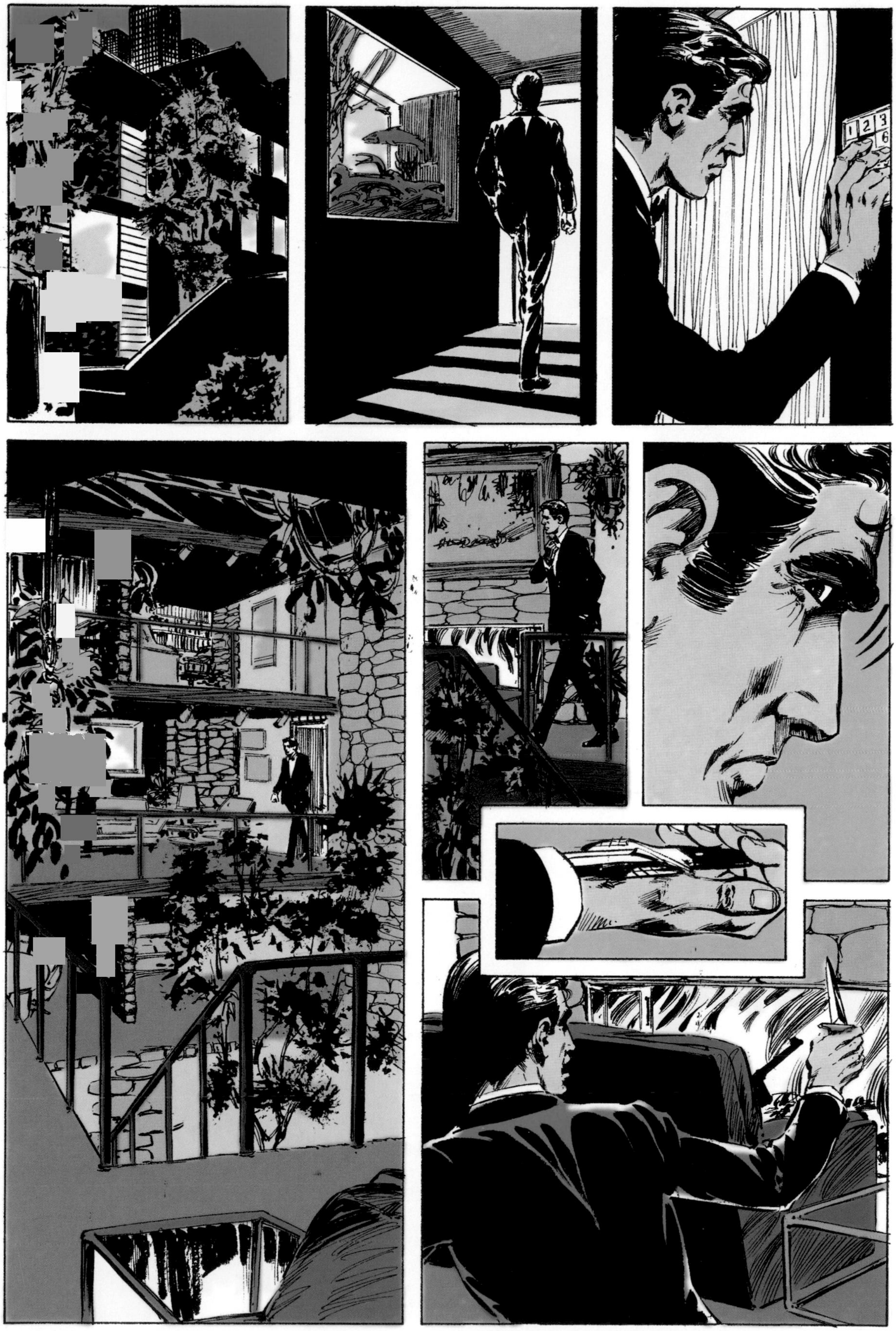
1 2 3
6

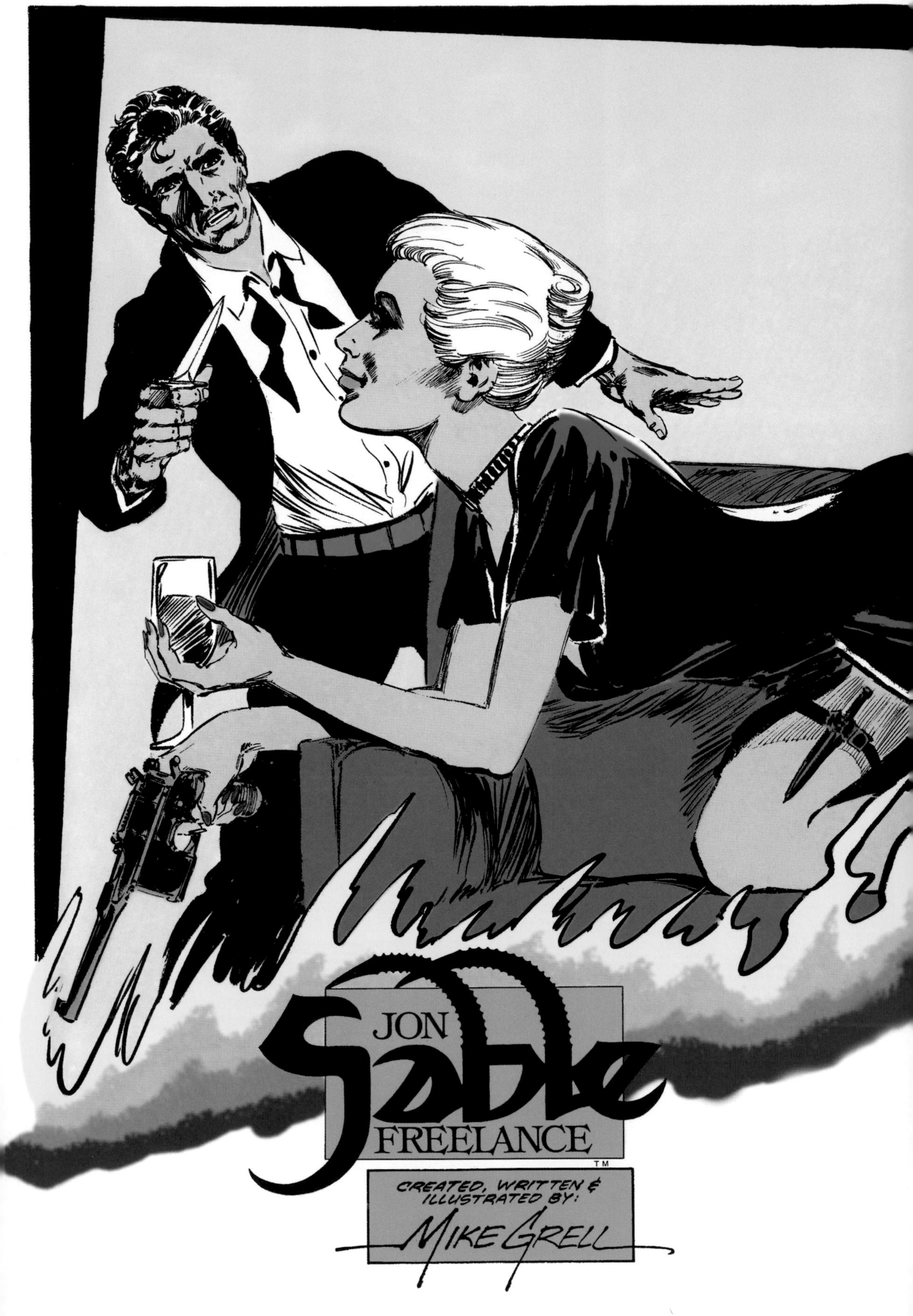

JON
Sable
FREELANCE
TM
CREATED, WRITTEN & ILLUSTRATED BY:
MIKE GRELL

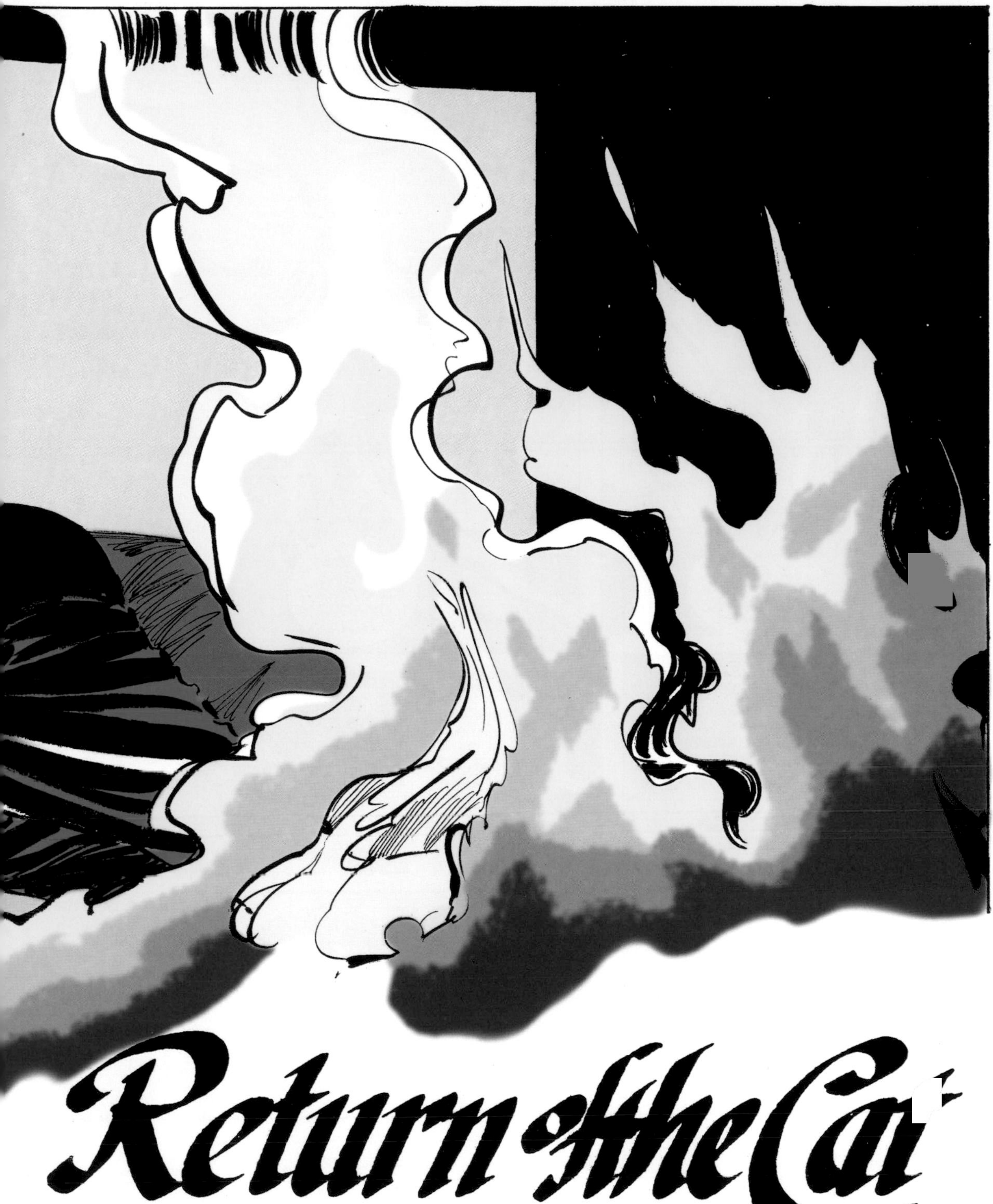

Return of the Cat

lettered by
KEN BRUZENAK

colored by
JANICE COHEN

edited by
MIKE GOLD

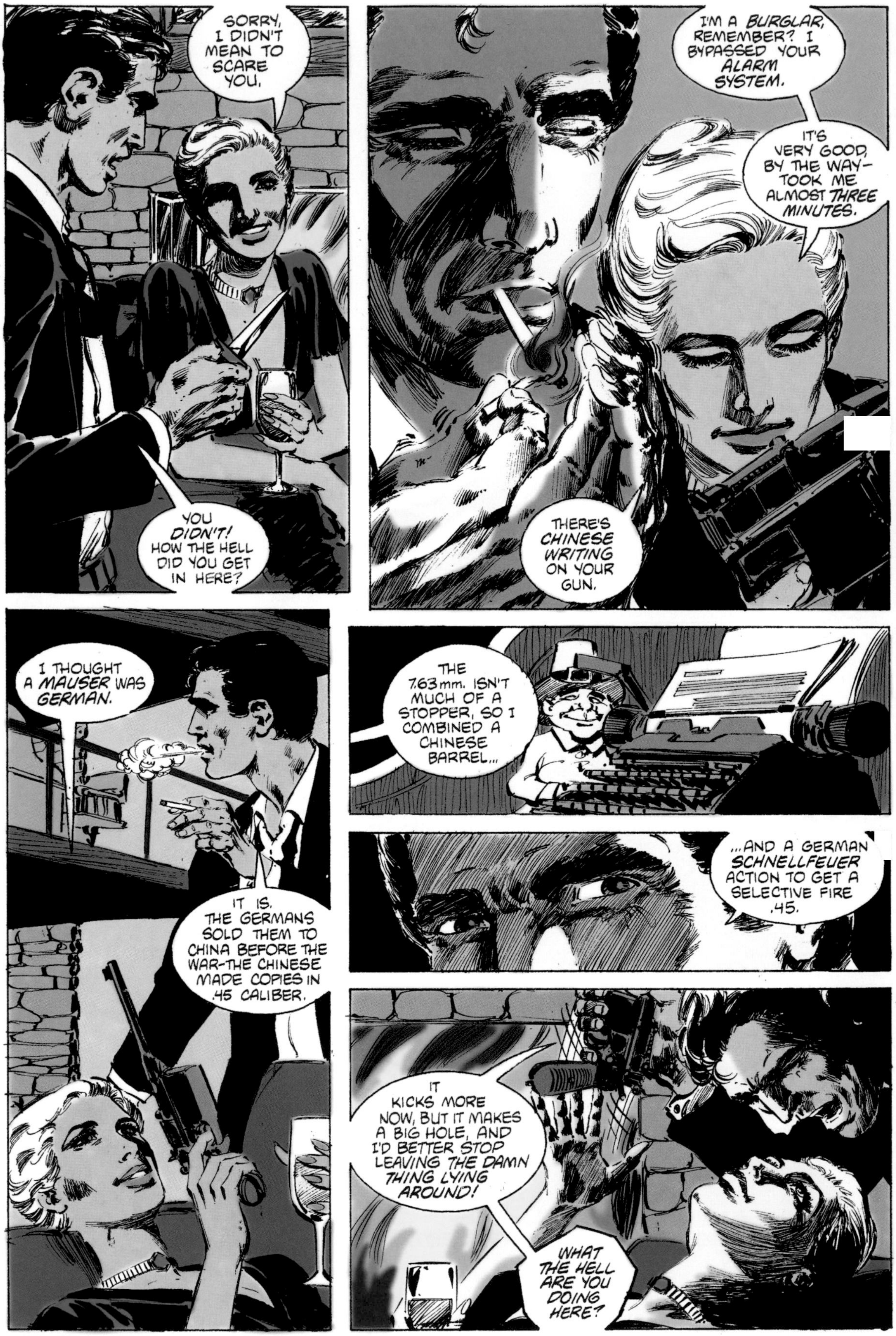
SORRY, I DIDN'T MEAN TO SCARE YOU.
YOU DIDN'T! HOW THE HELL DID YOU GET IN HERE?
I'M A BURGLAR, REMEMBER? I BYPASSED YOUR ALARM SYSTEM.
IT'S VERY GOOD, BY THE WAY- TOOK ME ALMOST THREE MINUTES.
THERE'S CHINESE WRITING ON YOUR GUN.
I THOUGHT A MAUSER WAS GERMAN.
IT IS. THE GERMANS SOLD THEM TO CHINA BEFORE THE WAR-THE CHINESE MADE COPIES IN .45 CALIBER.
THE 7.63 mm. ISN'T MUCH OF A STOPPER, SO I COMBINED A CHINESE BARREL...
...AND A GERMAN SCHNELLFEUER ACTION TO GET A SELECTIVE FIRE .45.
IT KICKS MORE NOW, BUT IT MAKES A BIG HOLE, AND I'D BETTER STOP LEAVING THE DAMN THING LYING AROUND!
WHAT THE HELL ARE YOU DOING HERE?

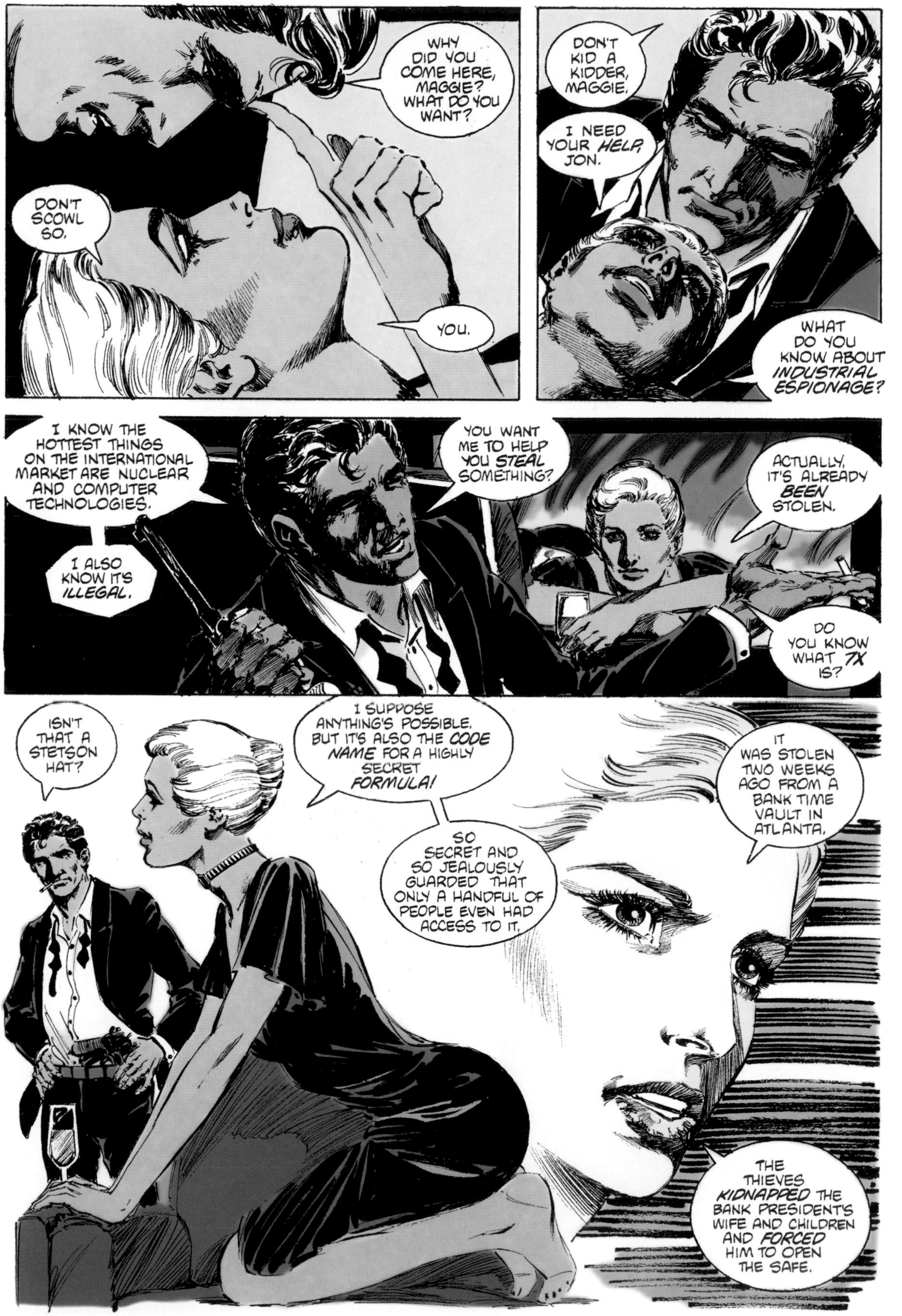
WHY DID YOU COME HERE, MAGGIE? WHAT DO YOU WANT?
DON'T SCOWL SO.
YOU.
DON'T KID A KIDDER, MAGGIE.
I NEED YOUR HELP, JON.
WHAT DO YOU KNOW ABOUT INDUSTRIAL ESPIONAGE?
I KNOW THE HOTTEST THINGS ON THE INTERNATIONAL MARKET ARE NUCLEAR AND COMPUTER TECHNOLOGIES.
I ALSO KNOW IT'S ILLEGAL.
YOU WANT ME TO HELP YOU STEAL SOMETHING?
ACTUALLY, IT'S ALREADY BEEN STOLEN.
DO YOU KNOW WHAT 7X IS?
ISN'T THAT A STETSON HAT?
I SUPPOSE ANYTHING'S POSSIBLE. BUT IT'S ALSO THE CODE NAME FOR A HIGHLY SECRET FORMULA!
SO SECRET AND SO JEALOUSLY GUARDED THAT ONLY A HANDFUL OF PEOPLE EVEN HAD ACCESS TO IT.
IT WAS STOLEN TWO WEEKS AGO FROM A BANK TIME VAULT IN ATLANTA.
THE THIEVES KIDNAPPED THE BANK PRESIDENT'S WIFE AND CHILDREN AND FORCED HIM TO OPEN THE SAFE.

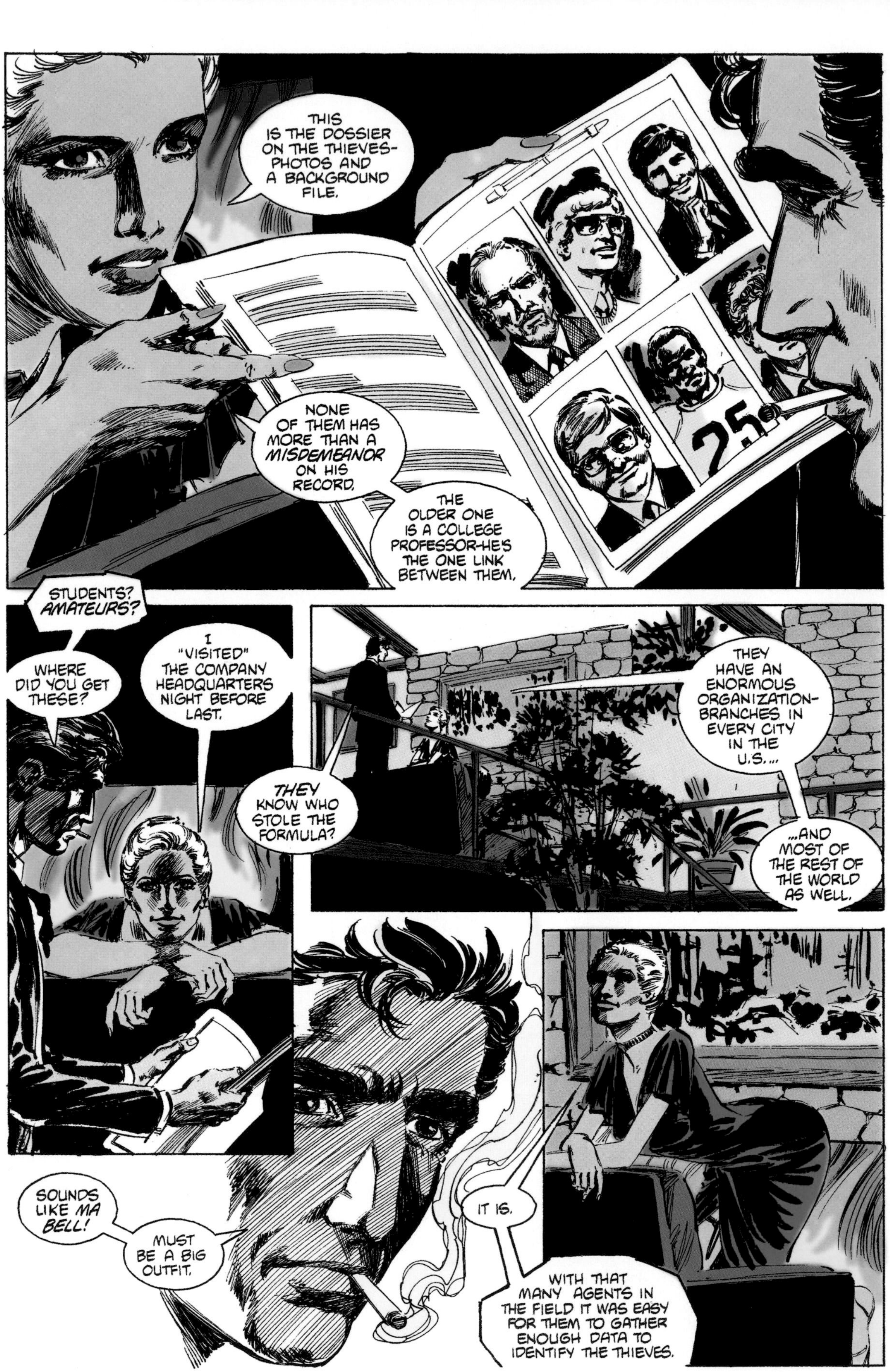
THIS IS THE DOSSIER ON THE THIEVES- PHOTOS AND A BACKGROUND FILE.
NONE OF THEM HAS MORE THAN A *MISDEMEANOR* ON HIS RECORD.
THE OLDER ONE IS A COLLEGE PROFESSOR-HE'S THE ONE LINK BETWEEN THEM.
STUDENTS? *AMATEURS?*
WHERE DID YOU GET THESE?
I "VISITED" THE COMPANY HEADQUARTERS NIGHT BEFORE LAST.
THEY KNOW WHO STOLE THE FORMULA?
THEY HAVE AN ENORMOUS ORGANIZATION- BRANCHES IN EVERY CITY IN THE U.S....
...AND MOST OF THE REST OF THE WORLD AS WELL.
SOUNDS LIKE *MA BELL!*
MUST BE A BIG OUTFIT.
IT IS.
WITH THAT MANY AGENTS IN THE FIELD IT WAS EASY FOR THEM TO GATHER ENOUGH DATA TO IDENTIFY THE THIEVES.

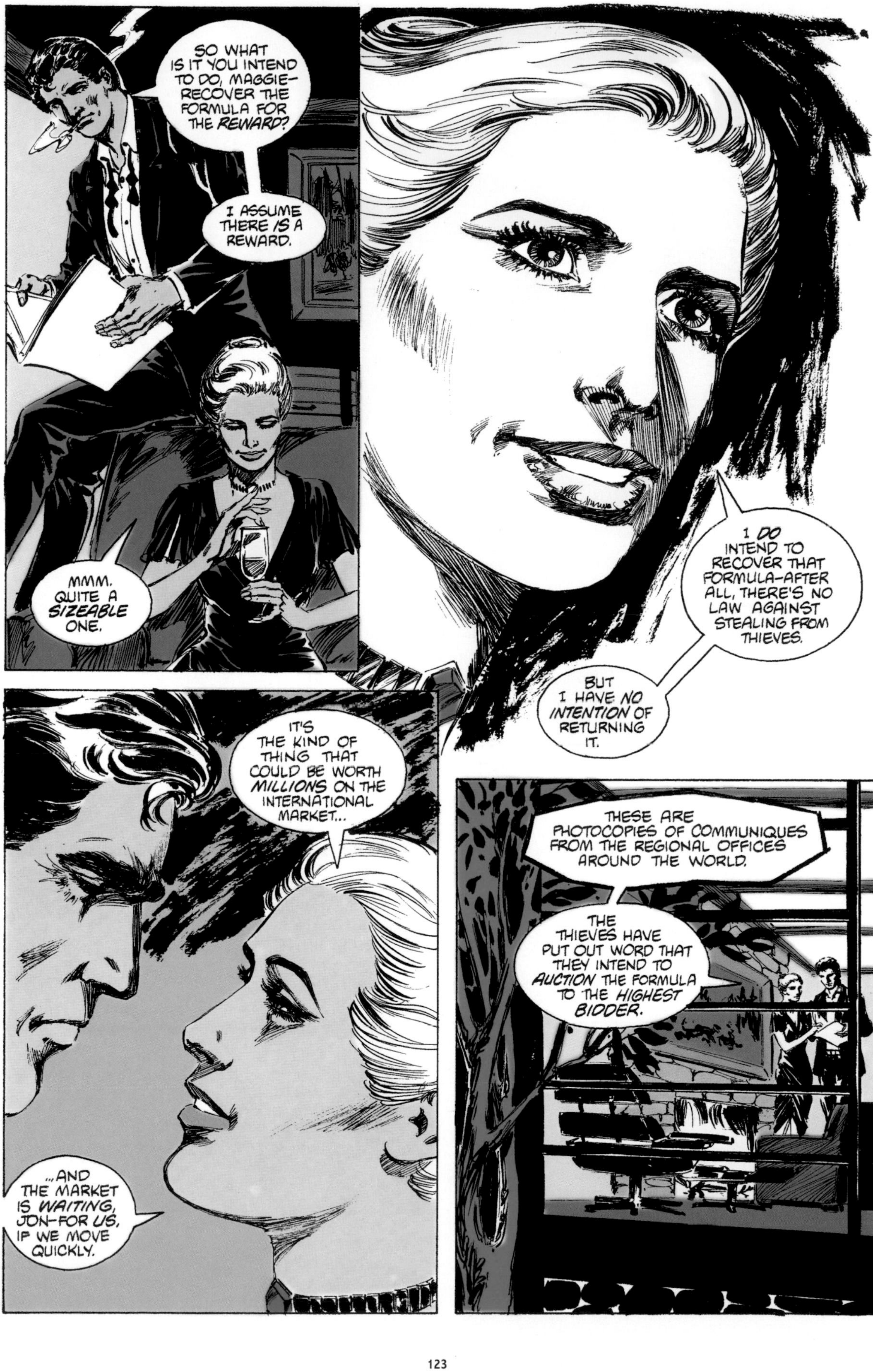
SO WHAT IS IT YOU INTEND TO DO, MAGGIE- RECOVER THE FORMULA FOR THE *REWARD?*
I ASSUME THERE *IS* A REWARD.
MMM. QUITE A *SIZEABLE* ONE.
I *DO* INTEND TO RECOVER THAT FORMULA-AFTER ALL, THERE'S NO LAW AGAINST STEALING FROM THIEVES.
BUT I HAVE *NO INTENTION* OF RETURNING IT.
IT'S THE KIND OF THING THAT COULD BE WORTH *MILLIONS* ON THE INTERNATIONAL MARKET...
...AND THE MARKET IS *WAITING,* JON-FOR *US,* IF WE MOVE QUICKLY.
THESE ARE PHOTOCOPIES OF COMMUNIQUES FROM THE REGIONAL OFFICES AROUND THE WORLD.
THE THIEVES HAVE PUT OUT WORD THAT THEY INTEND TO *AUCTION* THE FORMULA TO THE *HIGHEST BIDDER.*

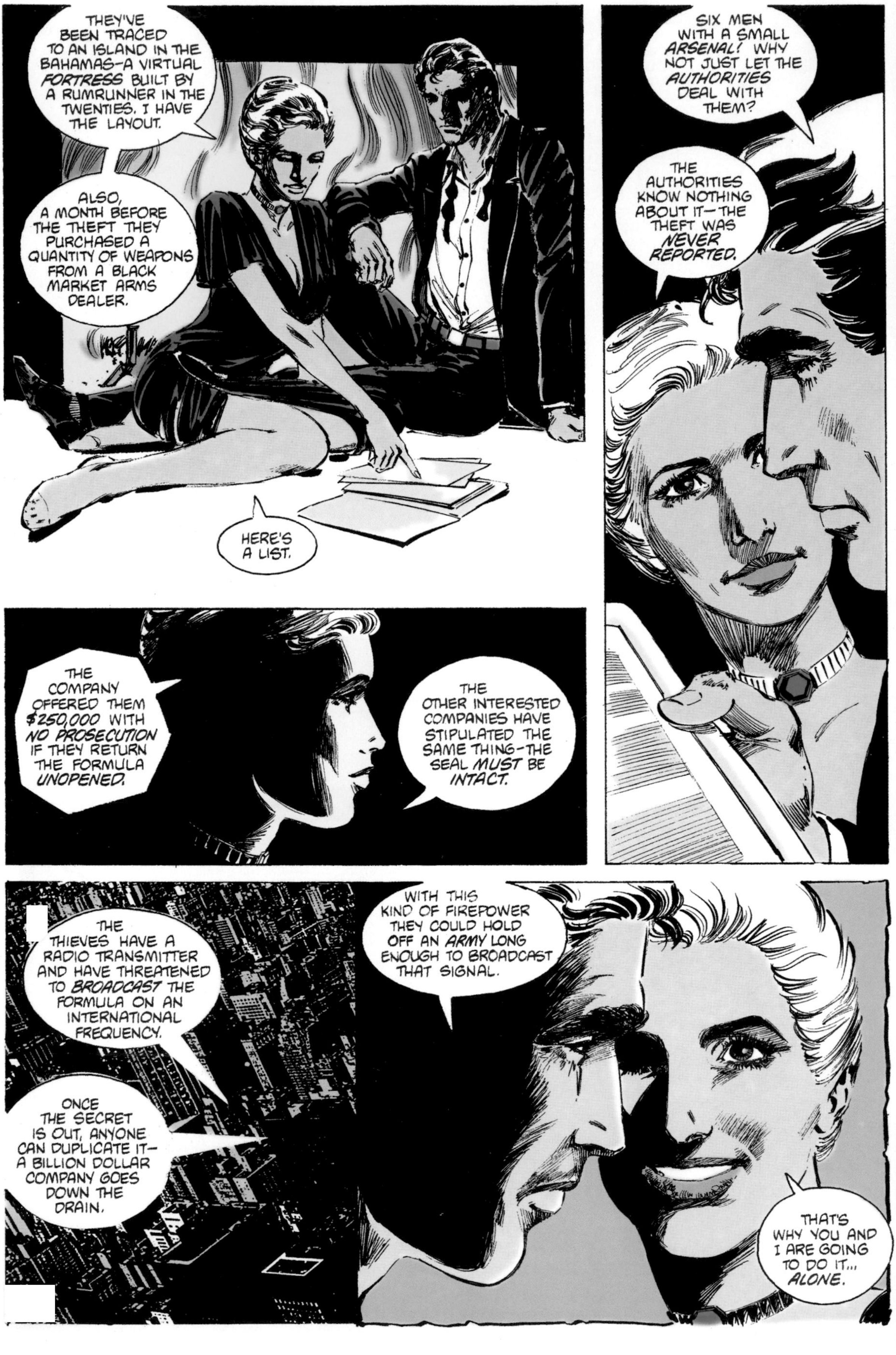
THEY'VE BEEN TRACED TO AN ISLAND IN THE BAHAMAS—A VIRTUAL FORTRESS BUILT BY A RUMRUNNER IN THE TWENTIES. I HAVE THE LAYOUT.
ALSO, A MONTH BEFORE THE THEFT THEY PURCHASED A QUANTITY OF WEAPONS FROM A BLACK MARKET ARMS DEALER.
HERE'S A LIST.
SIX MEN WITH A SMALL ARSENAL! WHY NOT JUST LET THE AUTHORITIES DEAL WITH THEM?
THE AUTHORITIES KNOW NOTHING ABOUT IT—THE THEFT WAS NEVER REPORTED.
THE COMPANY OFFERED THEM $250,000 WITH NO PROSECUTION IF THEY RETURN THE FORMULA UNOPENED.
THE OTHER INTERESTED COMPANIES HAVE STIPULATED THE SAME THING—THE SEAL MUST BE INTACT.
THE THIEVES HAVE A RADIO TRANSMITTER AND HAVE THREATENED TO BROADCAST THE FORMULA ON AN INTERNATIONAL FREQUENCY.
ONCE THE SECRET IS OUT, ANYONE CAN DUPLICATE IT—A BILLION DOLLAR COMPANY GOES DOWN THE DRAIN.
WITH THIS KIND OF FIREPOWER THEY COULD HOLD OFF AN ARMY LONG ENOUGH TO BROADCAST THAT SIGNAL.
THAT'S WHY YOU AND I ARE GOING TO DO IT... ALONE.

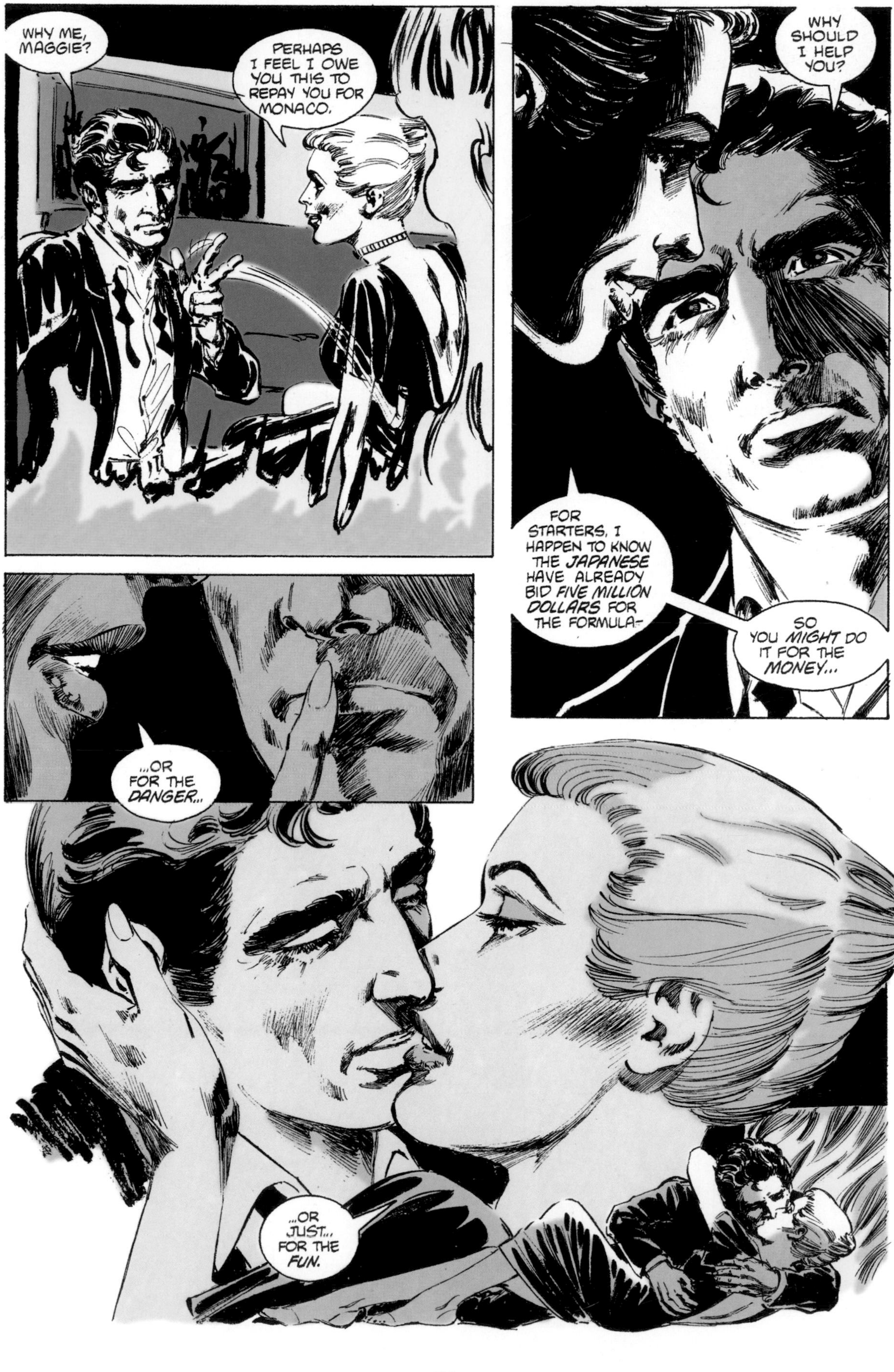
WHY ME, MAGGIE?
PERHAPS I FEEL I OWE YOU THIS TO REPAY YOU FOR MONACO.
WHY SHOULD I HELP YOU?
FOR STARTERS, I HAPPEN TO KNOW THE JAPANESE HAVE ALREADY BID FIVE MILLION DOLLARS FOR THE FORMULA--
SO YOU MIGHT DO IT FOR THE MONEY...
...OR FOR THE DANGER...
...OR JUST... FOR THE FUN.

JON...
JON...?
HOGAN'S ALLEY
ENTRY
JON?

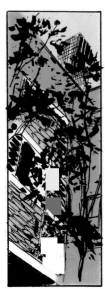

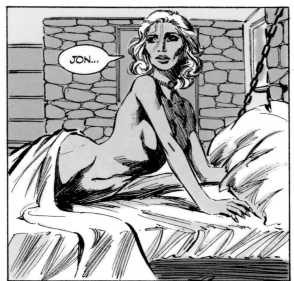

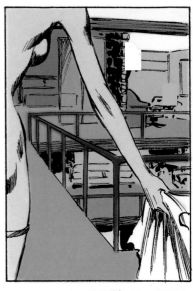

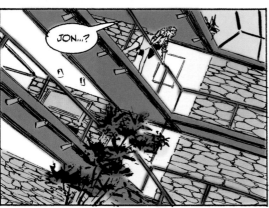

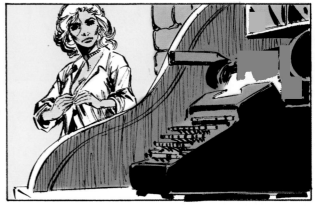

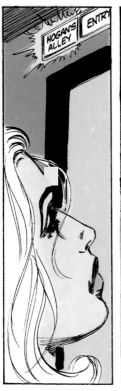

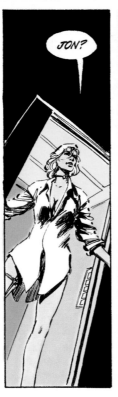

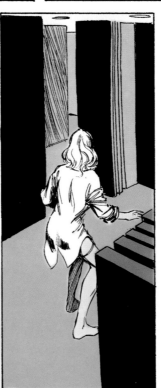

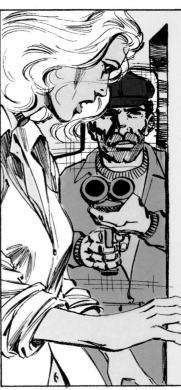

OW! YOU GOT ME!

CUTE.

WHO'S YOUR DECORATOR —HARRY CALLAHAN?

MORNIN'.

I'VE NEVER SEEN A GUN LIKE THAT.

IT'S NEW...

...BASICALLY, A .375. USES UP TO A 300 GRAIN SLUG...

...BUT IT DOES A WHOLE LOT MORE.

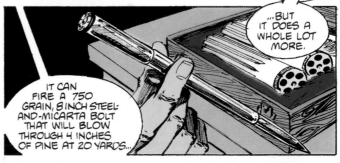

IT CAN FIRE A 750 GRAIN, 8 INCH STEEL-AND-MICARTA BOLT THAT WILL BLOW THROUGH 4 INCHES OF PINE AT 20 YARDS...

...UNDERWATER...

...IN VIRTUAL SILENCE.

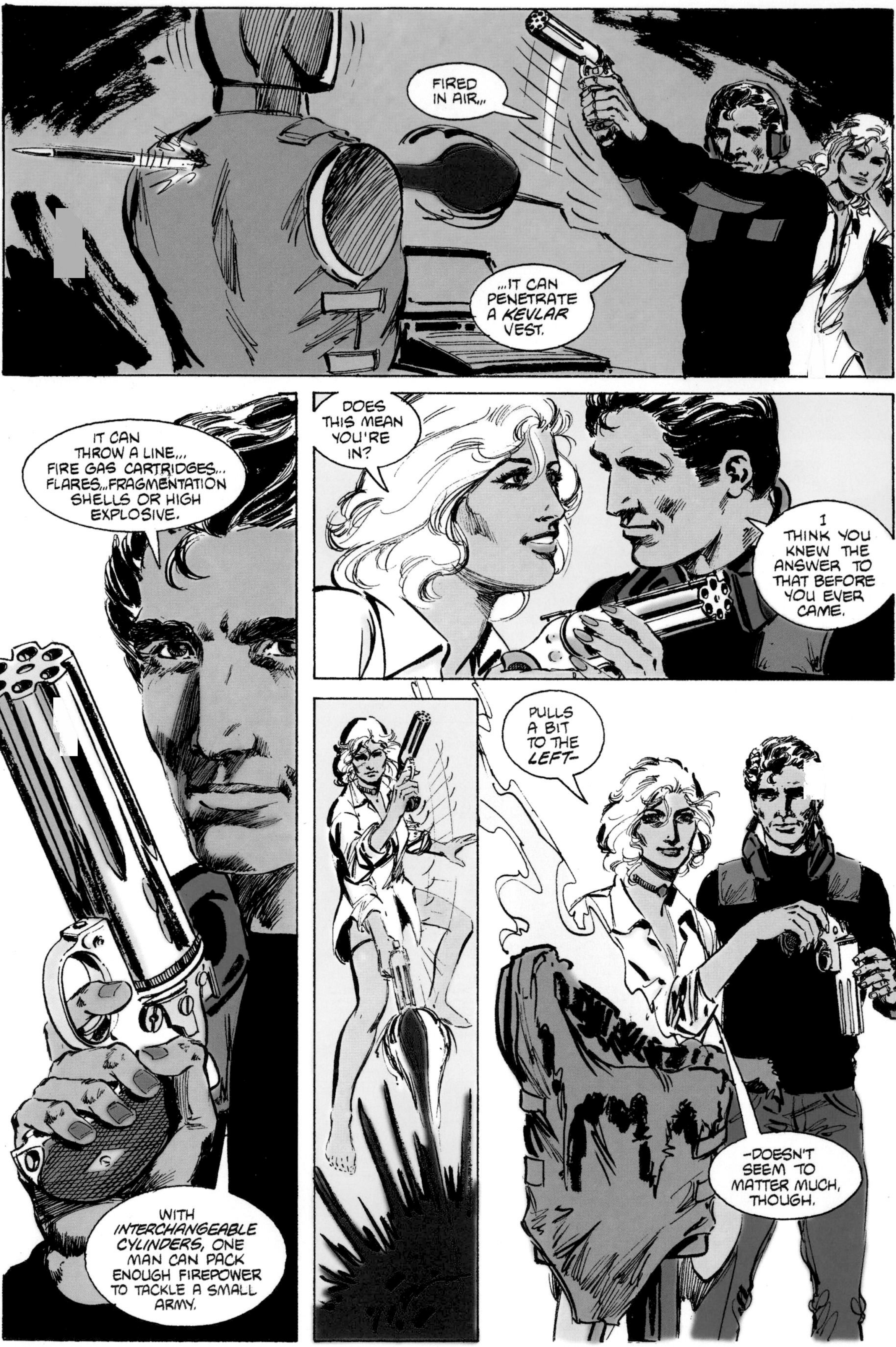
FIRED IN AIR...
...IT CAN PENETRATE A KEVLAR VEST.
IT CAN THROW A LINE... FIRE GAS CARTRIDGES... FLARES...FRAGMENTATION SHELLS OR HIGH EXPLOSIVE.
WITH INTERCHANGEABLE CYLINDERS, ONE MAN CAN PACK ENOUGH FIREPOWER TO TACKLE A SMALL ARMY.
DOES THIS MEAN YOU'RE IN?
I THINK YOU KNEW THE ANSWER TO THAT BEFORE YOU EVER CAME.
PULLS A BIT TO THE LEFT-
-DOESN'T SEEM TO MATTER MUCH, THOUGH.

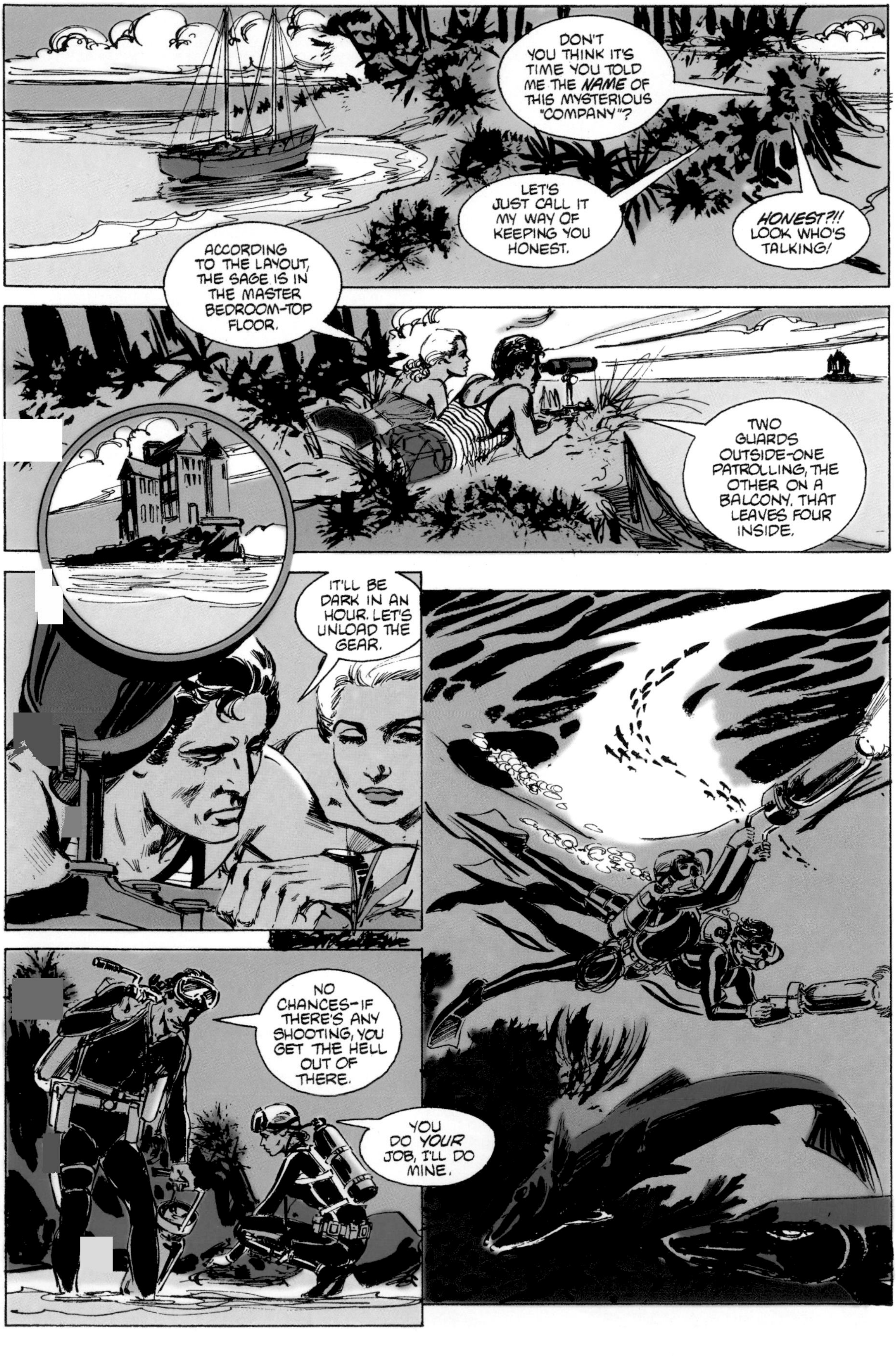

DON'T YOU THINK IT'S TIME YOU TOLD ME THE *NAME* OF THIS MYSTERIOUS "COMPANY"?
LET'S JUST CALL IT MY WAY OF KEEPING YOU HONEST.
HONEST?!! LOOK WHO'S TALKING!
ACCORDING TO THE LAYOUT, THE SAGE IS IN THE MASTER BEDROOM-TOP FLOOR.
TWO GUARDS OUTSIDE-ONE PATROLLING, THE OTHER ON A BALCONY. THAT LEAVES FOUR INSIDE.
IT'LL BE DARK IN AN HOUR. LET'S UNLOAD THE GEAR.
NO CHANCES-IF THERE'S ANY SHOOTING, YOU GET THE HELL OUT OF THERE.
YOU DO *YOUR* JOB, I'LL DO MINE.

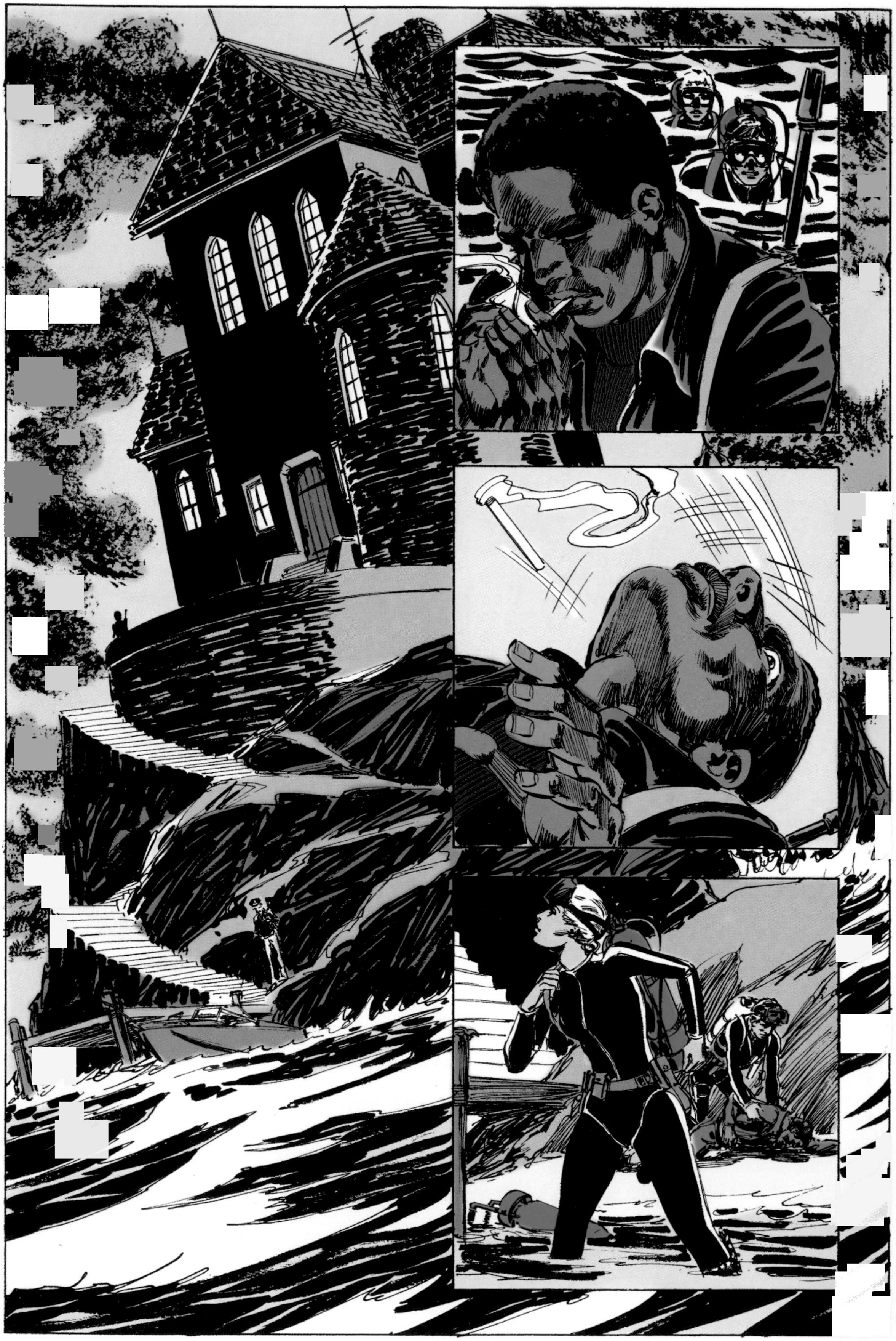

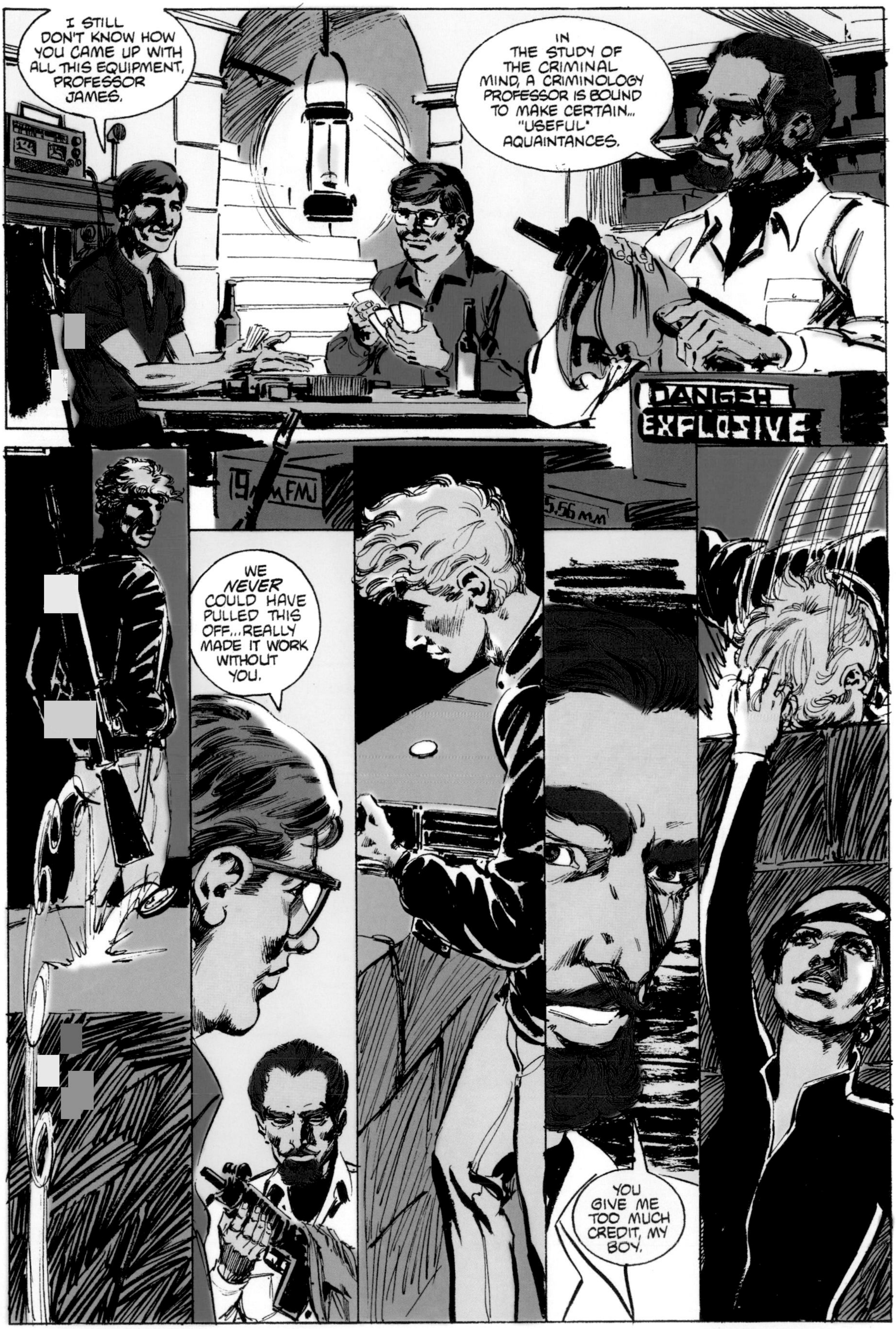
I STILL DON'T KNOW HOW YOU CAME UP WITH ALL THIS EQUIPMENT, PROFESSOR JAMES.
IN THE STUDY OF THE CRIMINAL MIND, A CRIMINOLOGY PROFESSOR IS BOUND TO MAKE CERTAIN... "USEFUL" AQUAINTANCES.
DANGER EXPLOSIVE
19mm FMJ
5.56mm
WE NEVER COULD HAVE PULLED THIS OFF... REALLY MADE IT WORK WITHOUT YOU.
YOU GIVE ME TOO MUCH CREDIT, MY BOY.

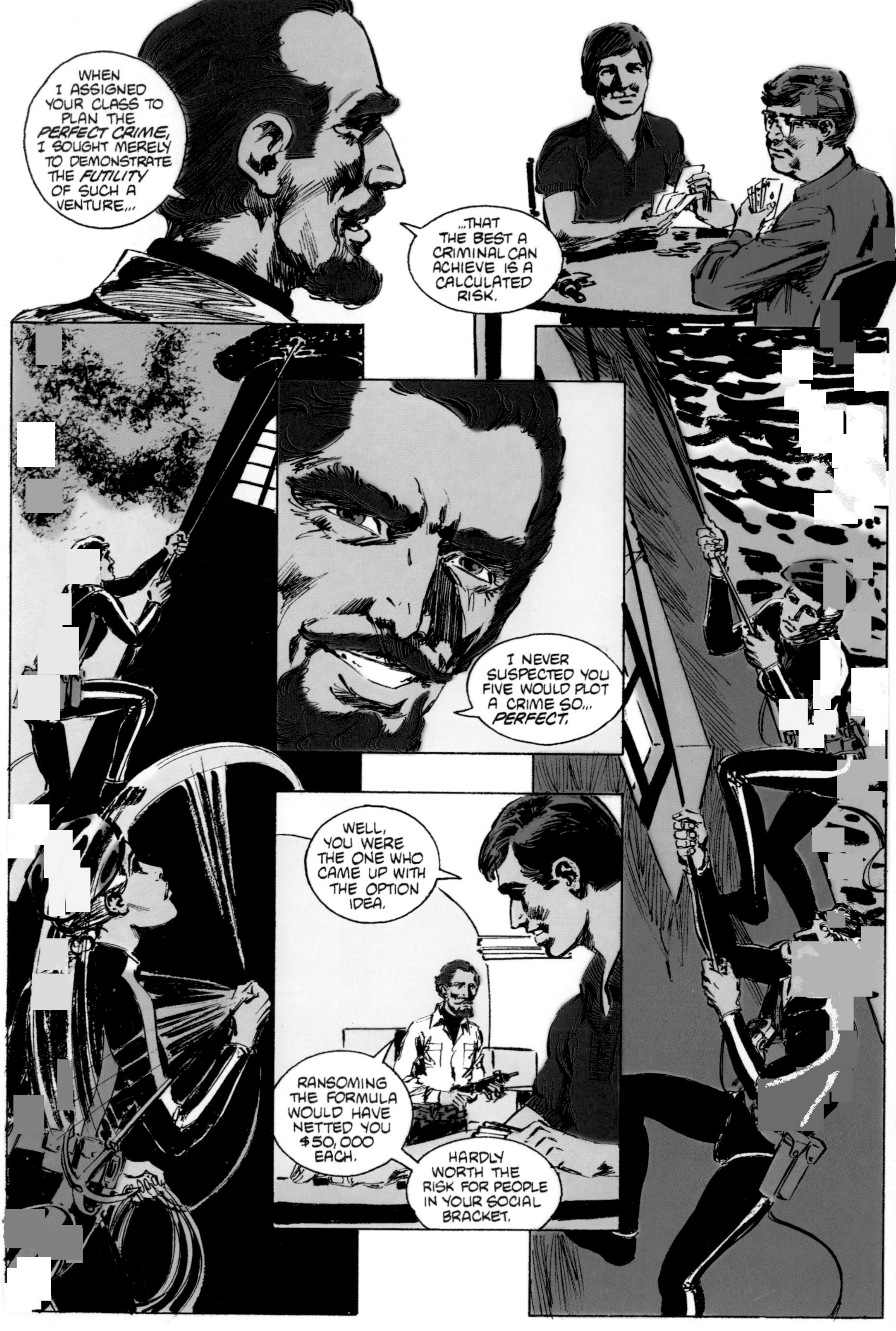
WHEN I ASSIGNED YOUR CLASS TO PLAN THE PERFECT CRIME, I SOUGHT MERELY TO DEMONSTRATE THE FUTILITY OF SUCH A VENTURE...
...THAT THE BEST A CRIMINAL CAN ACHIEVE IS A CALCULATED RISK.
I NEVER SUSPECTED YOU FIVE WOULD PLOT A CRIME SO... PERFECT.
WELL, YOU WERE THE ONE WHO CAME UP WITH THE OPTION IDEA.
RANSOMING THE FORMULA WOULD HAVE NETTED YOU $50,000 EACH.
HARDLY WORTH THE RISK FOR PEOPLE IN YOUR SOCIAL BRACKET.

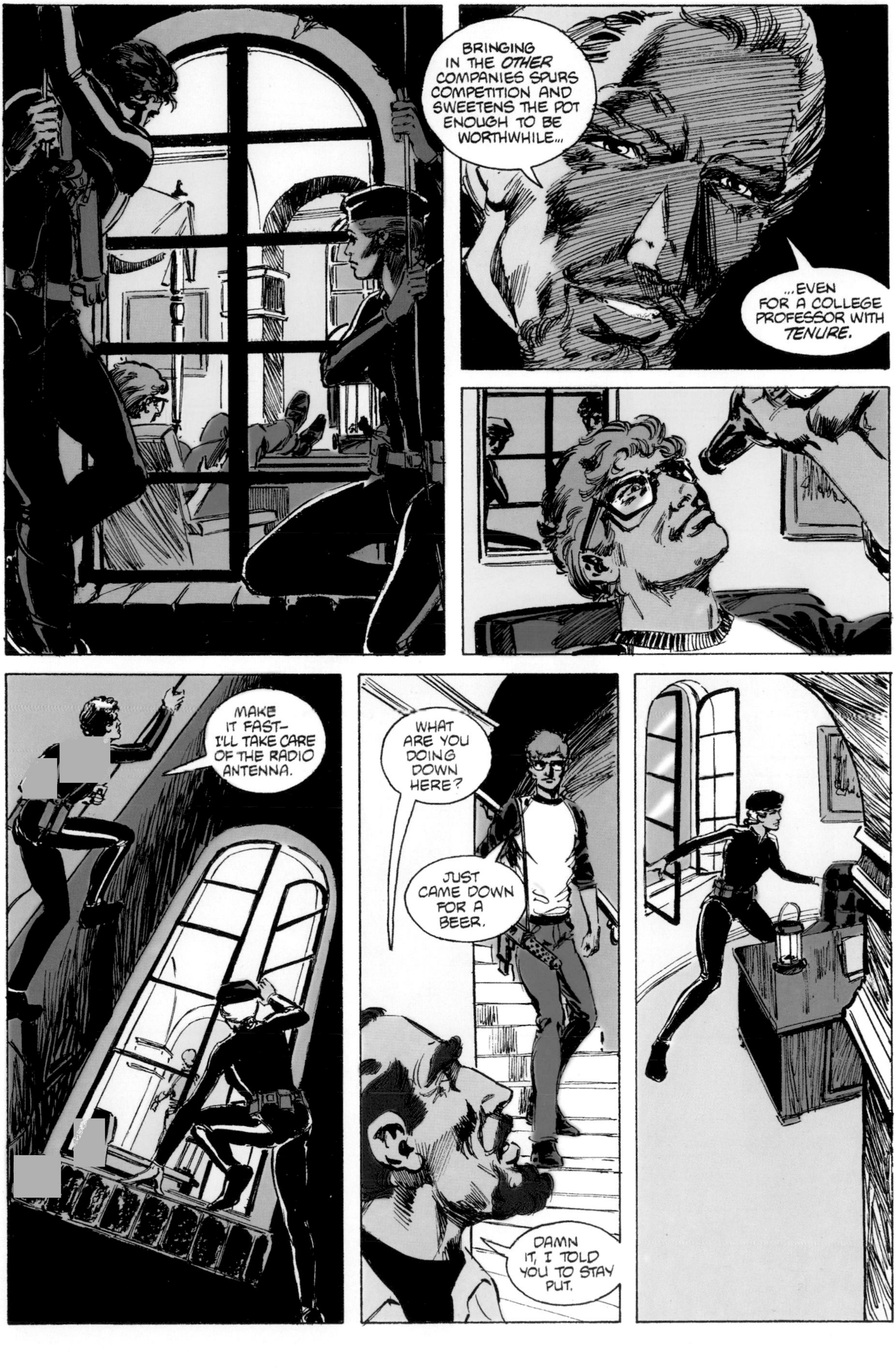
BRINGING IN THE *OTHER* COMPANIES SPURS COMPETITION AND SWEETENS THE POT ENOUGH TO BE WORTHWHILE...
...EVEN FOR A COLLEGE PROFESSOR WITH *TENURE.*
MAKE IT FAST– I'LL TAKE CARE OF THE RADIO ANTENNA.
WHAT ARE YOU DOING DOWN HERE?
JUST CAME DOWN FOR A BEER.
DAMN IT, I TOLD YOU TO STAY PUT.

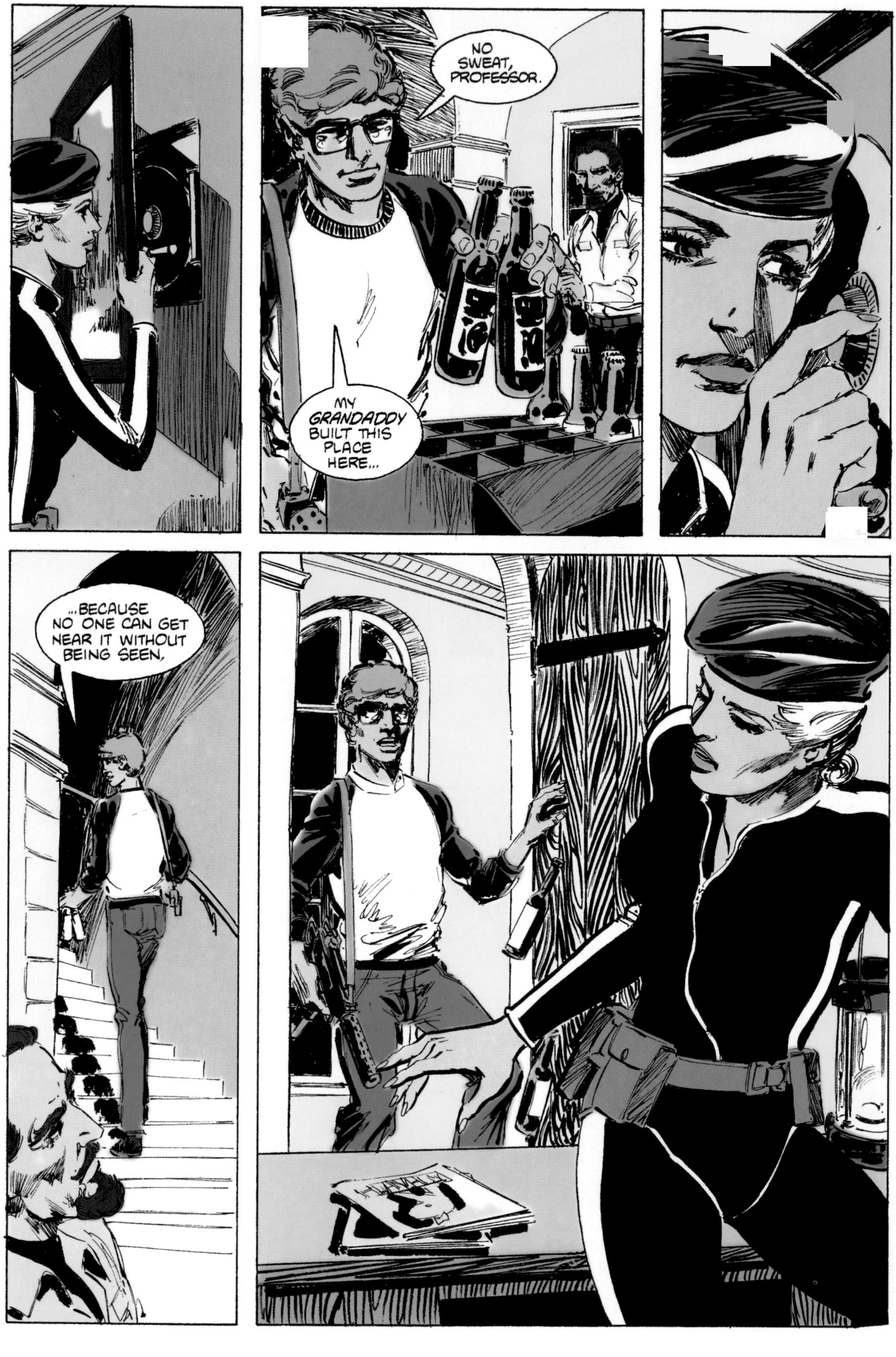
NO SWEAT, PROFESSOR.
MY GRANDADDY BUILT THIS PLACE HERE...
...BECAUSE NO ONE CAN GET NEAR IT WITHOUT BEING SEEN.

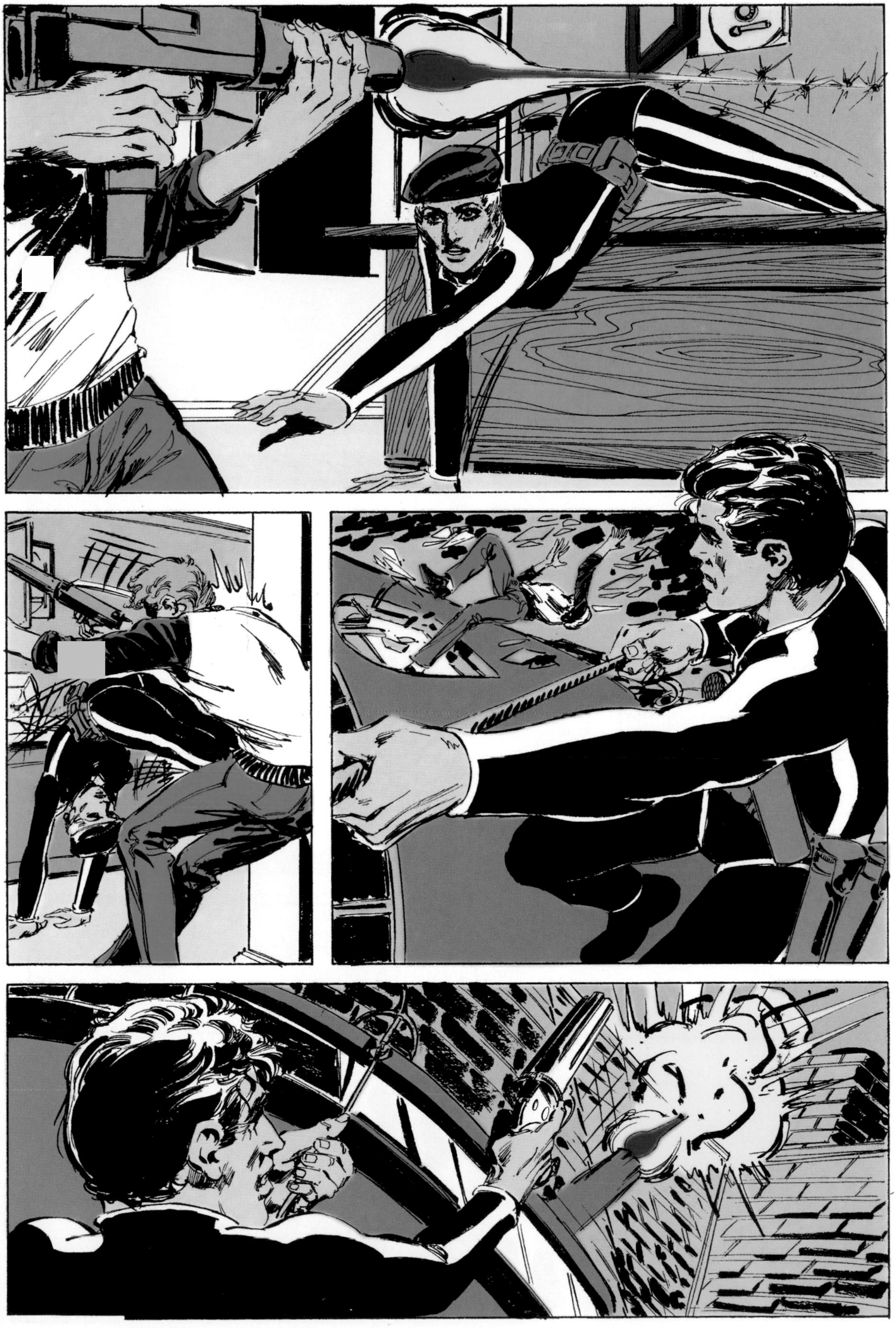

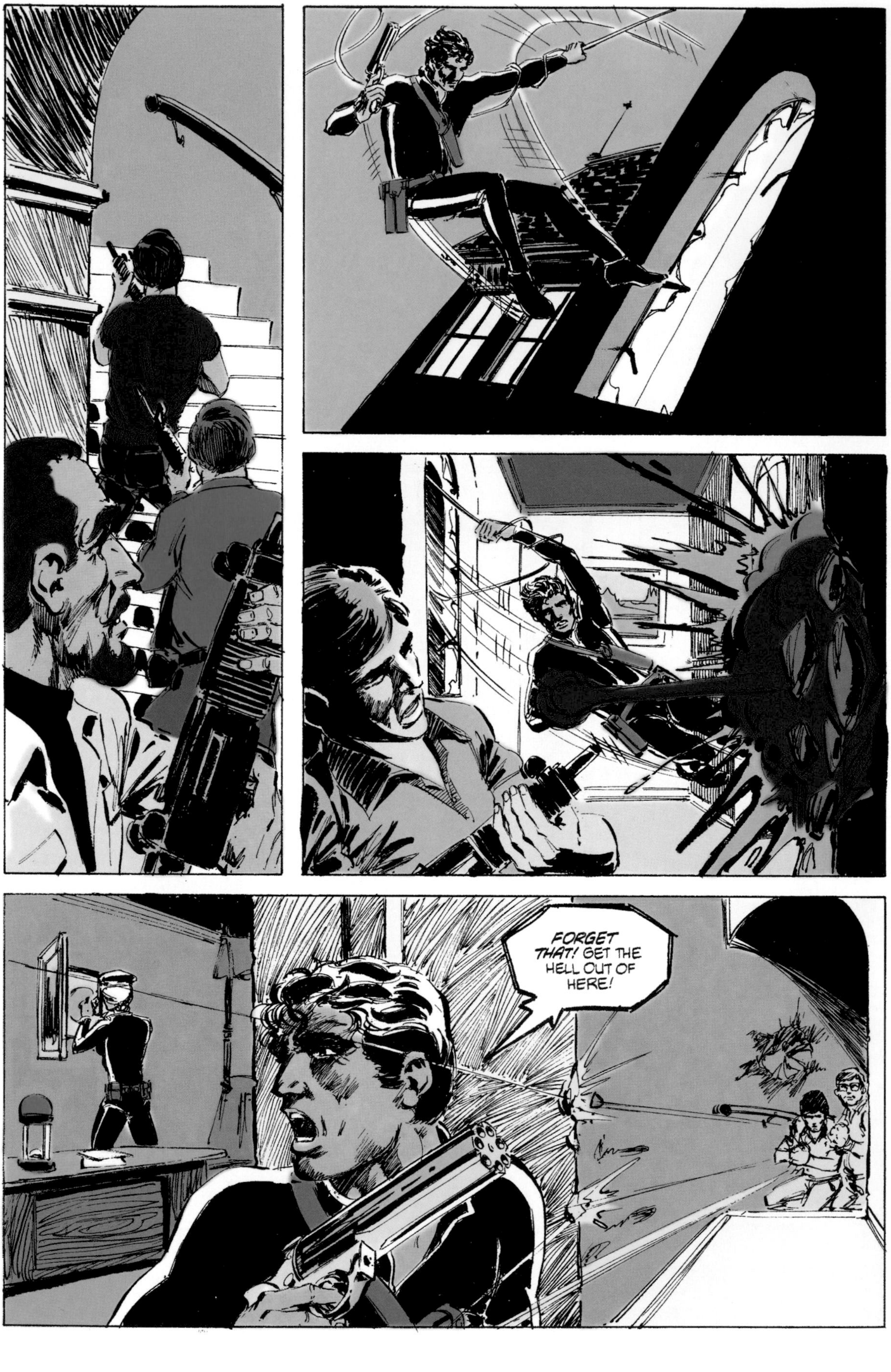
FORGET THAT! GET THE HELL OUT OF HERE!

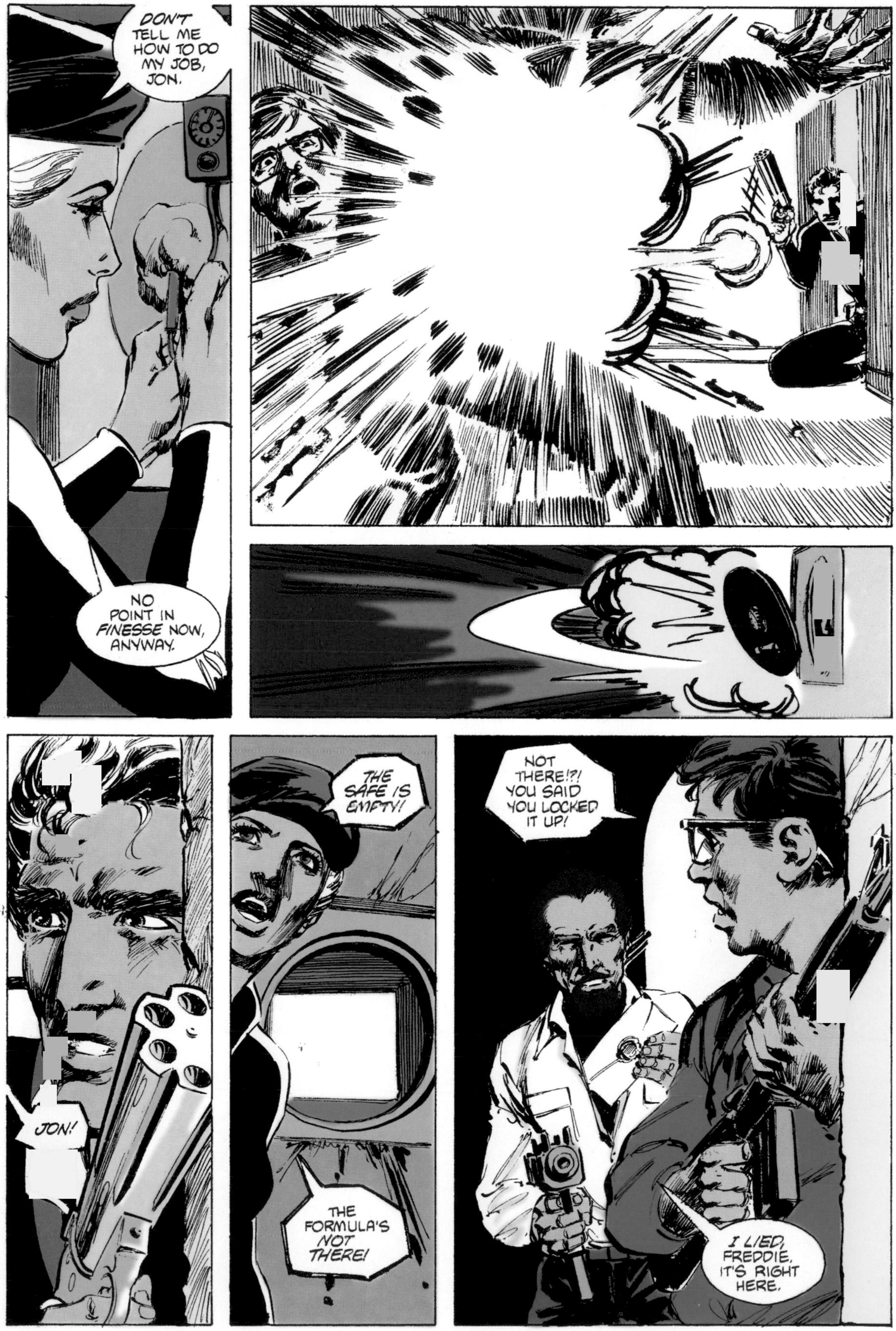
DON'T TELL ME HOW TO DO MY JOB, JON.
NO POINT IN FINESSE NOW, ANYWAY.
JON!
THE SAFE IS EMPTY!
THE FORMULA'S NOT THERE!
NOT THERE!?! YOU SAID YOU LOCKED IT UP!
I LIED, FREDDIE. IT'S RIGHT HERE.

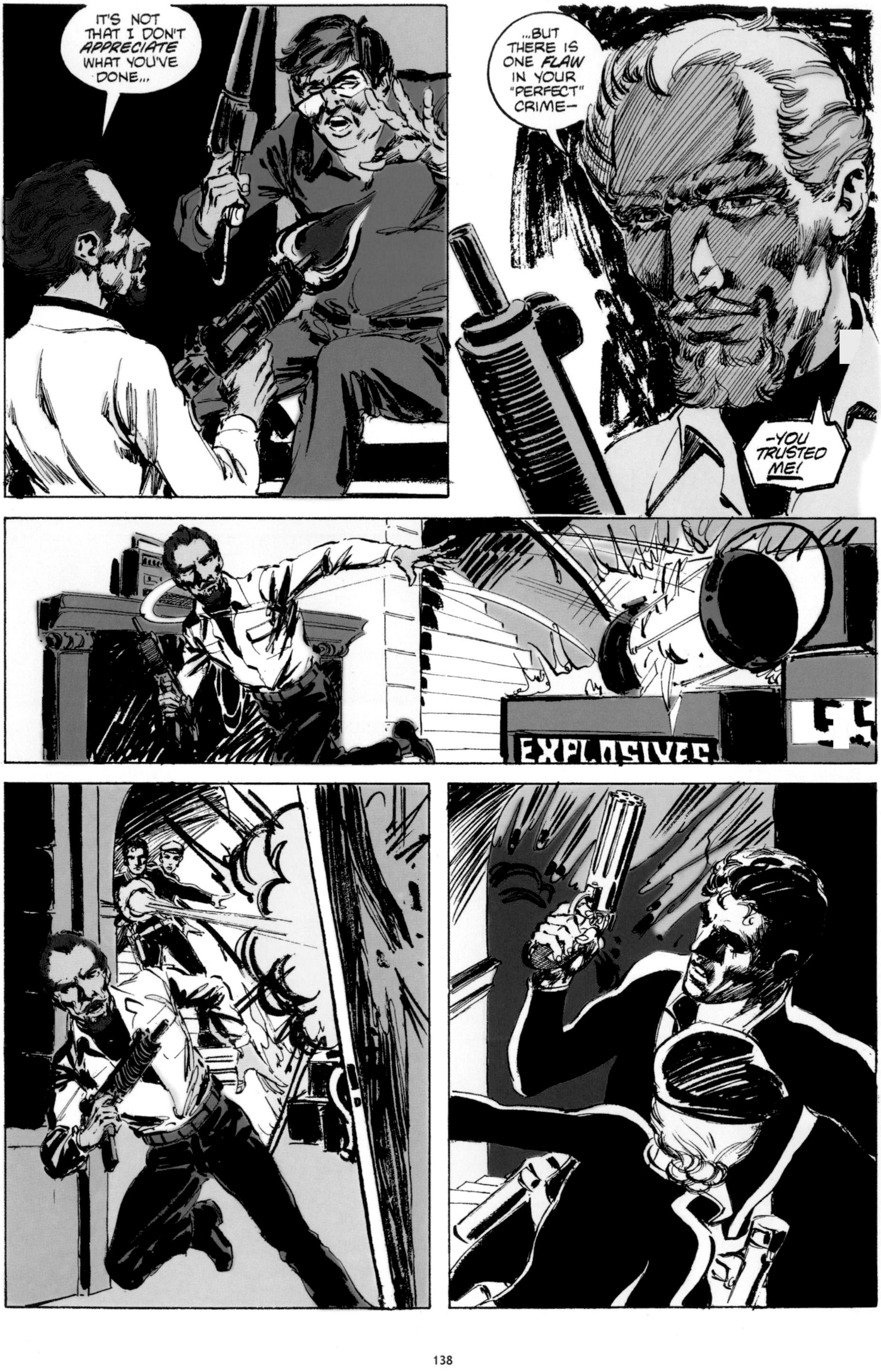
IT'S NOT THAT I DON'T APPRECIATE WHAT YOU'VE DONE...
...BUT THERE IS ONE FLAW IN YOUR "PERFECT" CRIME—
—YOU TRUSTED ME!
EXPLOSIVES

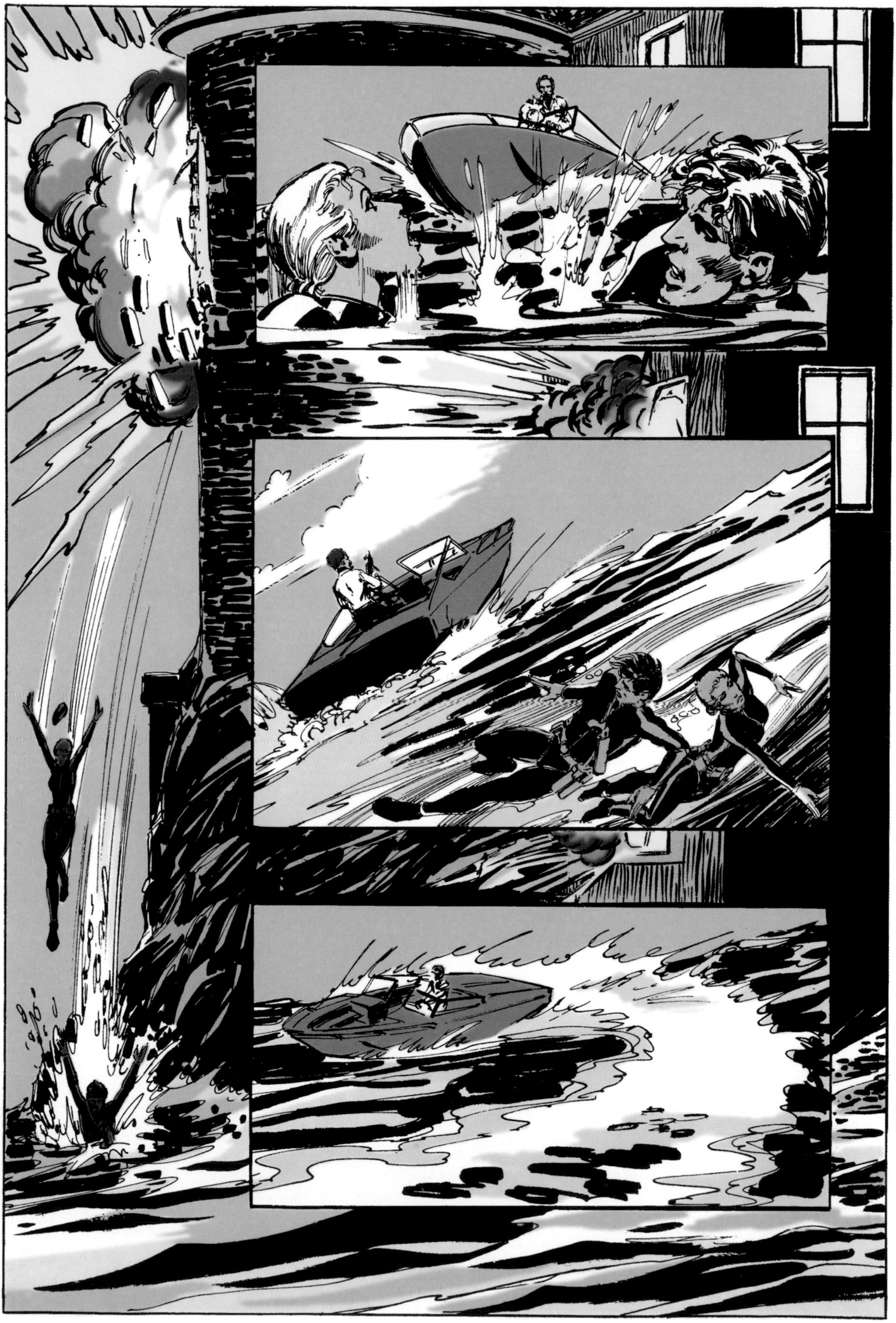

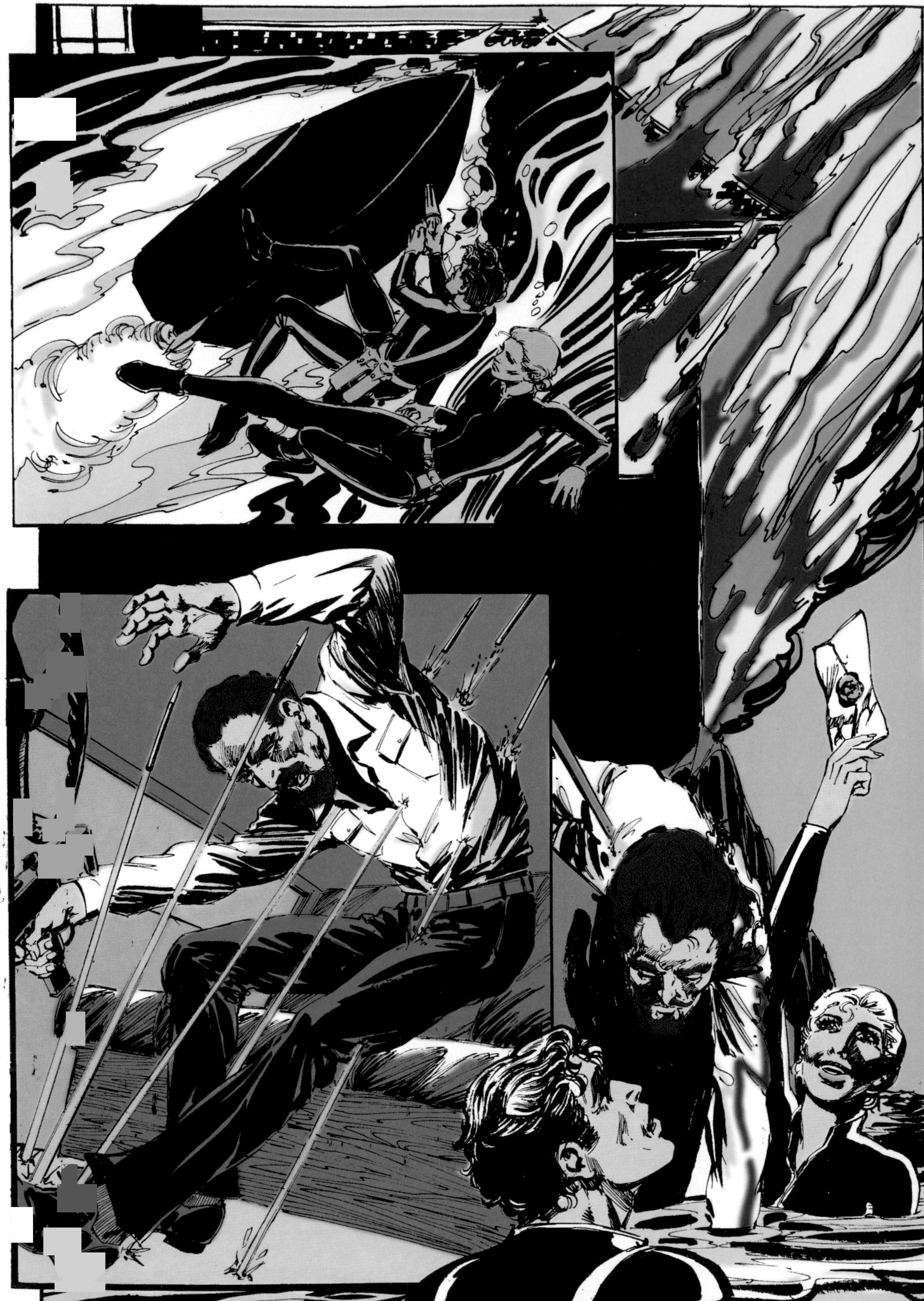

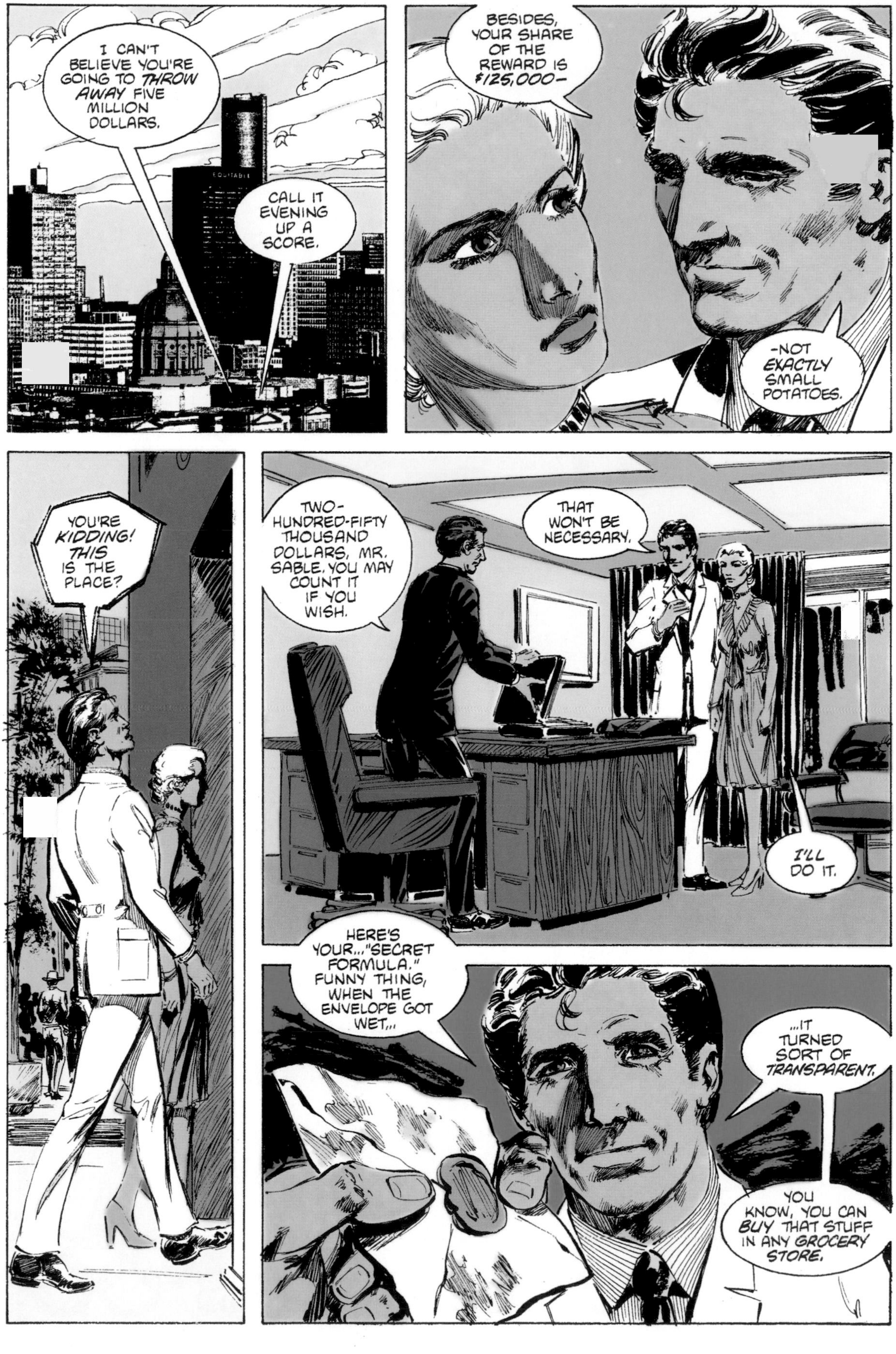
I CAN'T BELIEVE YOU'RE GOING TO THROW AWAY FIVE MILLION DOLLARS.
CALL IT EVENING UP A SCORE.
BESIDES, YOUR SHARE OF THE REWARD IS $125,000–
–NOT EXACTLY SMALL POTATOES.
YOU'RE KIDDING! THIS IS THE PLACE?
TWO-HUNDRED-FIFTY THOUSAND DOLLARS, MR. SABLE. YOU MAY COUNT IT IF YOU WISH.
THAT WON'T BE NECESSARY.
I'LL DO IT.
HERE'S YOUR..."SECRET FORMULA." FUNNY THING, WHEN THE ENVELOPE GOT WET...
...IT TURNED SORT OF TRANSPARENT.
YOU KNOW, YOU CAN BUY THAT STUFF IN ANY GROCERY STORE.

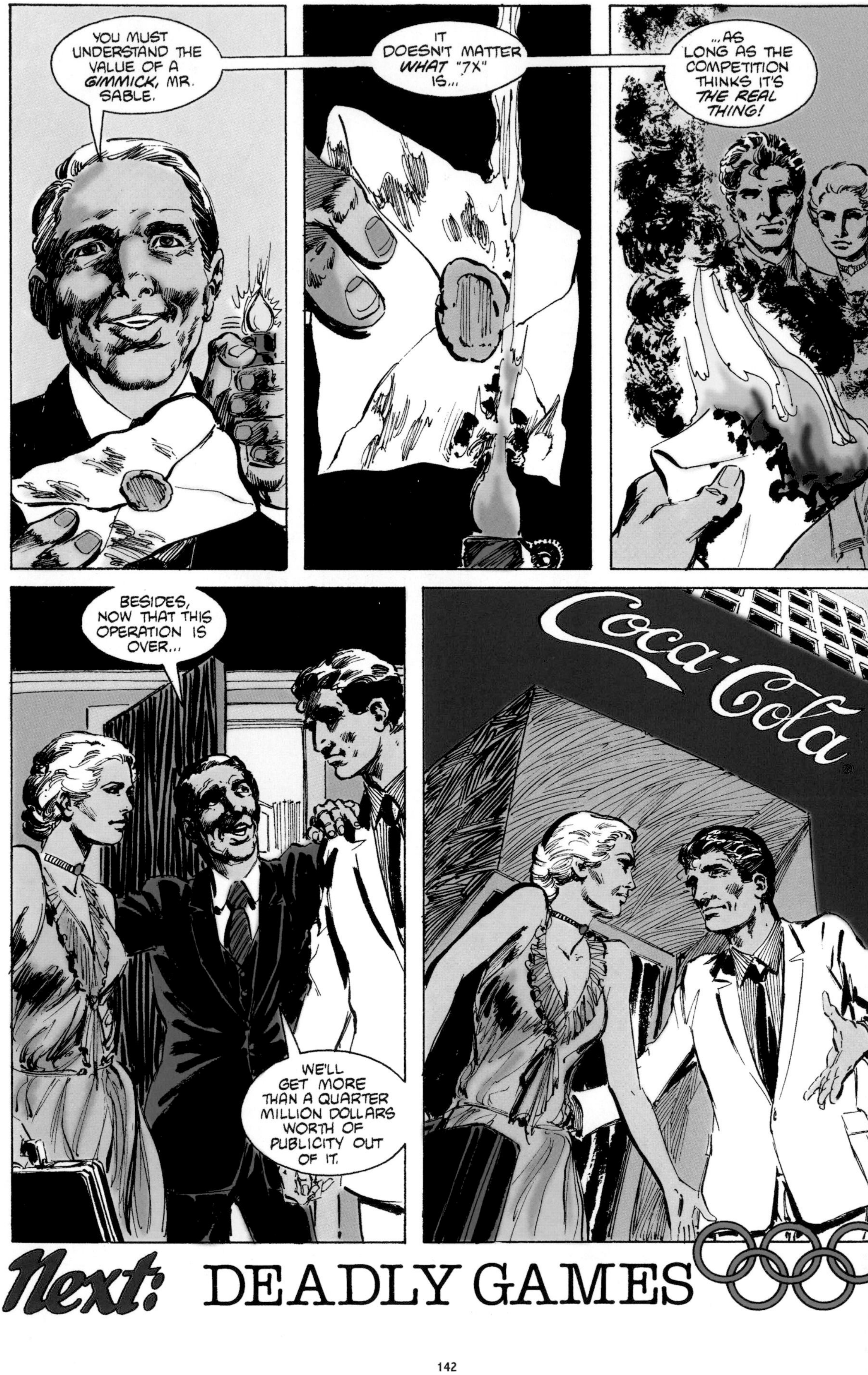
YOU MUST UNDERSTAND THE VALUE OF A GIMMICK, MR. SABLE.
IT DOESN'T MATTER WHAT "7X" IS...
...AS LONG AS THE COMPETITION THINKS IT'S THE REAL THING!
BESIDES, NOW THAT THIS OPERATION IS OVER...
WE'LL GET MORE THAN A QUARTER MILLION DOLLARS WORTH OF PUBLICITY OUT OF IT.
Coca-Cola

Next: DEADLY GAMES

Jon Sable, Freelance Cover Gallery

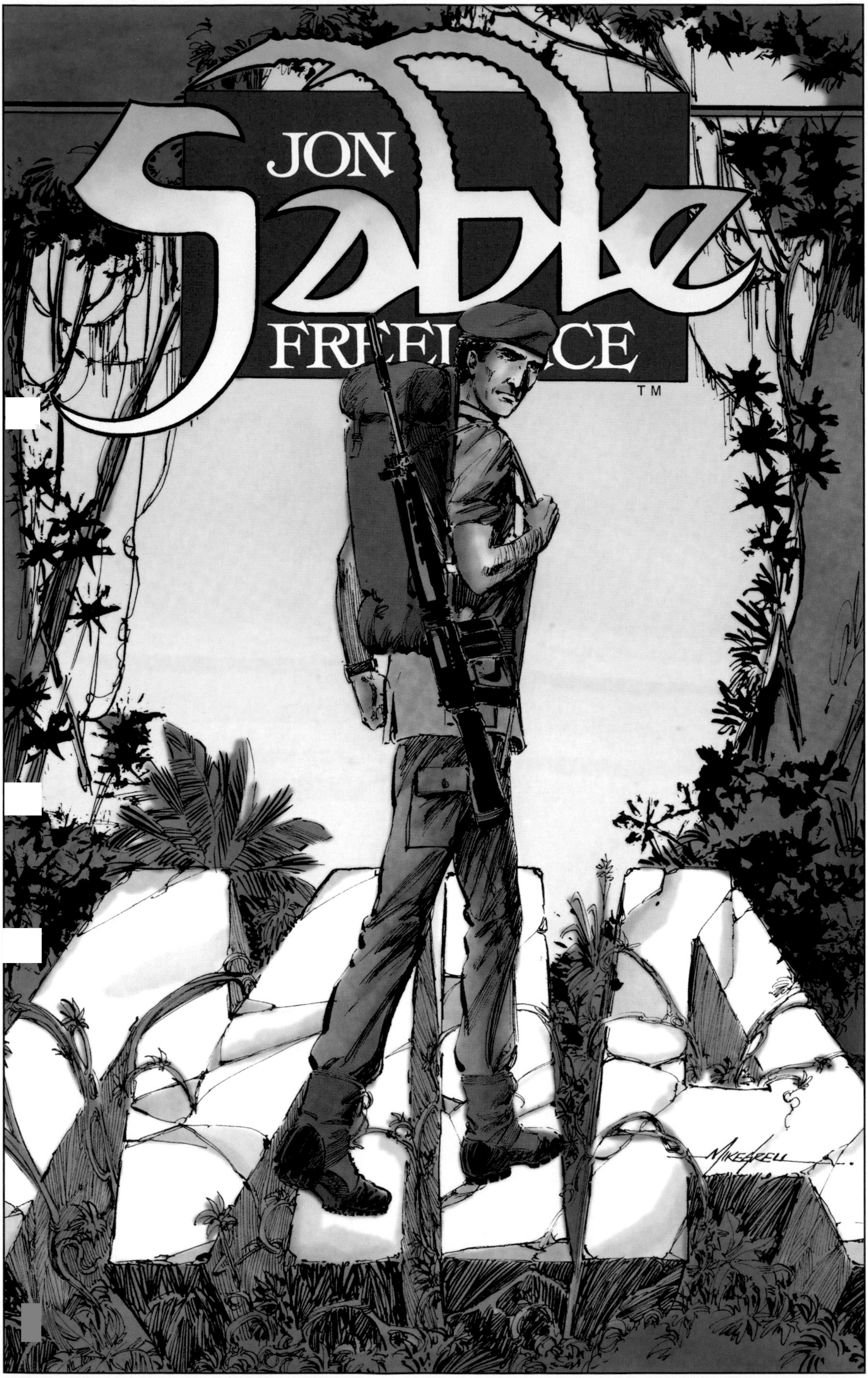
JON
Sable
TM
MIKEGRELL

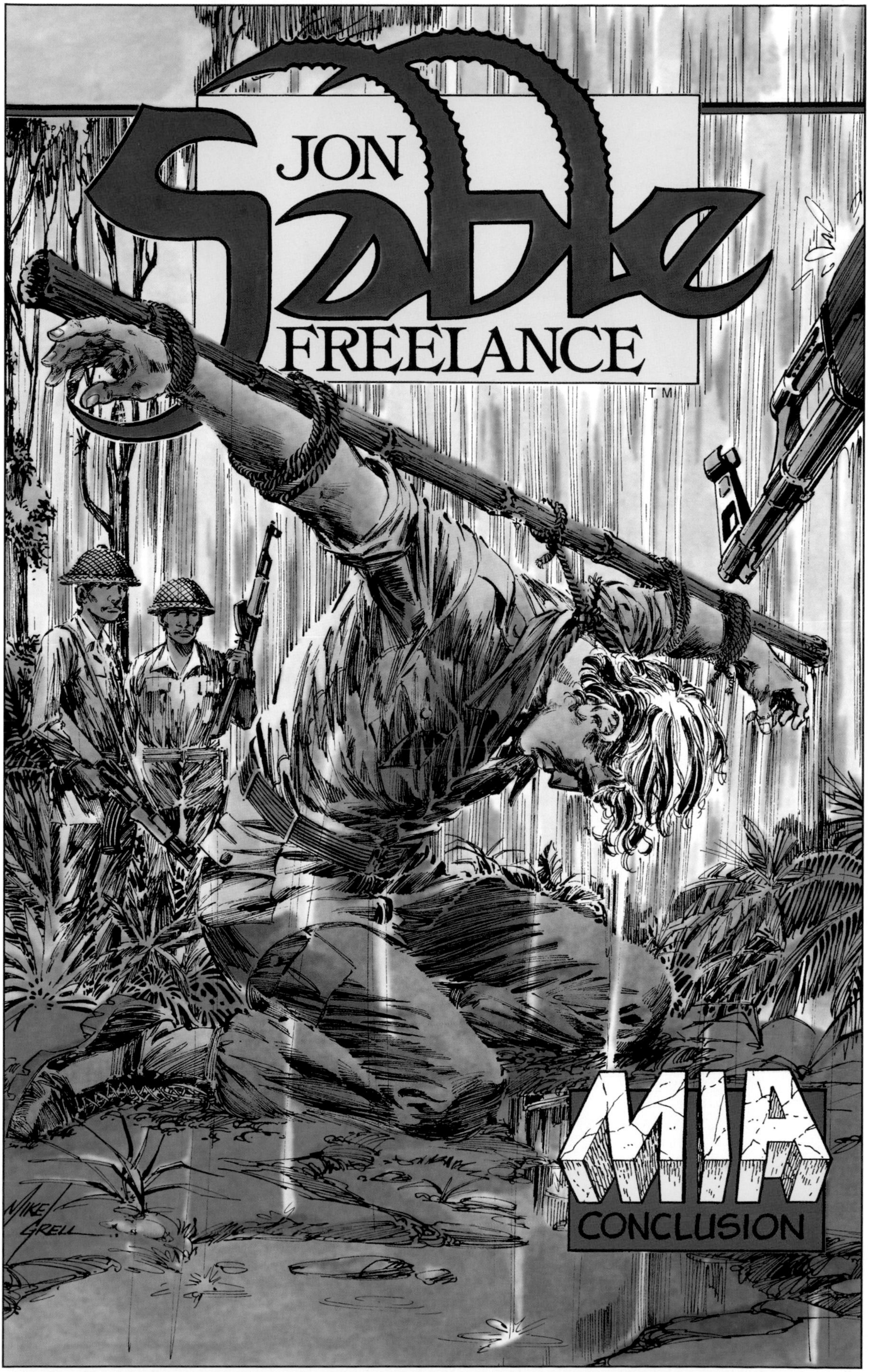
JON
Sable
FREELANCE
TM
MIA
CONCLUSION
MIKE GRELL

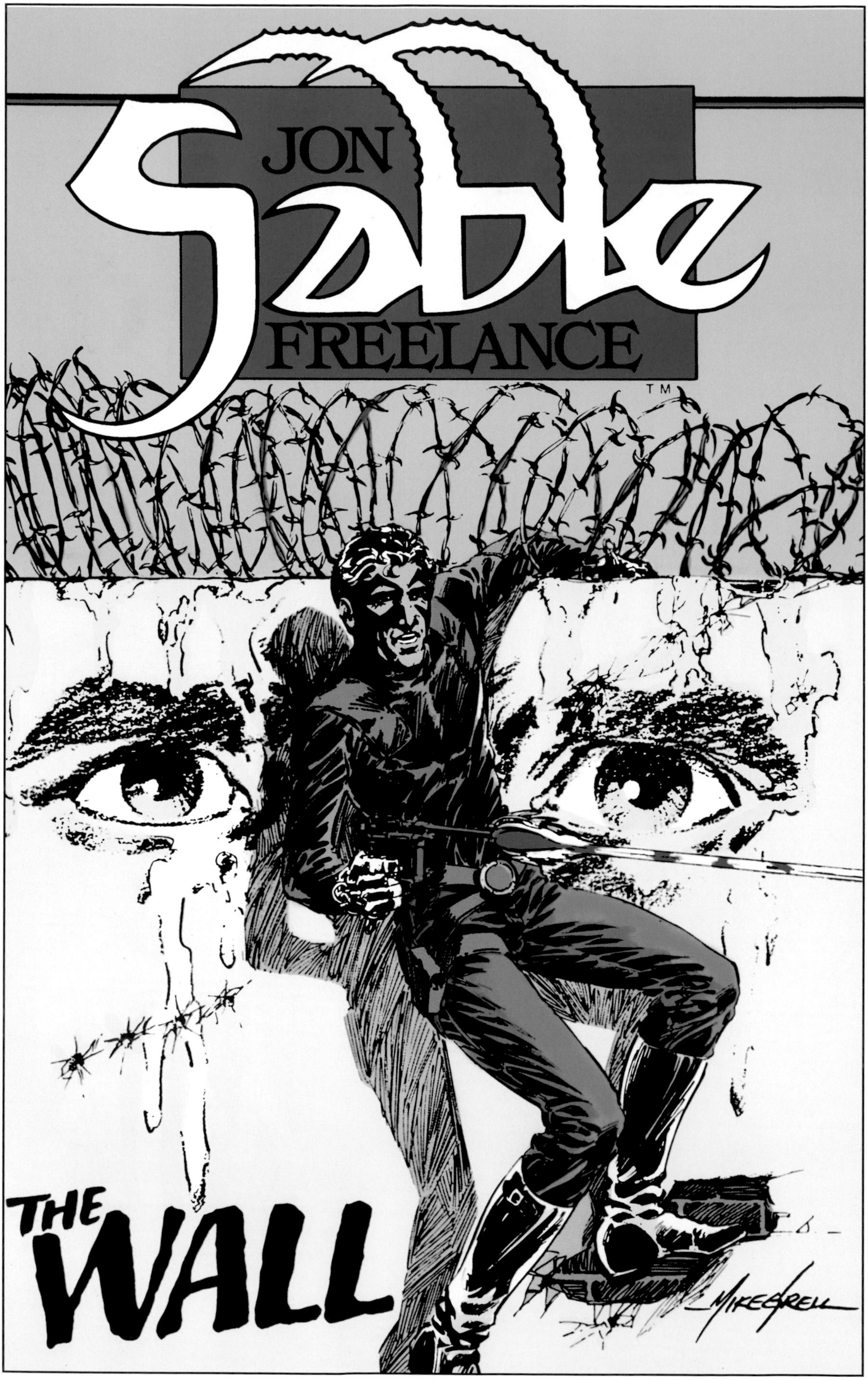
JON
Sable
FREELANCE
TM
THE
WALL
MIKE GRELL

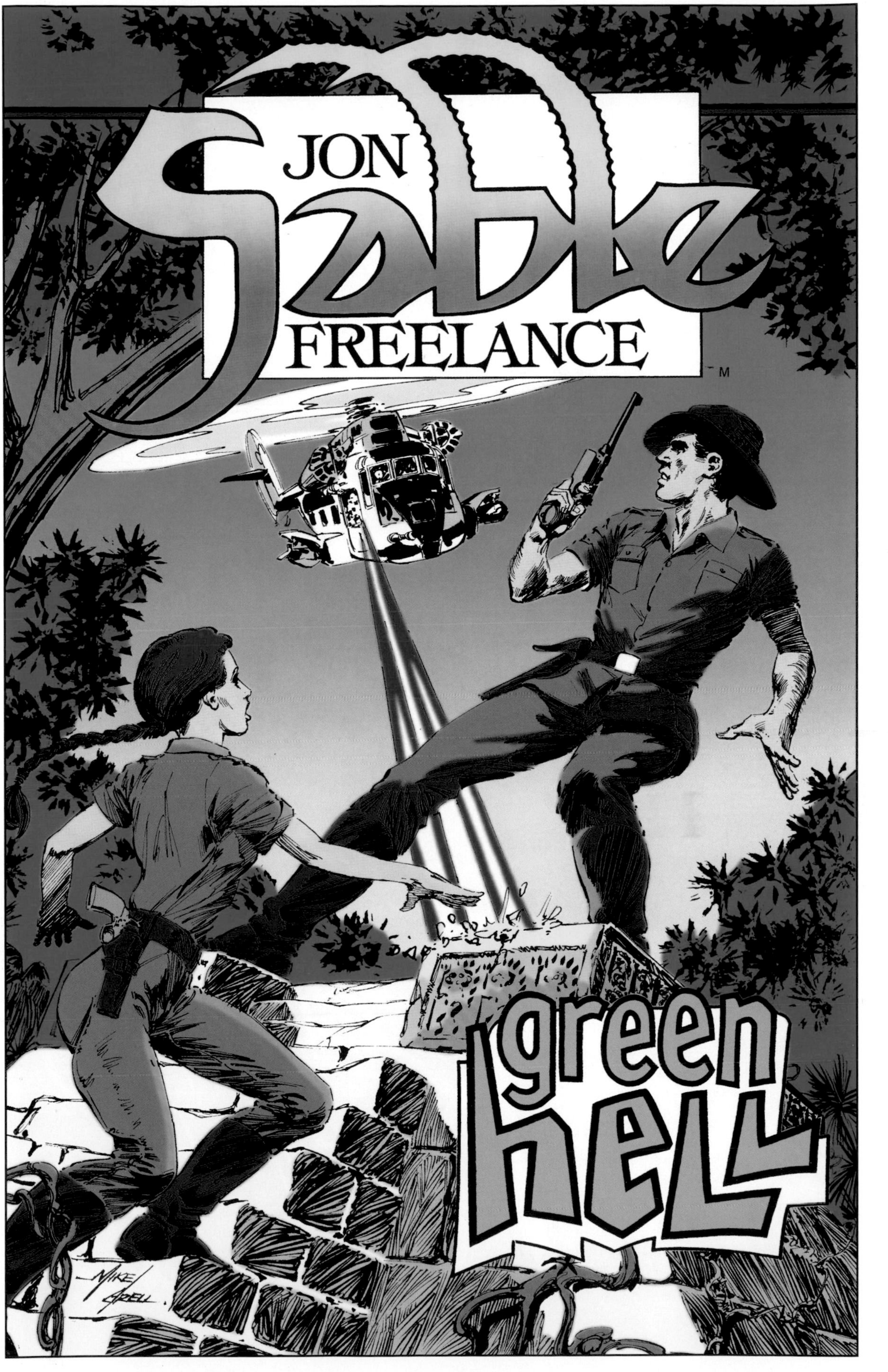
JON
Sable
FREELANCE
TM
green
hell
MIKE GRELL

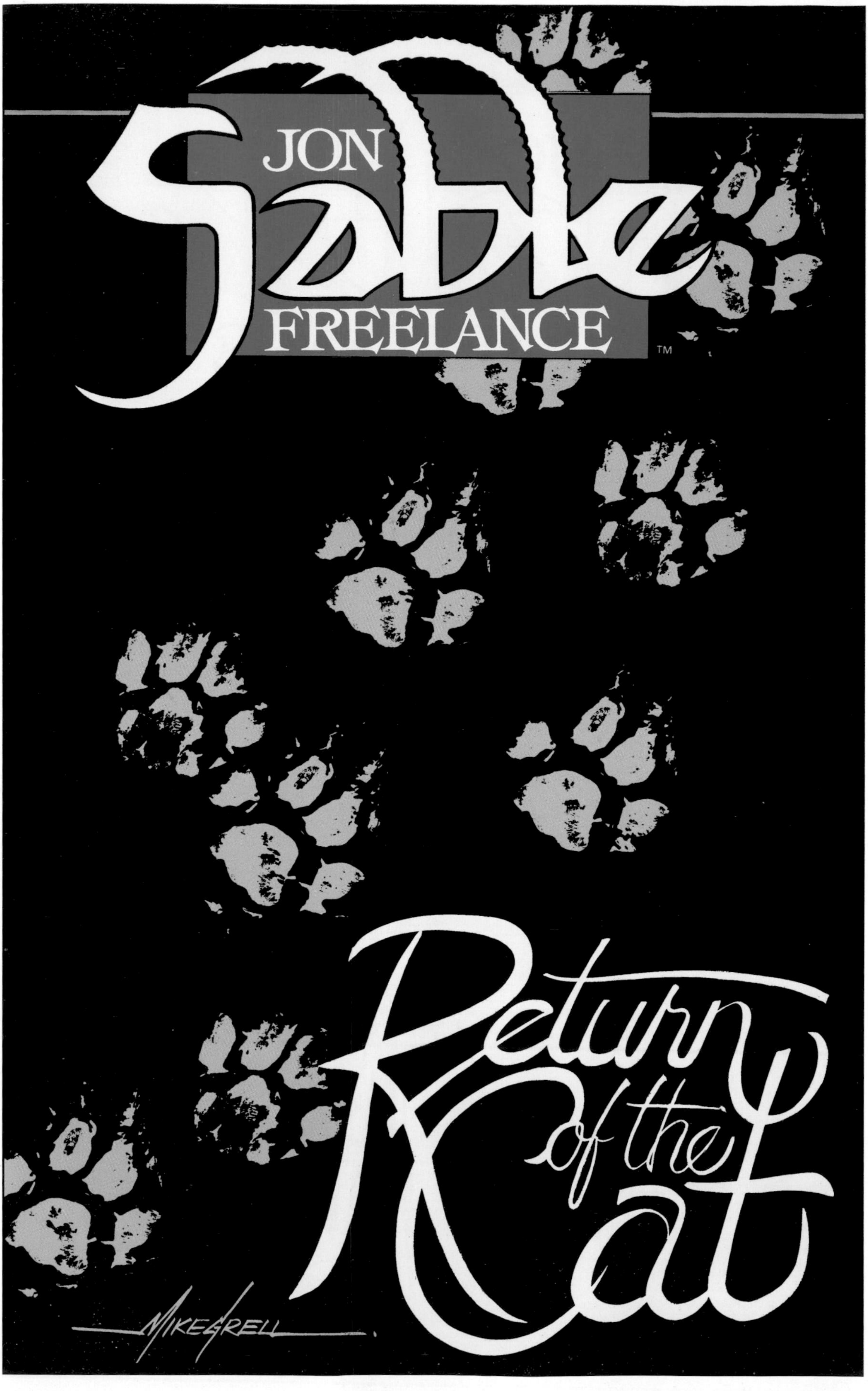
JON
Sable
FREELANCE
TM
Return of the Cat
MIKE GRELL